C000068677

© 2011 Venture Publications Ltd

ISBN 978 1905 304 43 1

All rights reserved. Except for normal review purposes no part of this book maybe reproduced or utilised in any form by any means, electrical or mechanical, including photocopying, recording or by an information storage and retrieval system, without the prior written consent of Venture Publications Ltd, Glossop, Derbyshire, SK13 8EH.

Dedicated to the Rev'd Eric Ogden
1934-2011

A fine example of Lancashire engineering showing a Massey-bodied Leyland Titan PD2/37 from the local Wigan fleet operating an enthusiasts' special service to the Cobham bus museum in Surrey. This can rightly be considered as representative of the best of traditional bus manufacture with front engine, half cab for the driver, and a forward entrance with sliding door to the saloon to keep passengers warm and safe. Number 140 was built in 1966 and withdrawn by GMPTE in 1983 after a spell as a driver trainer. It was purchased by the Wallace School of Transport in London, again for use as a driver trainer, before passing into preservation in 1991. (JAS)

The British Bus and Truck Heritage

Massey Bros
Coachbuilders

A history of the Company
and its products from 1904 to 1968

by

Phil Thoms

Computer Origination and Design: John A Senior

Venture *publications*

INTRODUCTION

This volume, the latest in the series of bodybuilders histories from Glossop, continues the work begun with a modest picture album of Northern Counties photographs way back in 1974. Access to manufacturers and their management allowed greater depth of coverage but throughout the 1980s the pace of closure of the British Bus and Coachbuilding industry was greater than the resources of the publisher and its authors could match.

Companies which had already gone out of existence took second place to those still trading, resulting in some – including Massey – being sidelined, either for lack of resource or for reasons of commercial viability. Eric Ogden and Harry Postlethwaite began to amass material for a Massey history in 1989 but various pressures caused the project to be put to one side for some years. More recently, we became aware that Phil Thoms had been working quite independently on the same project, unknown to the others, since 2004. His offer to take over the whole project was welcomed, and provided the necessary spark to reignite the concept. More research was necessary to bring the project nearer to completion for publication, with Phil now in the driving seat.

Sadly, Eric died on New Year's Day 2011 and so was not able to see the finished result, though we are sure he would have been proud of what has been accomplished. This book is, therefore, dedicated to his memory, as a tribute to the many years he spent researching and writing about matters pertaining to the bus industry. We shall miss him greatly.

Chester Corporation's ubiquitous No. 1 is a Guy Arab IV supplied in a batch of three in 1953. It ran in service for 22 years, subsequently being used as a driver trainer for a short time before being preserved. It was spotted at a rally in the late 'seventies shortly after leaving the Corporation's ownership. (JAS)

4

FOREWORD

Massey Bros. was one of the three principal Wigan bus bodybuilders, its well-rounded designs being instantly recognisable to the cognisant. Located in Pemberton, to the west of the town centre, it built bodywork for motor cars, light commercials, tramcars, buses and coaches – with occasional forays into railcars and hearses for good measure.

A family concern, it spread its connections to both Northern Counties, who eventually swallowed it up, and East Lancashire Coachbuilders, who managed to outlive both concerns, by the cross-fertilisation of personnel. Further afield, Leyland Motors Ltd also had former Massey personnel, and Leyland men went to Pemberton.

Whilst the Northern Counties album was being produced, David Cherry, Northern Counties Managing Director, very kindly invited Eric Ogden and John Senior to look round the Pemberton site which NCME had just acquired by the purchase of Massey Bros. in 1967. Mr Cherry was very conscious of the heritage of the area, and carefully took them through the former stables and showed the hay loft – both items dating from the original horse tram operation before Massey had moved in. Little did he, or they, realise that in that loft were many hidden gems which would only surface many years later, some of which would find their way into this book – sadly much was thrown away 'in the skip'.

There were still a handful of bodybuilders left at that time: Alexander was still a family concern in Falkirk; Burlingham had sold out to Duple; East Lancashire Coachbuilders were still on Whalley New Road, Blackburn; Eastern Coach Works, Park Royal and Roe had all been swallowed up by Leyland; Northern Counties was flourishing and expanding; Plaxton was still a family concern in Scarborough; Willowbrook had taken over Brush Coachworks. It is all so different now.

We hope that this long-awaited volume will bring equal measures of pleasure to those who remember the Pemberton products and to those who have only ever seen them in preservation. It may perhaps also facilitate the production of some more of those missing Company histories! We are always interested . . .

Former Birkenhead Transport No. 242 at a Brighton Rally in the early 'seventies. This Guy Arab 6LW was new in 1944 with a Massey utility body, as number 324 (BG 8557). It was rebodied by Massey in 1953 with a 7ft 9in wide body, possibly to stay within the weight limit. Oddly, the high radiator was retained, unlike many rebodied Guys at that time. (JAS)

CONTENTS

ACKNOWLEDGEMENTS

The Author and Publishers would like to record their sincere thanks to all those who have helped to make the production of this book possible. Many of the photographs from the official archives were rescued from the skip when the major reconstruction of the premises took place in the 1990s, and again when the NCME plant closed in 2005. It was amazing how many odd corners and forgotten drawers came to light!

We are particularly grateful to: Ted Jones, Martin Ingle, David Gray, Roy Tither, Ron Phillips, Graham Brindley, Geoff Lumb, Eric Ogden, Harry Postlethwaite, John Senior, Bob Rowe, Ian Stubbs, Scott Hellewell, and Ian Stopforth.

Also many thanks to Wilf Dodds, Charlie Martindale, Frank Darbyshire, Harry Wall, Peter Tulloch, Roy Marshall, GMTS Boyle Street, Ian Stewart, Ron Hall (Leyland Motors), Mike Sutcliffe (Leyland Society), Alan Pritchard, Margaret Moore, Richard Unsworth, Brian Lancaster, William and Valerie Price, Mike Booth, Alan Cross, Bob Downham, Mike Fenton, Graham Harper, Clifford Heap, Peter Jaques, Brian Lancaster, John Locke, Alan Mills, Owen Phillips, Ian Tyldesley, Garry Ward, Malcolm Wilford, Derek Winstanley, Ray Winstanley, Leslie Wormleighton and Wellington.

Books and magazines used for reference include: Bus & Coach; Motor Transport; Commercial Motor; Transport World; Buses Magazine; Classic Bus; Tramways of Wigan and PSV Circle Fleet Histories. Local newspaper extracts were supplemented from archives at the Wigan History Centre with assistance from Mike Haddon.

Items loaned from GMMTS and the Senior Transport Archive are gratefully acknowledged.

Bob Rowe kindly read the proofs and made several interesting observations which we were pleased to incorporate whilst Venture's regular proof readers David and Mary Shaw gave the whole work their usual thorough attention. Thanks to all three and apologies to anyone I have inadvertently missed out.

Phil Thoms
Sale
August 2011

IGMS

FRONTISPIECE

Looking resplendent in the colours of its former owner, this preserved lowbridge Leyland Titan PD2 sums up all that was so typical of Massey's later days. The curved upper-deck profile is seen to good advantage as are the clean lines of the whole bodywork. Number 36 had been delivered to the Welsh municipality in 1967, only months before production at Pemberton passed into the hands of Northern Counties following that Company's take-over of Massey Bros. (JAS)

CHAPTER I
In the beginning

Most enthusiasts in the bus world would recognise the curvaceous lines of a double-decker bodied by Massey Bros, but the roots of this well-known coachbuilder go back much earlier than their first vehicle-building venture after the Great War. Back, in fact, to 1904 when the three brothers Isaac, Thomas and William Massey formed a partnership to carry on business as timber merchants and building contractors in the small parish of Pemberton, about two miles to the west of Wigan town centre. Isaac, born in 1879, had trained as an accountant. Thomas was born three years later and became experienced in building and construction work. William, the eldest son who was born in 1877, worked in the coal mining industry and became a sleeping partner.

The original products were greenhouses, soon followed by terraced houses in and around Wigan, several of which may still be seen adjoining the firm's former location at Pemberton, Wigan. The business flourished, and contracts were obtained in 1906 for the construction of the Carnegie Library in Ashton-in-Makerfield and the following year the Enfield Spinning & Weaving Mill, next to their own premises in Enfield Street.

About 1908/9 Massey Bros became the official building and maintenance contractors for Eagle Picturedromes Ltd who owned and managed most of the cinemas in the Wigan area. Massey Bros started this contract with the building of the Pavilion Cinema in 1909, followed by the Palace Cinemas in Atherton and Platt Bridge, both completed in 1912, and the construction of the Gidlow Cinema in 1913. Contracts were beginning to come in thick and fast when the Company secured a large commission for what was, in those days, the princely sum of £30,000 for the building of Signal Cotton Spinning Mills. This was to be built adjacent to the huge Sandbrook Mills in Orrell, which, upon completion in 1914, employed more than 200 people. By the beginning of the First World War, cinema, or 'the flicks' as it came to be known, was firmly established as a popular entertainment and a spate of cinema building and conversions was taking place throughout the country. In 1916 the Queens Cinema in Pemberton was completed and the County Playhouse in Wigan town centre was started, but not completed until 1919 owing to lack of materials and manpower. It was reported in *The Times* newspaper in October 1919 "that some 20 million people a week saw 'the flicks' at picture palaces and theatres, thereby being an unrivalled means of communication."

The wedding of Isaac Massey and Elizabeth Taylor at Mount Zion Church, situated at the top of Enfield Street in Pemberton, in 1911.

In the picture left to right are: Miss Ellen Highton, Miss Lily Taylor, Mr Billy Massey, Miss Elizabeth Highton, Mr Isaac Massey, Mr Tom Massey, Miss Elizabeth Taylor, Miss Ellen Taylor and Mr Tom Taylor whose son Joe was the well-known director of Wigan RLFC.

Meanwhile, much maintenance work was arriving from Wigan Corporation and a substantial contract for £9,774 (worth about £450,000 today) was won in 1918 for the building of an extension and culvert at the Electricity Works.

Shortly after the end of the First World War, the temporary wartime restrictions on passenger transport operations were lifted, although some operators had been largely unaffected, and a period of considerable expansion took place. This provided good business for the coachbuilding industry, which manufactured bodies for new chassis, and also for reconditioned ex-war Department chassis. Many of these were purchased by ex-servicemen who had learned to drive and maintain motor vehicles in the armed forces, and using their gratuities, now wished to commence their own businesses as local carriers of both goods and passengers.

For some reason, perhaps nothing more substantial than coincidence, Wigan – which was already an important railway wagon building location – was to become quite a centre for the supply of bus bodywork. Santus had started trading in 1906 as wheelwrights and turned to coachbuilding around the beginning of the First World War. Their last buses and coaches were built in 1953 and the Company is one of many which is now almost forgotten. Wigan Motor Bodies Ltd was established in 1916 at the Old Haigh Foundry site but went out of business after only a couple of years. The Haigh Foundry was initially opened in 1810 for manufacturing engines and pumping equipment for the mining industry and later became involved in the building of locomotives. In 1919/20 both Massey Bros and Northern Counties Motor & Engineering Co. commenced their operations in the vehicle bodybuilding industry following the end of The Great War.

Map taken from a 1955 Ordnance Survey plan of the Pemberton area showing buildings owned by Massey Brothers and departmental usage for each phase of their coachbuilding production:-

A	Finishing shop (known as 'Stalag')
B	Paintshop
C	Upstairs – Trimming, seats and flooring
C	Downstairs – Wood Machining
D1	Lower deck bodybuilding shop
D2	Top deck bodybuilding shop (known as 'Winter Gardens')
D3	Stores

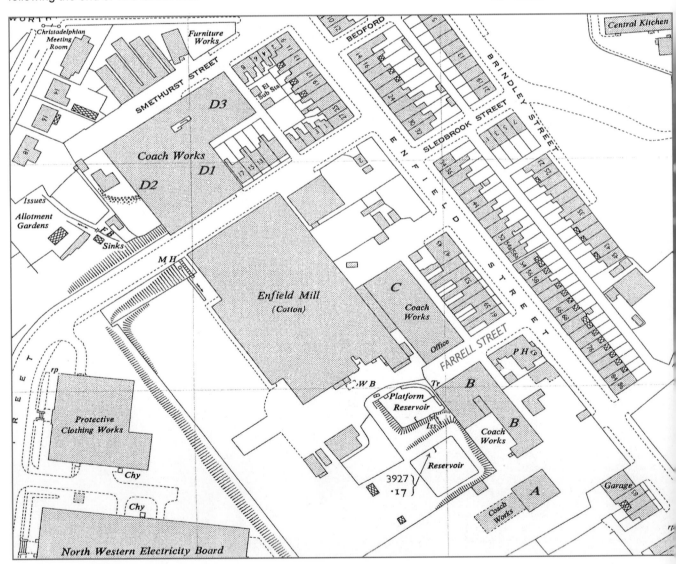

George Danson, seen bare-headed and with a confident smile, outside the Barton & Danson works in 1925, the date that this Leyland C7 model was bodied by the company and delivered to Royal Blue Line of Great Eccleston. (ELCB)

Early in 1920 Massey Bros bought the Wigan Corporation tramcar repair depot in Enfield Street (originally home to horse, steam and then electric tramcars) together with some adjoining land from Lord Ellesmere for £3,000. This was to be Massey Bros base until their demise in 1967. Their registered office was actually in Farrell Street, off Enfield Street, until it was finally registered as being in Enfield Street, after rebuilding work on the site.

Massey Bros advertised in all the local newspapers from the beginning of 1920, and became agents for Tilling-Stevens petrol-electric vehicles, the American Columbia six-cylinder cars and Ford motor cars and landaulettes (see adverts on pages 19, 21 and 25). They were also advertising nationally in the *Commercial Motor* for 1s 6d (7.5 pence) per week and *The Motor Trader*.

Passenger vehicle bodies built by Massey Bros at this time were almost always small normal-control buses and charabancs, but many other types of vehicle were built, adapted, repaired and rebodied. Bodies for such vehicles as light lorries, furniture vans, saloon cars, sports cars, taxis and even hearses were built and a selection can be seen on page 13.

During this early period, Massey Bros employed two particularly notable people, Harry Barton and Bill Danson, who, after a disagreement with the Massey brothers, left to start their own coachbuilding business trading as Barton & Danson which was based in Orrell, a mile west of Pemberton. Harry Barton was also a director of the bus operating side of Cadmans Services, also based in Orrell, which started in May, 1930. Their services operated west of Wigan and they stopped trading in August, 1935 when the business was sold mainly to Ribble Motor Services and partially to Wigan Corporation. It was stated (by his nephew) that Harry Barton returned to Massey Bros sometime during the early 1930s probably after the cessation of Barton & Danson at the end of 1931. Bill Danson's son George was also employed by Massey Bros as an apprentice draughtsman and it is believed that he also spent a short time at Barton & Danson. He would later leave to start the reconstituted East Lancashire Coachbuilders in Blackburn, as detailed later.

Building and maintenance activities continued with the building of a screening plant for Wigan Corporation and the construction of more cinemas, this time

Isaac Massey, right, photographed whilst officiating at the Induction of Rev'd Parker Johnson at St Matthews Highfield in 1937.

a few miles away in Tyldesley and in Atherton which was the home of Lancashire United Transport, the principal passenger transport operator in the area since 1905, later developing into Britain's largest independent bus operator. More houses were built, along with schools and industrial premises, and further maintenance contracts were secured for many of the mills in the Wigan environs, including the large Eckersleys Mill and Clifton Mill. Some semi-detached houses were built off Enfield Street in the late 'thirties. During this period Isaac Massey designed and built his own detached house named Somerville on Billinge Road not far from the Pemberton works. He also built Plane Cottage a little further along Billinge Road for his daughter Clara.

Much property repair work was carried out during and after the Second World War because of extensive bombing, notably in Liverpool. After the Second World War, Isaac Massey employed a certain Mrs Louisa Merrifield in the position of housekeeper but she was sacked after only a short time. A few years later in 1953, Mrs Merrifield was convicted of a murder in the Blackpool area and duly hanged.

During the 1940s contracts were won, initially from the colliery companies and after 1948 from the National Coal Board, for work in Rochdale and Wigan and also for work at the Beech Hill Royal Ordnance Factory plus many smaller companies; more houses were also built. A special lift shaft was built at Eckersley's Mill in 1958 and three churches were built for The Church of the Latter Day Saints.

In 1962 new houses were built in Chiswell Street, Conway Street and Linden Street, all in Pemberton. At the end of 1962 all such building activity ceased and thereafter Massey Bros concentrated solely on bus-bodying.

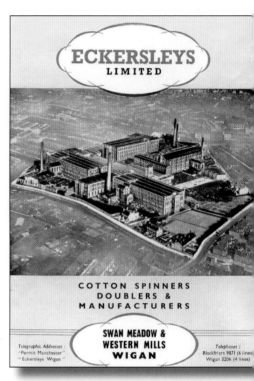

ECKERSLEYS
LIMITED

COTTON SPINNERS
DOUBLERS &
MANUFACTURERS

Telegraphic Addresses :
"Permit Manchester"
"Eckersleys Wigan"

SWAN MEADOW &
WESTERN MILLS
WIGAN

Telephones :
Blackfriars 9871 (6 lines)
Wigan 3206 (4 lines)

The cotton mills were enormous, employing thousands and the contracts to maintain them must have been both lucrative and welcome, providing a steady income until the slump in the cotton trade put many of them out of business.

This dual-door single-decker was an early example of Massey bus bodybuilding on wartime reconditioned chassis, the rear artillery wheels giving the game away. Note the long rear overhang, typical of buses at that time using a fairly short wheelbase chassis. Other operators, including Barton Transport and Liverpool Corporation, were noteworthy for operating buses with a considerably longer overhang – road holding and ride quality must have been considered dubious at best.

The images shown here were taken from engraving blocks found in a skip by the foreman-trimmer, Brian Stopforth, outside the Massey works at the time of the takeover by NCME. Sadly, Brian died in 2004 and his son Ian invited the Author to inspect the blocks together with some old photographs which we are pleased to reproduce.

All of the vehicles shown were built for local operators except for the small bus shown third down on the left which was a Ford, registered in 1920 in South Shields for non-psv use. This miscellany typifies the variety of bodies produced by Massey Brothers in the early 1920s.

CHAPTER 2
Coachbuilding and the 'Twenties

In the early 'twenties many charabancs and small buses were built for the growing number of local operators, together with major customers such as Wigan Corporation and Cumberland Motor Services Ltd. As far as is known the connection between Cumberland Motor Services and Massey Bros started after the Meageens, who were the majority shareholders of CMS, and the Massey family, had met on holiday and would spend many holidays together in and around the Lake District. It is also known that Tom Meageen, son of the founder Henry Meageen, was a regular visitor to Enfield Street until his death in 1949. There were also orders from many independent operators in the wider reaches of Lancashire and the north-west plus Yorkshire, the North Midlands, North Wales and Isle of Man.

Wigan Corporation was obviously keen to support local industry as examples of all three major local bodybuilders (Massey, Northern Counties and Santus) featured in the bus fleet almost from the outset. Massey Bros bodies were first purchased in 1920, the year after the commencement of Wigan's bus operations, and were fitted to six Tilling-Stevens petrol-electric normal-control chassis. The vehicles, numbered 4 to 9, contained seats for 32 passengers. Four of them lasted for only two years, the other two being withdrawn in 1927 and 1928.

The holding of a Ford agency ensured a steady flow of bodies of varying types, passenger and non-passenger, on that model, and other small vehicles were fitted to imported Berliet and Fiat chassis. Full-sized buses were usually found on former ex-war department subsidy chassis such as AEC or Daimler Y-types, Leyland RAF models, and, less frequently, Thornycrofts from the Basingstoke builder. When Wigan Corporation disposed of four of its Tilling-Stevens models a Thornycroft bus was one entrant to the fleet in their place.

Manufacturers were promoting their wares by the construction and demonstration of their latest models and Massey Bros. were among the many bodybuilders entrusted with this work. Strangely, perhaps, both Massey and nearby Northern Counties found themselves bodying Albion chassis for this purpose – was there a connection other than geographical location?

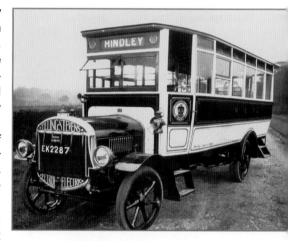

Wigan Corporation's Tilling-Stevens petrol-electric chassis were fitted with dual-doorway bodies as seen here, but had short lives as noted in the text. The half-open rear was quite common at the time being favoured by several bodybuilders. Note the high floor, requiring steps for access, due to the straight-framed chassis – a normal feature until cranked chassis were introduced later in the 1920s.

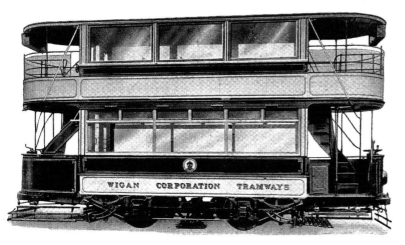

welve double-deck tramcars were ordered from
Massey Bros. by Wigan Corporation in 1920, the
rst car going into service in June 1921, though the
rder was not completed until April the following
ear. These cars were identical to the six English
lectric cars supplied in 1920 and were probably
uilt from the same drawings, or possibly sub-
ontracted from the Preston firm. They were
ithdrawn in March 1931 when Wigan abandoned
s tramway system.

The Tilling-Stevens and Thornycroft buses for Wigan have been mentioned and Massey Bros. were to continue building bodies for Wigan Corporation until 1967 when the takeover by Northern Counties occurred. Also ordered by Wigan in 1920 were twelve double-deck tramcar bodies to be built on English Electric trucks. The four-wheel, single-truck cars with electrical equipment also by English Electric, and numbered 81 to 92, were, as far as is known, the only complete tramcars ever built by Massey. The Wigan tramcar bodies were identical to an earlier batch of English Electric-bodied cars, so much so that EK Stretch who wrote several books covering tramway operations in and around this area considered that these must have been built from the same drawings. This was not an unusual situation but equally it might have been an order sub-contracted from the Preston firm to Pemberton.

A notable addition to these early customers – Cumberland Motor Services Ltd – has already been mentioned. The first bodies were supplied to this operator in 1923 and began an association which lasted until 1948, when Tilling Group policy required operators to take Bristol chassis with Eastern Coach Works bodies, thus terminating the association with both Massey and Leyland Motors Ltd. Interestingly, Cumberland had forward-ordered a large number of Leyland chassis which Tilling were obliged to take, but though some went to CMS others were dispersed in the Tilling Group.

A change of General Manager in the nearby Salford Tramways undertaking around this time was shortly to have a marked effect at Pemberton. James Scott Duncan Moffet had been Manager at Belfast from 1916-23, joining Salford after the departure of GW Holford in 1923. Mr Holford had been with Salford since 1886, Manager since 1905, and left to go into commercial activities – rumoured to be with Karrier Motors of Huddersfield.

As the 1920's progressed, heavier-weight chassis with forward-control were introduced, where the driver was situated alongside the engine instead of, as previously, behind it, thus increasing the passenger carrying capacity. Massey Bros business began to switch to this type of vehicle as fewer operators ordered normal-control chassis. This variety of chassis configurations led to a wider number of body designs being produced.

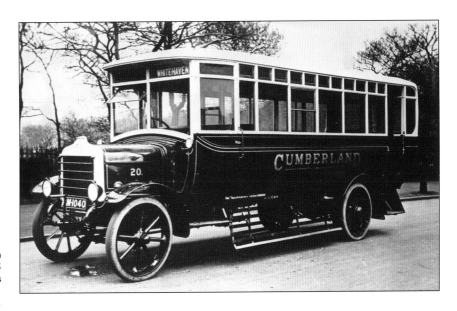

Cumberland Motor Services had a long association
with Massey Bros, commencing in 1923. This 1925
Daimler Y-type, RM 1040 and numbered 20, was
ne of a batch of six. (HSPC)

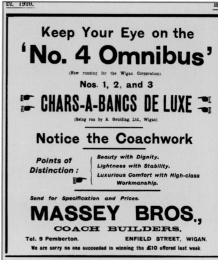

22, 1920.   11

Keep Your Eye on the
'No. 4 Omnibus'
(Now running for the Wigan Corporation).

Nos. 1, 2, and 3
CHARS-A-BANCS DE LUXE
(Being run by A. Goulding, Ltd., Wigan)

Notice the Coachwork

Points of Distinction : | Beauty with Dignity.
Lightness with Stability.
Luxurious Comfort with High-class Workmanship.

Send for Specification and Prices.

MASSEY BROS.,
COACH BUILDERS.
Tel. 9 Pemberton.   ENFIELD STREET, WIGAN.
We are sorry no one succeeded in winning the £10 offered last week.

Taken on a trip to Southport this unidentified charabanc, above left, was owned by Lancaster's of Pemberton who were related to the Massey family. Note the Massey motif on the door. Most of the charabancs in this fleet doubled as coal lorries during the week, which was frequent practice at the time.

Whilst many early photographs were taken in and around the works, local photographers used more suitable backgrounds when they were commissioned to take official views – standing outside Wigan Grammar School was a popular spot as here on the left. Cumberland Motor Service No. 5, AO 6652, was one of four ex-war department Daimler Y-types fitted with a passenger body with seats for 32 passengers in the early months of 1923.

Two examples of advertising from the early 'twenties. The display version on the right appeared in *The Motor Trader* whilst that on the left was one of a series of cards produced by the company to be given away as promotional material and highlighting local contracts. (RMC)

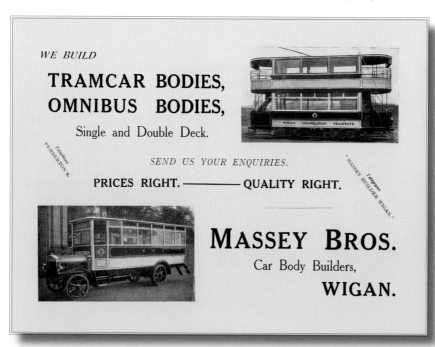

WE BUILD

TRAMCAR BODIES,
OMNIBUS BODIES,

Single and Double Deck.

SEND US YOUR ENQUIRIES.

PRICES RIGHT. ———— QUALITY RIGHT.

MASSEY BROS.
Car Body Builders,
WIGAN.

Telephone PEMBERTON 8.   *Telegrams "MASSEY BUILDER WIGAN."*

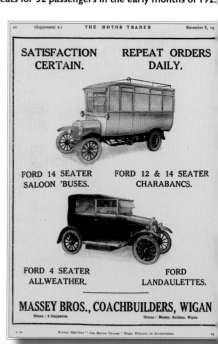

10   (Supplement x.)   THE MOTOR TRADER   November 8, 19

SATISFACTION   REPEAT ORDERS
CERTAIN.   DAILY.

FORD 14 SEATER   FORD 12 & 14 SEATER
SALOON 'BUSES.   CHARABANCS.

FORD 4 SEATER   FORD
ALLWEATHER.   LANDAULETTES.

MASSEY BROS., COACHBUILDERS, WIGAN
Phone : 9 Pemberton   'Grams : Massey, Builders, Wigan.

Facing page: One of several adverts used during the early 1920s in both the Wigan Observer and Wigan Examiner newspapers. Number 4 presumably refers to the first saloon bus, EK 2287, whilst the charabancs presumably included the example shown at the left carrying the Massey Bros. scroll and garter. The significance of the £10 prize will have to remain a mystery.

Right: This Karrier WDS, registered EH 2684, with seating for 24 passengers, was supplied in May 1921 to Cooke, Robinson & Company, one of the major independent bus operators in the Potteries, and based in the town of Hanley. They were later taken over by BET's Potteries Motor Traction company.

Note the solid-tyres, artillery wheels at the rear, the dual-doorway bodywork with both acetylene side and electric head lamps and the steps giving access to the saloon on this typical high floor chassis of the period. The coachbuilder's transfer will be seen below the fleet number 4.

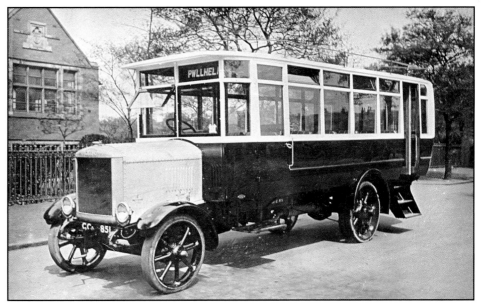

Another Karrier, this time a K3 model delivered to The Tocia Motor Omnibus Company Ltd in December 1921. Tocia were based in Pwllheli on the Lleyn Peninsula, North Wales, and were eventually taken over by Crosville in 1934. The outward-opening door with single step was clearly not intended for normal passenger use.

A roof luggage pen is provided, and there would be steps at the rear to allow access for loading and unloading. Headlamps are in position but sidelights remain to be fitted.

Local furniture remover Richard Moorfield bought this Daimler Y-type furniture van in 1921, and it doubled as a charabanc at the weekend when the box van body was quickly and easily lifted from the chassis. This dual-usage was common practice at the time and occasionally resulted in the passenger body, charabanc or small saloon, surviving with the company as a store or small office. Of such finds have come some splendid restoration projects.

This Daimler B-type started life in London before being purchased by Royal Blue in Llandudno, North Wales, and fitted with a charabanc body a seen here in Rhyl. The robust, if somewhat rudimentary, chassis, was capable of more than seasonal summer excursion work, of course, and like many others purchased in the early post-war years was soon rebuilt as a saloon bus. This example was rebodied with a Massey 32-seat body a seen below in May 1922 for new owners Brookes Brothers based in Rhyl. Trading as White Rose Motors the firm grew to an impressive size and became a considerable thorn in the side of the Crosville Motor Company until the takeover after the LMSR investment in Crosville. The company had considerable charisma and one of its mid-'twenties Leyland-bodied Leyland SG-types has been lovingly restored by Mike Sutcliffe, the Leyland specialist, ensuring this splendid livery and much-loved operator will not be forgotten. (STA upper)

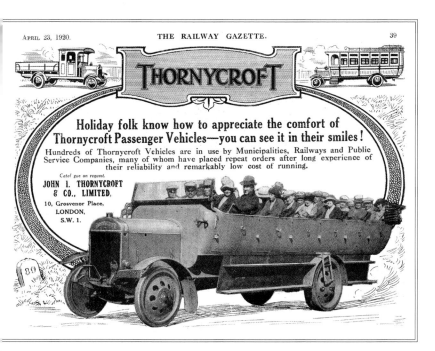

April 23, 1920. THE RAILWAY GAZETTE. 39

THORNYCROFT

Holiday folk know how to appreciate the comfort of Thornycroft Passenger Vehicles—you can see it in their smiles!

Hundreds of Thornycroft Vehicles are in use by Municipalities, Railways and Public Service Companies, many of whom have placed repeat orders after long experience of their reliability and remarkably low cost of running.

Catalogue on request.

JOHN I. THORNYCROFT & CO., LIMITED.
10, Grosvenor Place,
LONDON,
S.W. 1.

Thornycroft vehicles would appear in the Wigan bus fleet in 1924, as seen on page 21. Note the primitive metal passenger step over the rear wheel. (STA)

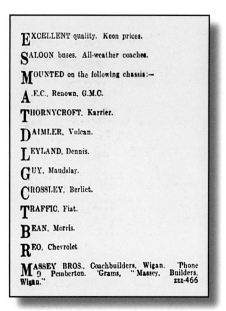

EXCELLENT quality. Keen prices.

SALOON buses. All-weather coaches.

MOUNTED on the following chassis:—

A.E.C., Renown, G.M.C.

THORNYCROFT, Karrier.

DAIMLER, Vulcan.

LEYLAND, Dennis.

GUY, Maudslay.

CROSSLEY, Berliet.

TRAFFIC, Fiat.

BEAN, Morris.

REO, Chevrolet

MASSEY BROS., Coachbuilders, Wigan. 'Phone 9 Pemberton. 'Grams, "Massey, Builders. Wigan." zzz-466

A typical example of advertising from *Commercial Motor*. (STA)

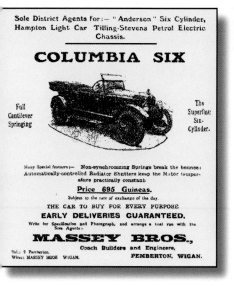

Sole District Agents for:— "Anderson" Six Cylinder, Hampton Light Car Tilling-Stevens Petrol Electric Chassis.

COLUMBIA SIX

Full Cantilever Springing

The Superfine Six-Cylinder.

Many Special features:— Non-synchronizing Springs break the bounce: Automatically-controlled Radiator Shutters keep the Motor temperature practically constant.

Price 695 Guineas.

Subject to the rate of exchange of the day.

THE CAR TO BUY FOR EVERY PURPOSE

EARLY DELIVERIES GUARANTEED.

Write for Specification and Photograph, and arrange a trial run with the Sole Agents:

MASSEY BROS.,

Coach Builders and Engineers,

Tel.: 9 Pemberton.
Wires: MASSEY BROS WIGAN.
PEMBERTON, WIGAN.

There was a demand for American motor cars after the end of the First World War and Massey responded by taking an agency for Columbia, bodying them as required by their clients. Nearby, Northern Counties were bodying Moon cars, also from America. (STA)

Above right: An Albion PE24 demonstrator with 20-seat body completed by Masseys in August 1923 and believed to have been exhibited at the London Olympia show. It was later sold to J Huie of Campbelltown. It was photographed in the works yard and the distinctive office block in the background lasted until the major redevelopment after Northern Counties had gone into receivership.

Number 1 in the St Helens & District Motor Service Co Ltd fleet was this Daimler B, newly rebodied in 1922 with this attractive 26-seat body. It had previously operated as a PSV for County Carriers, also from St Helens, from 1914. St Helens & District was taken over by the Corporation in 1927.

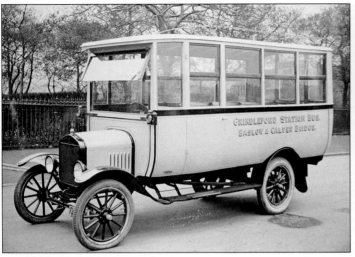

Top left: Maurice Kenyon bought this neat 14-seat Ford Model TT in 1922 for his connection service from Grindleford Station to Baslow via Calver Bridge in the Peak District. The service, when taken over by Hulley's of Baslow in 1939, had been in operation for over 40 years.

Centre left: An early 1923 pre-delivery shot of a Fiat with 14-seat bus body, registered WY 6897, for Barrett & Thornton of Otley, in the West Riding of Yorkshire. Note that the opening door is in the second bay on this vehicle and the one above.

Top right: Another view taken outside Wigan Grammar School is this Guy model A (NT 2033) for the fleet of Davies of Worthen in Shropshire. This neat 20-seater was supplied in November 1922 for the 20 mile Chirbury to Shrewsbury service.

Centre right: H Brook & Co. of Stranraer operated three Berliet's similar to the above; this one with Massey bodywork was registered OS 1358 and dates from 1925. Harry Brook had first operated a bus service in Morpeth before moving across the border to Galashiels where he started a partnership operating as Brook & Amos. In 1924 Harry moved on to Stranraer and established the business of H Brook & Company which ran under the name 'The Pilot' (visible on the vehicle behind) in the south west of Scotland and in some operations in Northern Ireland.

'The Pye bus that never was'. Masseys completed the body of this Berliet at the time of the takeover of John Pye (Heswall) by Crosville in 1924. Intended to be No. 21 in the Pye fleet it was not required by Crosville, and was then registered in Wigan as EK 3622 and sold through an agent to Blue Bus Service of Bridlington. It was photographed outside Wigan Grammar School as were many of the vehicles of this period.

After its experience with the Tilling-Stevens TS3 models Wigan Corporation turned to Basingstoke builder Thornycroft for their replacements, with two BT models being purchased, one bodied by Massey in 1924 and the other, numbered 3, in the following year. This vehicle, built on a Thornycroft BT chassis, was the second bus to receive fleet number 1 in the space of only 5 years, the earlier number 1 having been a locally-built Pagefield model.

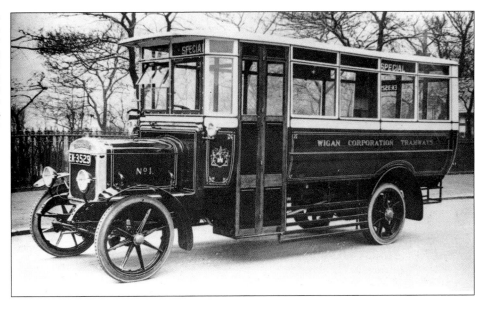

BODIES.

FORD OWNERS, AGENTS AND IN-TENDING PURCHASERS.—WE supply Ford 12 and 16 seater Bodies, also ALL WEATHER char-a-bancs Bodies, to seat 10 persons.—Send for particulars to the specialists, Massey Bros., Coach-builders, Wigan. (xx)

STA)

Cumberland No. 67, RM 2049, was an AEC 411 with seating for 29 passengers delivered in November 1925. It was later traded in to the dealership arm of Leyland Motors and then sold by them to Miller of Edinburgh. Note that although the radiator and bonnet line have dropped appreciably the body design has not taken advantage of this. (CMS)

By 1924 the growth of the various business activities became such that it was decided to create a limited company to handle the building and maintenance aspects (Massey Brothers Ltd – Company Number 197363) whilst the coachbuilding continued as a partnership (Massey Bros) and as the administration side of the business needed to keep pace, a Mr George Chapman was employed as shorthand typist and clerk and the employees of both organisations reported to the same office. In later years Mr Chapman was promoted to Company Secretary, a role he would retain until his retirement in the mid-'sixties. Also during this early period Mr Alfred M Alcock joined Massey Bros as works foreman/designer and also acted as part-time salesman. He had previously worked for Northern Counties in Wigan Lane.

In addition to supplying the small independent operators the Pemberton factory was also now supplying the needs of the companies which would grow to become major and well-respected names in the industry. One such was Westmorland Motor Services Ltd, formed in 1925 by the Meageen family of Cumberland Motor Services Ltd – the family also having business interests in the Isle of Man – and the first new buses purchased for this venture were three AEC Renowns with Massey single-deck bodies. The chassis was the first AEC model to have a name beginning with R, but this first use of the name 'Renown' is not to be confused with the later and much better-known examples featuring three axles. The 411 Renown broke new ground among forward–control AEC models in having pneumatic tyres as standard from new.

The family connection between this vehicle and its cousin alongside are clearly apparent – same chassis, same body design, same livery, same lettering style – and, of course, the same family ownership. (CMS)

Lambsfield Motors Ltd of Lancaster became part of Lancashire and Westmorland, seen on the previous page, and operated this Leyland G6 with Massey 32-seat body which was new in June 1924. It is believed that it became No. 384 in the Ribble fleet when it passed into that company's stock after Ribble took over L&M in 1927. The high bonnet line and even higher radiator top tank severely restricted the body designer's scope but clever use of livery could mollify the effect as demonstrated by the Hebble vehicle on page 24.

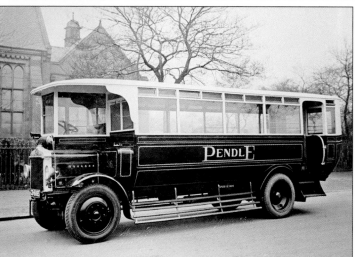

Since 1974 the name 'Pendle' has been associated with the Burnley and Pendle undertaking previously known as Burnley, Colne and Nelson though, of course, it actually refers to Pendle Hill with its legendary Lancashire Witches. In early 1926, when this vehicle was delivered, Pendle Motor Services was the trading name of Lancashire Industrial Motors of Blackburn who were taken over by Ribble later that year. This vehicle was one of six supplied on AEC 413 chassis and became Ribble No. 214. Note the more curvaceous rear and the prominent canopy supports, reminiscent of tramcar practice – such brackets would often be formed from decorative wrought iron scrollwork.

Decorated for a local carnival is Cumberland No. 57, RM 306, a Massey-bodied Daimler Y-type dating from 1924. It is shown in Central Square, Workington. (HSPC)

The next development in bus design came in the mid-'twenties when passenger carrying chassis were finally separated from goods models and the chassis frames were cranked to lower them over the rear axle, giving a lower floor line. Arguably, the most famous passenger vehicles of this period were from the Leyland L-range: Lion, Lioness, Leveret and Leviathan. The PLSC Lion quickly established itself as a simple and reliable vehicle and large numbers were produced, with the later longer model PLSC3 becoming an industry favourite.

Doug Jack, in his book *The Leyland Bus,* records that Leyland Motors bodied some 50% of all Lions built, and this gives a pointer to what was happening elsewhere. Operators wanting the Leyland body had four choices – join the wait for the Lancashire built product; purchase a lookalike built to Leyland patterns; purchase a genuine approved alternative via Leyland from one of its sub-contractors – or go elsewhere for something different. This situation would recur when the even-more popular T-range was introduced at the 1927 Commercial Motor Show as we shall see. Bodybuilders producing Leyland-look a likes, or sub-contracting included Massey, Ransomes, Short Brothers, Vickers and Chas Roberts among others, Vickers factory at Crayford in Kent was geared up for the mass-production of machined frames, in addition to building complete bodies as a Leyland sub-contractor.

Bodies on the PLSC chassis were supplied to British Automobile Traction Co subsidiaries Cumberland Motor Services and the-then Cumberland-controlled operator on the Isle of Man, Manxland Bus Services Ltd, which also received bodies on ADC Chassis that had been ordered originally for the Cumberland concern. Massey bodies on the Leyland Lion chassis supplied to Cumberland in 1927 were built to the standard Leyland design; however, Massey Bros own

Two views showing Salford trams before and after rebuilding by Massey at the corporation's Frederick Road workshops. The design is directly based on the Moffet trams for Belfast, where JSD Moffet had been Manager from 1916-23, joining Salford after the departure of GW Holford in 1923.

At this time Salford operated a fleet of 225 trams of which 96 were small open-top single-truck cars, many dating back to the beginning of electric operation in 1901/2, as seen by No. 25 below.

Moffet persuaded the Tramway Committee to allow him to completely rebuild 55 of the earliest cars by removing the top deck fittings, platform bearers and staircases, and fitting the remaining lower-deck 'cabin' with conventional rear-ascending staircases, enclosed platforms and enclosed top-covers as shown in the lower view. The work was carried out by Massey's employees at Salford's main Frederick Road depot between 1926 and 1928, leading to a design very similar to trams Mr Moffet had operated in Belfast.

The last of the reconstructed Salford trams remained in service until 1939, a testament to the soundness of the new bodies and confirming the wisdom – and financial value – of the exercise. (STA both)

design, although similar to that of Leyland, did possess its own character, the most noticeable difference being a slightly sloping rather than a vertical windscreen, and a fully-rounded rear dome, thus producing a rather more modern appearance. Later Massey bodies as fitted to Leyland Tiger chassis also had similarity to the contemporary Leyland design, and in addition to being fitted to new chassis this basic design was used in 1932 to rebody a batch of 1926 Leyland Lions – once again for Cumberland Motor Services.

Despite all this activity at Pemberton in connection with buses large and small, high and not-so-high, there was other work going through the factory. When Mr Moffet (mentioned in the caption above) arrived in Salford he found a fleet of 225 trams of which 96 were small open-top single-truck cars, many built by GF Milnes and dating back to the beginning of electric operation in 1901/2. At the time Manchester were rebuilding large numbers of small trams in their own car works, converting them into fully enclosed bogie trams. Moffet may then have been made aware of Wigan's top-covered four-wheelers fitted with top covers manufactured by Massey Bros.

He persuaded his Committee to allow him to completely rebuild 55 cars by fitting the lower-deck 'cabins' with conventional rear-ascending staircases, enclosed platforms and enclosed top-covers as illustrated. The contract was placed in 1926 and the work was carried out by Massey's employees at Salford's main Frederick Road depot between 1926 and 1928 producing a design very similar to

trams Moffet had operated in Belfast. The price was £630 per car including £50 for contingencies. It is believed that there was a family connection in middle management between the two concerns, explaining this otherwise unusual contract.

As this work continued into 1927, Massey Bros received another order from Salford Corporation, for single-deck bodies on twelve Karrier three-axle chassis. Though almost all subsequent deliveries were on Leyland double and single-deck chassis this was the first of several orders for bus bodies from this operator in the pre-World War Two period and may be significant in view of the suggestion that Mr Holford had moved to Karrier Motors from Salford in 1923. A Massey advertisement of 1934 featuring a bus body built for Salford Corporation also included the statement, 'Salford use Massey tramcar bodies' and, comparing the original Victorian tramcars with the then-modern conversions, Massey no doubt felt fully justified in making that statement.

James Moffet died in harness in 1933 but Massey continued to supply bus bodies to the undertaking until 1937 when Salford changed its policy to purchasing only metal-framed bodies, and Massey's connection then ceased.

The twelve Massey-bodied Karrier WL6's supplied in 1927 were numbered 25-36 and similar in appearance to two Hall, Lewis models supplied a few months earlier. Note the title of the undertaking painted on the lower side panel is 'SALFORD CITY TRAMWAYS'. The very prominent frontal protuberance is the arrangement for the Gruss air springing, popular for a while in the late 'twenties and 'thirties. The glazed front door used as the passenger exit was an attempt at passenger flow.

Karrier chassis were known for their prodigious consumption of lubricating oil, but after an unrelated accident in Wallasey where a prop shaft snapped and came through the floor, causing a fatality in the saloon, many operators withdrew them prematurely.

One of these monsters survives in preservation, having been completely rebuilt by Karrier expert Geoff Lumb, and carries a clerestory-roofed English Electric body from the Ashton under Lyne fleet. The opportunity to see, and hopefully ride, in that vehicle, will really be something special. (STA)

A Tilling-Stevens demonstrator built in 1926 and believed to be of type B9A. Massey had bodied eleven Tilling-Stevens by then, this became the twelfth.

This is one of a number of 26-seater coaches which Garlick, Burrell and Edwards, Ltd., have supplied to R. Barr (Leeds) Ltd. The body, which is equipped with a removable top cover, is by Massey Brothers, Wigan, and is mounted on a Tilling-Stevens "Express" chassis.

How to Make Motor Transport Pay.

Buy a TILLING STEVEN'S PETROL ELECTRIC.

The Finest Investment You Can Make.

SPECIAL FEATURES :-
Economy in Petrol. Quick and Smooth Acceleration. Silent Running. No Gears to Change or Clutch to Operate.

May we send you Full Details. A Demonstration with Pleasure.

AUTHORISED AGENTS :-

MASSEY BROS.,
Coachbuilders, Pemberton, Wigan.

Tel. 9 Pemberton. Wires: Massey, Wigan.

pposite: Hebble No. 14, (CP 4897), was an Albion K26 with 26-seat body photographed in July 1926 nd shows that some operators were still happy o stay with the normal control body useful for ne-man-operation with the driver in the saloon mongst the passengers. Note the folding door nd the very high entrance – perhaps there was a lding step which is not visible. The makers badge visible, however, adjacent to the doorway at the oot of the side panel. By 1929 Massey had bodied 5 Albions for this operator.

The Proof of a Good Job is the Regular Sale it Commands.

The Tilling Steven's Petrol Electric Chassis

Has been chosen on its merits by the

Aberdeen Suburban Tramways.
Birmingham Corporation.
Bradford Corporation.
Bournemouth Corporation.
Caerphilly Urban District Council.
Capetown Electric Tramways.
Chesterfield Corporation.
Douglas Corporation.
Durban Municipality.
Johannesburg Corporation.
Leeds City Tramways.
Liverpool Corporation Tramways.
Londonderry Corporation.
Morecambe Corporation.
Newcastle Corporation.
Oldham Corporation Tramways.
Pietermaritzburg Municipal Tramways.
Pretoria Municipality.
Sheffield Corporation.
Walsall Corporation.
Warrington Corporation
Wigan Corporation.
Wellington, N.Z.
West Bromwich Town Council
Widnes Corporation.
Wolverhampton Corporation Tramways.
Allen Omnibus Co., London.
Anlaby Motor Omnibus Co., Hull.

Birmingham and Midland Motor Omnibus Co., Ltd.
Brighton, Hove, and Preston Omnibus Co., Brighton.
Eastern Counties Road Car Co., Ltd., Ipswich.
East India Tramways, London.
East Kent Road Car Co., Ltd., Canterbury.
Greenock and Port Glasgow Tramway Co., Greenock.
Isle of Thanet Electric Trams and Lighting Co., Ltd.
Lisbon Electric Tramways Co.
Loughborough Road Car Co., Loughboro.
Maidstone and District Motor Services, Ltd.
Mansfield and District Tramways, Notts.
Potteries Electric Traction Co., Stoke-on-Trent.
Pickfords, Ltd., Brixton, S.W.
Penryn and Falmough Motor Co., Cornwall.
Scottish General Omnibus Co., Larbert.
Standerwick, Blackpool.
Southdown Motor Services, Ltd.
Thomas Tilling, Ltd., Peckham.
Trent Motor Traction Co., Ltd., Westminster, S. W.

If it's good for them, it's good for you.

Send for particulars to Sole District Agents,

MASSEY BROS., WIGAN.

Tel. 9, Pemberton. 'Grams, Massey, Wigan.

In the late 1920s, there was increasing demand for double-deckers and Massey Bros made tentative moves into that market. Meageen influence continued when Cumberland Motor Services purchased a Guy FCX three-axle chassis in 1927 which was fitted with a Massey lowbridge body. This body was unusual in that it incorporated two sunken gangways, one at each side of the upper-saloon, this arrangement being necessary at that time to avoid infringement of the patent of the Leyland design with sunken offside gangway as fitted to the lowbridge Titan. It was Cumberland's first new double-decker and gained a reputation of 'not being very good at climbing hills', which must have been something of a handicap in a place like Whitehaven. When, many years later this point was put to Algie Corlett, a retired Cumberland Works Superintendent, his reply was, "It was good for nowt". His remarks obviously referred to the chassis, rather than the body, as many more Massey bodies were purchased but no more Guy FCX chassis, apart from three second-hand from Morecambe and Heysham Corporation for a works service during the war, which had very short lives with the company.

Cumberland Motor Services No. 74 was built in 1927 with a lowbridge body and delivered with seating for 56 passengers, being modified to 52 before entering service. The upper-deck seating arrangement was single back-to-back bucket seats along the centre, leaving two aisles, one on either side as can be seen in the ceiling in the lower photograph whilst the builder's transfer can be seen above the rear window. The vehicle was withdrawn in December 1933.

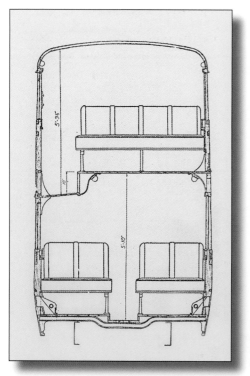

Left: The patented Leyland Motors side gangway layout, designed by GJ Rackham, which reduced the height of the lowbridge Titan TD1 to 12ft 10in and revolutionised the double-decker market. Competitors were obliged to use alternative layouts, as above with Cumberland's Guy or, later, pay Leyland a royalty for use of the design. (STA)

ooking decidedly old-
shioned in 1929 when
ompared to the Leyland
itan of two years earlier
 this Tilling-Stevens type
S17A supplied to Widnes
orporation and given
eet No. 25 (TE 9052). The
assey transfer can be
early seen on the panel
ext to the front wheel,
 practice used by them
ntil 1967. Extending the
pper-deck forward of
e bulkhead behind the
river was another of the
itan's attributes.

The long majestic bonnet clearly identifies this as a Leyland Lioness, and this LC1 model was purchased new by Workington Motors Services in 1927, being numbered 55, (RM 3872), in their fleet. It passed to Cumberland Motor Services in 1932. It has sometimes (wrongly, of course) been thought to e a vehicle from the fleet of Brookes Brothers White Rose Motors of Rhyl because of the motif on one of the doors. This vehicle is one of Leyland's range which included the PLSC Lion and the Leviathan, the latter having many similarities to Massey's double-decker design as seen above.

Massey Bros. had bodied only a handful of Dennis chassis – around ten in eight years – when, in 1929, the Guildford manufacturer commissioned a double-deck body on an HS chassis for demonstration purposes. This was the prototype for the HV series and went on hire to Sunderland Corporation who bought it in June 1930. Sunderland purchased three Dennis HVs later the same year. The demonstrator was withdrawn in 1935 and converted to a tower wagon. The body style is very similar to that fitted to the Widnes TSM 17A around this period, and the Guy FCX in 1927, and only the third double-decker body (apart from the Wigan trams) built by Massey up to this time. It was the fourth demonstrator built, but the first for Dennis.

Manxland Motor Services Limited was, in 1927, placed under the control of Cumberland Motor Services Limited whose influence was soon to be seen in choice of vehicles. This Massey-bodied Leyland Lion No. 26 (MN 5106) was one of two dating from 1927 and diverted from a Cumberland order. Sister vehicle No. 27 was used as a tree lopper by Isle of Man Road Services, after withdrawal in 1951 until 1967, giving 40 years of service. (HSPC)

Below: Cumberland No. 65 was one of two Leyland Lion PLSC3 models bodied by Massey and is pictured here with Mr J Clements and his son outside Arlecdon outstation. Mr Clements built the garage and operated his own bus service before selling out to Cumberland with whom he became a driver. After takeover Cumberland rented the garage from Mr Clements. (HSPC)

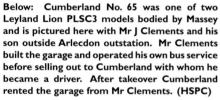

eyland **PLSC Lion** number 31 was pictured in
he twilight of its long life which began in 1928
ith Manxland. It was transferred to the Isle of
lan Railway Co in 1929, thence to the Isle of Man
oad Services in 1930. It was spotted in Douglas
1951 being closely followed by a 1947 Leyland
itan **PD1A** with Leyland bodywork. Still looking
ood after 23 year's service it was withdrawn a
hort time after this photograph was taken and
as eventually scrapped in 1954. (ABC)

bove right: Cumberland's number 31 was a
eyland **Tiger TS2** with Massey body, supplied in
929. It was rebodied in 1939 with a luxury coach
ody by Massey and fitted with a Cov-Rad radiator
onversion at the same time. Photographs after
he conversion can be found on page 53.

ight: Number 113 was one of a further four
eyland **Tiger TS2** models supplied to Cumberland
ith Massey bodywork as shown in 1930. All were
ebodied by Myers and Bowman in 1938, and Cov-
tad radiator conversions were fitted at the same
ime.

In February 1929, the works foreman/designer Alfred Alcock, seemingly in a freelance capacity, entered into an agreement with the Leeds-based bodybuilder Charles H Roe. This agreement allowed Roe, under licence, to build double-deck bus bodies with both a rear staircase and entrance for access to the upper-deck, and a front staircase and door for means of exit from the upper-deck. The agreement licensed Roe to construct and sell bodies of this type to the Mexborough & Swinton Traction Company (though in fact none were supplied) and 13 municipal undertakings, and also stated that Massey Bros were excluded from supplying these 14 customers.

However, later in 1929, Massey Bros announced their own design for a two-stairway double-decker which was detailed in the September 1929 issue of the *Motor Transport* magazine. Massey produced a body for Merseyside on a Tilling-Stevens TS15A petrol-electric double-decker to this specification, as shown. It cannot be a coincidence that Alfred Alcock's unusual design, with its nearside forward-ascending staircase, mimicked the very Salford trams which Massey had just finished converting from reversed-stair layout to conventional rear-ascending. The unusual design was featured in the trade press, as shown, This vehicle was one of only two of this chassis type to be built. Wolverhampton Corporation ordered the other one with a Dodson 66-seat rear-entrance highbridge body which was then featured in the 1929 Commercial Motor Show before entering service. Three months later, in the same magazine, details were shown of a 'clever dual-purpose' single-deck design from the drawing boards of Massey Bros

The Merseyside Touring Company was a regular customer (through its Liverpool based agent Garlick, Burrell & Edwards) from 1928 until 1930 when it was taken over by Ribble Motor Services Ltd.

Merseyside also had bodies on Bristol and Tilling-Stevens chassis which seemed very like those of the Burlingham design of the time, perhaps another case of using other makers' drawings. Other notable clients during the late 'twenties were Hebble Motor Services, and Holt Brothers of Rochdale (better known as Yelloway). Although Ribble Motor Services only ever ordered two new bodies from Massey Bros (in 1928 on PLSC Lions) they were acquiring local operators in the counties of Lancashire, Cumberland and Westmorland, many of which had vehicles with Massey bodywork.

SINGLE AND DOUBLE DECK
OMNIBUS BODIES
ARE OUR SPECIALITY.

Write for particulars, stating your exact requirements.

MASSEY BROS.,
CAR BODY BUILDERS,
WIGAN.

(STA)

This Tilling-Stevens double-decker, supplied to the Merseyside Touring Co in December 1929, was the subject of a full page article in September 1929 *Motor Transport*, as reproduced opposite. The small illustration of the Salford tram is a reminder that the staircase layout, whilst unusual on a bus, was commonplace on contemporary tramcars. In fact Massey Bros. had 110 sets of these staircases on their hands from the Salford contract to rebuild the 1901 cars, and it surely cannot be just coincidence that Alcock chose this layout for his tour-de-force.

Just how little the intrepid tram driver could see on his nearside is amply demonstrated here. By leaning well forward he could, just, see round. To assist him further there was a set of small holes in one riser, at eye level. (STA)

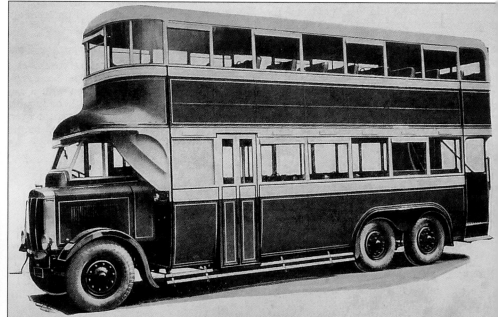

MOTOR TRANSPORT   December 2, 1929.

Service Bus
or
Long-distance
Coach

A Clever Dual-purpose
Body Design by Massey
Bros., of Wigan

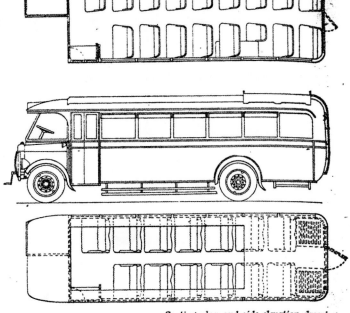

Seating plan and side elevation drawings of the Massey convertible passenger vehicle.

THE idea of constructing a body that can be used either for ordinary service bus work or, with a few alterations, for long-distance coach jobs, is not new, but in the latest dual-purpose body designed by Massey Bros., of Wigan, certain difficulties that have been met with in the past are largely overcome. For the past two years the firm has been experimenting with various types of bodies in order to arrive at a design that would allow the complete change-over to be easily made in five hours and would afford maximum comfort when the body was accommodating long-distance passengers. In connection with this latter provision it was considered necessary to incorporate a simple foolproof sunshine hood.

The body has been built on a forward-control type Tilling - Stevens B.10A chassis, and its external appearance is quite normal. It was made to the order of the Merseyside Touring Co., Ltd., of Liverpool, who operate on both service and long-distance routes. As a service bus the body provides seats for 32 passengers all facing forward. The seats are of blue leather with spring squabs and rolls, and, in place of the usual two seats (facing each other) over the wheel arches, there is a single seat facing forward over each arch; the arches themselves are covered with a mahogany tray. Except for those over the wheel arches the windows are of the adjustable type. Luggage nets are provided under the side domes extending the full length of the body. The nets of blue mesh are suspended from a blue Doverite-covered rail carried on the usual brackets. The body is of the single front-entrance type with an emergency door at the rear. The interior finish has been carried out entirely in polished wood arranged in light panels set in dark mahogany framing. This gives a pleasing effect, and has the merit of being easily polished up to give the nice appearance for long-distance work. A clock is let into the bulkhead partition. Interior lighting is provided by ten lamps set in the side domes. The lamps are by Gabriels, of Birmingham, with rims coloured blue and white, and having opaque glass.

The Roof

Although the roof is detachable for the greater portion of its length, there is nothing to suggest this to the casual eye; the detachable portion of the roof has the usual hand rails and straps attached, while the interior of the roof is carried out in panelled oak and mahogany. Three Airvacs are used, the grilles being finished mahogany colour. Altogether, the interior appearance of the roof is very neat.

When it is intended to use the body as a long-distance coach the detachable portion of the roof can be lifted off from immediately behind the bulkhead partition as far as the second window from the rear, giving an opening in the permanent roof of 16ft. by 6ft. The remaining (undetachable) portion of the roof carries a large luggage box, access to which is gained by a rear ladder.

The hood used to replace the detachable roof is of entirely new design, and it is operated easily by means of a handle and gear box contained in the bulkhead partition. There are no chains or sprocket wheels used in the arrangement of the hood control. When the hood is in the open position it remains in the fixed rear portion of the roof under the luggage box. It is not necessary to remove the hood when the bus is being used as a service vehicle, as it is housed in such a way that it does not interfere with the general symmetry of the dome. At the moment a full description of the operating mechanism of the hood cannot be given.

Naturally, two sets of seats are provided; those for long-distance work are of the armchair type with headrests covered in red leather, and provide accommodation for 26 persons all facing forward. It is estimated that the time taken to change from one set of seats to the other is five minutes per seat. Underneath the floor covering are bolted longitudinal plates to which are welded a series of nuts spaced out to receive the bolts holding down the seat legs. This allows the seats to be taken out without any work underneath the chassis.

Commendable arrangements are made for carrying long-distance passengers' luggage. The two seats on either side of the rear emergency door (in the service bus layout) are replaced by two luggage racks giving accommodation for 26 average-size suitcases; these racks can be conveniently loaded through the emergency door. The exterior of the body is furnished in the red and white colours of the Merseyside Touring Co.

B 36

Reprinted from **MOTOR TRANSPORT** *September 2, 1929*

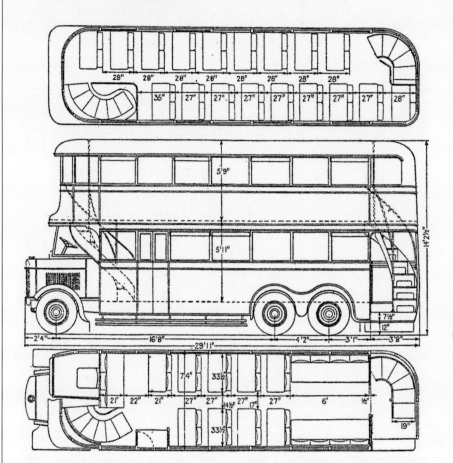

A Two-stairway Double-decker

Massey Bros. Design a Clever Sixty-four Seater on a Rigid Six-wheeled Chassis

Showing principal dimensions and general arrangement of the Merseyside Touring Co.'s six-wheel double-deck bus with two stairways.

ONE of the objections to a large capacity two-deck body on heavy traffic routes is that a great deal of time is wasted in picking up and setting down passengers when, as is usual, there is only one entrance to each deck. Two-stairway double-deckers have been designed, however, to speed up loading and unloading, the latest being one under construction by Massey Brothers, of Pemberton, Wigan, to the order of the Merseyside Touring Co. The chassis of the vehicle is a rigid six-wheeled Tilling-Stevens, and the introduction of the second stairway has not reduced the possible seating capacity to any great extent, there being, in fact, seats for 64 passengers, 29 downstairs and 35 on the top deck.

Seating and Stairways.

The lower saloon is divided into two compartments. The rear compartment is over the rear wheels, and the ten seats in it are arranged longitudinally. In order to furnish easy accessibility to the rear axles the seats are on hinged boxes. The seats in front of the rear compartment are of the orthodox type facing forward, with the exception of three seats behind the bulkhead partition which face rearwards.

The rear platform and stairway is of standard design with roomy entrance to lower saloon and stairway. The stairway is of very easy rise and has exceptionally wide treads. The top tread is turned inwards to land the passengers immediately on the centre gangway of the top saloon. The front stairway, which is intended for exit passengers only from top deck, has received careful attention. It has been built with a landing immediately above the driver on the top deck and carried downwards above the engine bonnet, and through the front bulkhead partition, on to the lower saloon floor at the front nearside and at a convenient point to the front exit door which is intended to be operated by the driver or passengers.

In the lower saloon the head-room is 5ft. 11in. and on the top 5ft. 8½in. The building out of the front stairway over the bonnet has not seriously restricted the driver's vision, and it has not in any way interfered with engine accessibility.

The top deck seats face forwards in pairs on both sides of a centre aisle.

The upper saloon is bow-fronted, there being two bent glass windows on either side of a large centre window. Flush-fitting interior operated direction indicators are built at the front and rear of the

vehicle. The driver's cab is fully floating and thin, but very strong steel support pillars for the upper part of the cab ensure that the driver's vision is not restricted.

To Save Weight.

With regard to actual constructional details all pillars are flitch plated and timbers hollowed out for lightness. Aluminium brackets are fitted to pillars and bolted through the roof sticks. The flitch plates are let into the roof sticks. The roof is of plywood, with aluminium at the front and rear. Considerable use of aluminium has been made in order to keep weight down.

The overall height unladen is 14ft. 2½in., while the weight is 2 tons 13 cwt. Ventilation has received a good deal of attention, the lower saloon having seven drop windows with louvres fitted above each. Other means of ventilation are by a side louvre of the collector type above each window, and the insides of these have been finished in a pleasing manner. The top saloon has eight drop windows and louvres, whilst the front centre light is made to lower some 6in., the top of this being fitted with a deep glass louvre vent which admits a good supply of fresh air.

Printed in Great Britain by The Cornwall Press Ltd., Paris Garden, S.E.1.

Warrington Corporation purchased two 30ft long AEC Renown chassis which were intended for London Transport. Massey Brothers supplied the 65-seat dual entrance/exit bodywork and No. 39 (ED 5880) is shown in the Warrington livery of Munich Lake (Maroon) and Citron (Yellow) at the corner of the A56, opposite the Walton Arms, in April 1930. The two vehicles remained in service until 1937, and whilst the design looks strange, even dangerous perhaps, it was no more so than the hundreds of tramcars then in use throughout the country with their equally restrictive layout as seen on page 30. Nevertheless, the front staircases were fairly soon removed, possibly following an inspection under the new 1931 Road Traffic Act. This was Massey's first order from Warrington; the operator took six Titan TD1s in 1931 but never patronised the Pemberton factory again. Had the body design been a step too far, closing the door on any future prospects? (STA)

CHAPTER 3
The double-decker predominates

We have seen in the previous chapter that double-decker production was minimal at Pemberton in the '20s. By December 1929 only four such vehicles had been produced: Guy FCX in 1927, and finally a Dennis demonstrator and the TSMs for Widnes and Merseyside Touring in 1929. Yet just a few miles away at Leyland the new Leyland Titan double-decker – launched at the 1927 Commercial Motor Show – had swept the board and Leyland's bodyshop could not keep up with demand. Various bodybuilders were appointed as sub-contractors for this new design with its distinctive 'piano-front' but where possible Leyland kept these orders away from its home territory, frightened that it might lose valuable skilled staff to its competitors when it was desperately short of such tradesmen.

Thus, it came about that the model was produced by United in East Anglia, Vickers at Crayford in Kent, Charles Roberts in Wakefield, Short Brothers in Rochester, Ransomes in Ipswich and others. Massey's first foray into bodying this chassis came in 1931 when it supplied Warrington with six bodies on TD1 chassis. The two AEC Renowns supplied to the same operator in 1929 had mimicked the piano front, but there the resemblance had ended as we have seen. The piano-fronted Leyland-designed body associated with early Titans was also built under licence by a number of other bodybuilders including Massey Bros, Northern Counties Motor & Engineering Co. and HV Burlingham to the specific requirements of certain operators, including Wigan Corporation, long after it had been discontinued by Leyland Motors and on later Titan chassis where it was clearly outdated.

Massey Bros also had their own design of body which was fitted to early Titans and other makes of chassis. Although similar in general outline to the Leyland design, the frontal treatment was different in that the vertical portion of the front upper saloon panelling was taken higher and then carried back horizontally to form a 'shelf' below the front windows.

West Bromwich, Widnes and Sunderland joined the growing number of municipalities placing orders at the end of the 'twenties. Widnes had taken the earlier box-like double-decker, actually only Massey's fourth double-deck body, where the upper-deck sat on a flat-roofed saloon and stopped short at the front bulkhead, leaving the area above the driver's cab unused. West Bromwich

West Bromwich No. 38 was one of three Dennis HVs with lowbridge bodies delivered in July 1930 with the body again following the then contemporary Leyland Titan 'piano-front' design. This was destined to be the only order from West Bromwich ever received by Massey Bros. (OS)

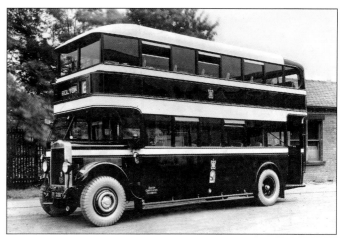

Wigan Corporation No. 74, one of ten Leyland Titan TD1s with 48-seat Massey-built lowbridge body to the Leyland design, which was delivered in 1931.

Nearby Bolton Corporation had bodies by Charles Roberts of Wakefield, better known as railway rolling stock builders, fitted to their TD1s, and No. 6 is seen by the weighbridge house at Horbury. It would take a keen eye to detect differences from a Leyland-built example. (STA)

Leigh Corporation, like Wigan, took piano-fronted bodies long after they had gone out of fashion, and fitted them to later (new) Titan TD3 chassis in 1933. Number 47 is seen in these two views on a dismal day in Leigh town centre in 1934. (STA both)

Photographed in St Margaret's Bus Station, Leicester in June 1948 was this Leyland TD1 of Brown's Blue of Markfield acquired from Warrington Corporation in December 1946. It was originally Warrington's No. 45 (ED 464) and was one of a batch of six highbridge vehicles dating from 1930/31. It was withdrawn in December 1949 and scrapped a short while later.

Birkenhead Corporation withdrew their 1932 batch of five Daimler CH6 deckers with Leyland-style lowbridge bodywork in 1939 and two were sold to Blair & Palmer of Carlisle. B & P No. 14 is seen shortly after entering service, complete with wartime headlamp masks. It lasted in service until October 1948 when it was withdrawn and scrapped.

and Sunderland each ordered three Dennis HV chassis with lowbridge and highbridge bodies respectively, but these, like the Warrington vehicles shown, were more akin to the Leyland design. Two of the bodies from the West Bromwich vehicles were later transferred to other chassis in the independent fleet of Green Bus of Rugeley, who themselves undertook the rebodying in the post-war period.

Perhaps not surprisingly Warrington did not repeat the order for the 65-seat design body fitted to its Renowns, but as mentioned took further more-conventional Massey bodies on Leyland Titan TD1 chassis in 1930 and 1931. Massey Bros provided four similarly unusual bodies for Bury Corporation in 1930, a layout on which this operator standardised at the time, (also taking Roe bodies in 1933, mounted on AEC Regent chassis similar to the Warrington Renowns in that they featured a front door with an open rear platform and were of dual-staircase configuration). As the 1930s progressed, the majority of Massey bodies ordered were double-deckers and this prevailed for the rest of the company's history.

Use of the piano-front body design was not restricted to Leyland chassis, as an AEC Regent demonstrator was fitted with a Massey version in 1931. This was to be expected as GJ Rackham, designer of the Titan, was by now working at AEC and as such also took a very keen interest in body design, piano-front designs appearing on his new Regent double-decker, being the counterpart to the Leyland Titan. The AEC demonstrator was registered in Cumberland and after a period of hire to Cumberland Motor Services was purchased by the operator, becoming No. 47 in the fleet, until 1936 when it was sold for further service with Western SMT. Birkenhead Corporation also employed this design.

The similarity of outline with the standard Leyland body design is evident in this view of Cumberland No. 47 a Massey-bodied AEC Regent dating from 1930. Originally built as a demonstrator and purchased by Cumberland in 1931, number 47 was unique in the fleet but was replaced after sale in 1936 by another Regent, also numbered 47, and one of a pair from the Southall manufacturer. Note the lower projection around the destination box; Massey's own version was much deeper.

Having successfully placed a fleet of Leyland-bodied Titans in service in 1929, consideration was being given by Wigan Tramways Committee in the following year to replace their tram system. It was not surprising that Leyland Titans were again the committee's choice. The Leyland Society, in its history *The Leyland Buses of Wigan Corporation*, records that after agreeing a repeat order for Leyland-bodied Titans, it was provisionally agreed that Leyland would supply 20 further Titan chassis for bodying by local coachbuilders, who would mount bodies to a design that would not infringe the patent rights held by Leyland. These buses were required for delivery by March 1931. Subsequently, it was agreed in a meeting attended by representatives from Massey Bros, Northern Counties and Santus, that bodies would be built to the Leyland design at a cost of £750 per body. Leyland Motors agreed to

Wigan Corporation 62-seat tram No. 90 at the Abbey Lakes terminus shortly before the abandonment of the tramway system in 1931 which brought more Leyland Titans – but now with Massey bodies – into the fleet. Massey also built the bodies on these trams which, as described in the text, were then fitted to English Electric equipment. Note the method of securing the top deck cover to the canopy bend above the conductor's head.

a special concession in the case of these vehicles which were to be built for the Corporation, by allowing the local coachbuilders to copy the 'Titan' design on payment of £1 instead of the usual charge of £50. This concession was a special one acknowledging the Corporation's wish to maximise local employment. From this point on Wigan Corporation only ever ordered Leyland chassis (apart from wartime allocations) and bodywork was always built in the county of Lancashire, and more often than not, supplied by Massey Bros or Northern Counties from Wigan. Of particular note was a batch of piano-fronted bodies as late as 1938 for Wigan Corporation shared by Northern Counties and Massey Bros and built on Leyland Titan TD5 chassis.

A break from the supply chain to municipalities had occurred in 1932 when Wirral independent, Macdonald & Co (Maxways) of Birkenhead, placed an order for six AEC Regal coaches for long distance work. These vehicles were acquired along with the Maxways business by Crosville in December 1934.

At the same time Massey Bros produced a glossy pamphlet entitled *Inspiration* which illustrated the conversion of open rear-staircases on double-deckers to the conventional enclosed type. This resulted in a contract for Birkenhead Corporation for the conversion of 15 Leyland-bodied Titan TD1s (fleet Nos. 79-93). Three years later, similar projects for Crosville Motor Services were undertaken on 13 Leyland-bodied TD1s (fleet Nos. 325-36 and 414) and for Millburn Motors of Preston who had acquired five ex-Bolton Corporation Leyland-bodied TD1s (fleet Nos. 52-6); these were promptly sold to other operators, four of which lasted into the mid-'fifties.

As detailed in the text above, Maxways ordered six AEC Regals with 32-seat rear entrance bodywork for their North Wales coastal service. Here we see BG 617 posing for the camera prior to delivery in June 1932. (STA)

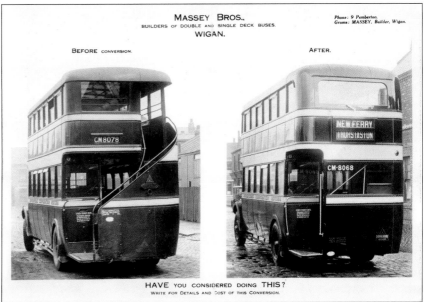

The original Leyland Titan TD1 models featured this open staircase arrangement which, within a matter of months, had been superseded by the enclosed version seen on the right. Massey Bros. had been building the enclosed version for Wigan to Leyland's design and quickly realised that there was a market for converting the earlier models – which clearly had many more years life left in them – into the by-then more commonly used enclosed version. By chance a Bolton vehicle was converted back to open staircase format when it was saved for preservation, and can be seen in the LVVS museum at Lincoln. (STA)

This Leyland Lion LT5, (DE 8942), with 31-seat Leyland-style body, complete with arched windows, entered service in July 1932 with Greens Motors Ltd of Haverfordwest and is seen parked in Tenby in the late 'thirties. Although the chassis specification had been upgraded the old-fashioned frontal arrangement with short radiator made the vehicle seem quite dated. Note the roof-mounted luggage carrier and marker light above the indicator.

By contrast, the later LT7 model looked very much more modern with the deep radiator and flush frontal alignment. Caught in the summer sunshine is Widnes No. 38 (ATD 682) a 35-seat vehicle with Massey body which lasted in service until 1952. Sister vehicle No. 37 was destroyed in a whirlwind in 194 while No. 39 became a towing vehicle and was later preserved.

As the 'thirties progressed there was a general trend towards smoother, more curvaceous contours incorporating a sloping front profile rather than the previously almost universal piano-front, and Massey Bros attempts in this direction first appeared in 1934 with bodies on Leyland Titan TD3 chassis built for Birkenhead and Chester Corporations and, again, Cumberland Motor Services. Their new design incorporated smoother and more rounded contours and perhaps the most prominent feature was the steeply sloping driver's windscreen which, together with the deep valance under the driver's canopy, retained some Leyland influence. An exception to this progression, however, was a batch of seven bodies (five on Leyland Titan TD3 and two on Crossley VR6 chassis) for Salford Corporation in 1934 which were to follow the general outline of Park Royal and then Strachan-bodied Dennis Lances, delivered between 1930 and 1932, in which the sloping screen was surmounted by a vertical front destination panel above which the upper-deck front window was set well back and divided into three panels. It is believed that this upright front panel was an attempt to make the destination easier to read, avoiding the reflection on the sloping back aspect of the more modern curved outlines. Whereas the Park Royal and Strachans bodies were of five-bay construction, Massey stuck to its rather fussy six-bay formation, but nevertheless these vehicles possessed a majestic and imposing appearance in the Salford livery of bright red, lined out in gold, and a great deal of white. Generally, however, Massey Bros designs remained quite

Comparison of the vehicles shown in these Massey adverts reveals just how much of an advance the new curved profile of the Birkenhead vehicle represented when seen against the rather ugly Salford-inspired vehicle. Indeed, echoes of the Birkenhead design would be seen again in the 1960s as we shall see later in the story. (STA both)

alford Corporation may have shown it was capable of moving with the times when it modernised a large section of its tram fleet but it was definitely in a time warp with its bus fleet – the admittedly smart-looking Leyland TD3 delivered in September 1934 built by Massey and shown above, RJ 3008, was actually clearly related not just to the Dennis Lance models supplied between 1930 and 1932 but even further back, to the H types of 1929 as shown in this fine maker's view, right, of BA 7686 from that year. Progressive designers must have despaired at being asked to perpetuate such outdated models, but, as we all know, the customer is always right. Well, sometimes ... **(STA both)**

conservative until the late 1930s, though always with a willingness to meet operators' preferences as with the Salford and Cumberland orders.

A non-standard design was again used in 1935 for a batch of Leyland TB4 lowbridge trolleybuses for St Helens Corporation, whose tramway system was slowly being abandoned. These bodies incorporated five-bay construction and full-width front. Unusual features were triple upper deck front windows and a step directly on the rear platform instead of in the more usual place from the platform into the lower saloon. This latter feature also appeared in a batch of five single-deck trolleybuses delivered to The Tees-side Railless Traction Board, mounted on Leyland TB3 chassis, in 1936. St Helens Corporation continued to order Massey-bodied trolleybuses through to 1942.

Either someone couldn't spell or Masseys had also moved into the bridal business when these smart-looking trolleybuses were built for St Helens in 1935. (STA)

St Helens Corporation trolleybus No. 127 is seen turning at Denton Green during what appears to be a demonstration of the then newly introduced pedestrian crossings, complete with metal studs in the road surface, and flashing Belisha beacons named after Transport Minister Hoare Belisha. The vehicle is a lowbridge Leyland TB delivered in May 1935. The three window arrangement at the front of the upper deck was a popular feature on buses and trolleybuses at the time, being a legacy of the route number boxes placed in that position in a number of fleets. It would was give additional support for the overhead gantry and traction feed cabling seen here. Note the Bovril advert at the rear of the vehicle – some popular brand names still live on today. (STA)

Posed outside the main gates of Wigan's Haigh Hall in December 1936 having been towed from Massey's factory by the Leyland truck which would deliver it to Tees-Side is Leyland TB3 trolleybus No. 10, one of a batch of five, remaining in service until 1945 when they were bought by Southend Corporation for £250 each. The 'Scottish' style rear entrance is noteworthy. As is the continuation of the six-bay construction in contrast to the five-bay design of the St Helens models above. (STA both)

Chester Corporation fleet No. 7 (AFM 518) was one of three Leyland Titan TD4c (torque-convertor fitted) models which entered service in May 1936 and is seen at Enfield Street just before delivery. Chester's livery was green and cream at this time, as it had been in tram days. The vehicle was withdrawn by Chester in 1945 and bought by Bere Regis & District Motor Services along with sister vehicle No. 28, both remaining in service until the end of the 1950s.

This almost broadside view clearly shows the sharp lines of the front upper-deck, combined with the more rounded rear. Bolton number 33 was also a TD4c with torque-convertor transmission, this being popular with many operators replacing trams and making the transition easier from driving trams to driving buses. The deep housing on the front bulkhead (carrying the fleet number) is the combined Autovac and header tank for the fluid for the convertor.

Widnes Corporation bought their first of many Leyland double-deckers in November 1936. This is No. 42, BTD 123, and it was one of five Leyland Titan TD4 type with highbridge 52-seat bodies, again seen at Enfield Street prior to delivery.

Cumberland's AEC Regent demonstrator, number 47, was replaced by another AEC Regent when it was sold in 1936. Also numbered 47 and also bodied by Massey BAO 763 was one of a pair, 12 and 47, with the current lowbridge body design as shown here. (JFH)

In 1935 Massey Bros. had co-operated with Leyland Motors and the General Electric Company in a unique project for the building of a double-deck low-height trolleybus. It was mounted on a low-loading three-axle chassis and was exhibited on the GEC stand at the Commercial Motor Show held at London's Olympia later that year. The Massey body was of attractive, gently curving proportions, achieving an overall height of 13ft 6ins within an overall length of 30ft. Designated TB10, it was of very modern appearance for its time, featuring a set-back front axle allowing a folding door ahead of the front nearside wheel. There was also a conventional rear platform with a door to the lower saloon.

The low, flat floor was achieved ingeniously by employing two traction motors, each positioned on the outside of each chassis side member. The drive shafts from the motors also ran outside the chassis members to the differential casings mounted adjacent to the wheel hubs on each rear axle. A dropped front axle with underslung springs, and inverted springs at the rear, contributed to the low floor height. The body of composite construction accommodated 63 seats, 29 in the lower saloon and 34 above with two staircases, one at each end, with the entry being at the rear and the exit through the front door. The twin staircases and doorways made for quicker loading and unloading but at the expense of seven seats within the then legal length on three axles.

Testing took place on the local system of the South Lancashire Transport Company and it later went on loan to London Transport. The vehicle was then shown on the GEC stand at the Olympia Show. From London it travelled north to Derbyshire where it ran for several weeks with Chesterfield Corporation and was often referred to as the 'Queen Mary' because of its size in comparison with the small capacity trolleybuses in the town. By January 1936 it was on loan to Doncaster Corporation, and in February, a full technical description of it appeared in the trade press, but by March the vehicle had disappeared from view. Regrettably, this advanced vehicle was later dismantled by Leyland

The Leyland Lowloader being tilt-tested at Massey's and then towed out of the Enfield Street works on its way to Leyland for checking out and official photograph one of which is shown opposite.

Trials were carried out on the nearby SL system, as was normal Leyland practice and the lower view, opposite, shows the vehicle turning off the A6 at Swinton Church with SLT and Salford tram track visible. It is believed to have operated carrying fare paying passengers. (STA all

General Electric Co. Ltd.

STAND 118　　　　Magnet House, Kingsway, London, W.C.2.

Leyland-G.E.C. Low-Loading 3-axle Trolley Bus

HERE is another entirely new model, offering to the passenger vehicle operator the important advantages of an extremely low-loading line, low overall height, and a separate entrance and exit. It is a 3-axle double-decked outfit, and the chassis will be known as the TB10.

The floor of the lower saloon is only 14 in. above road level, and both the unloading

platform at the front and the loading platform at the rear are lower still, sloping up to floor level. Only one step, therefore, is necessary from the road to lower saloon floor level— an important feature from the safety view-point.

The body, which seats 63, is of the Hybridge type, and was executed by Massey Brothers, of Wigan. Unladen, its overall height to the top of the trolley gear is only 14ft. 4 in., while if the chassis is fitted with the Low-bridge body this figure can be reduced to

13 ft. 6 in. Similarly, if the forward staircase is done away with, and this can be done without sacrificing many of the other advantages of the vehicle, the seating accommodation would be increased to approximately 70 seats. The two staircase arrangement greatly reduces loading and unloading time under heavy traffic conditions. It also helps the conductor in his general supervision of the vehicle, particularly as the front exit door, electrically interlocked with the master control, is controlled by the driver, who becomes responsible for the safety of alighting passengers.

Maximum Economy

G.E.C. electrical equipment is provided, comprising two 40 h.p. motors arranged on either side of the frame. This has enabled series parallel motor operation to be provided with the addition of the usual field regulation to both motors, an arrangement giving maximum economy in energy consumption. The regulated fields enable a very low speed to be maintained on full series notch, an ideal arrangement for continuous running in dense traffic or fog, as the rheostats, not being in circuit, cannot become overheated.

The bogie is formed of two special fully-floating axles with separate worm drives at each end and with the centre beam dropped to permit of a low gangway.

The vehicle complete including all electrical equipment weighs 13 tons laden; it has a wheelbase of 15 ft. and a turning circle of 58 ft.

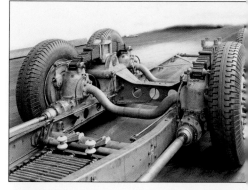

A selection of detail views of the body and chassis, together with an extract from The Leyland Journal for November 1935. The change in livery was effected in the Leyland studio with an airbrush, not in the workshops with a paintbrush. The view below really emphasises the extreme low level of the chassis and its various components. (STA all)

Motors and the overall concept never went into production. It was generally well received by staff and passengers alike, but no doubt it would have been expensive to manufacture because of the twin motor and transmission layout.

Also in 1936, the sloping body profile succeeded the near-vertical profile, first on the lowbridge body and then on the highbridge version. At the same time the pronounced curvature of the rear, which was to be a characteristic feature of Massey bodies for many years to come, began to take shape. The slope of the front was carried through to the bottom of the windscreen to present a neat and modern appearance. Another feature that began to appear at this time concerned the front side window of the lower saloon which incorporated a greater radius, the forerunner of the D-shaped window that was to become familiar on future Massey bodies.

A breakaway from the double-decker scene came in the same year when two interesting orders were received for single-deckers. A Leyland Cub SKP2 with 20-seat coach body was ordered by Edwin Box & Sons of Dewsbury; this vehicle was finished in Yorkshire Woollen District livery as that company had taken over the former before the body was built. The other vehicle was a six-wheel Leyland Tiger TS7T, a 40-seat bus for Thomas of Maesteg better known as Llynfi Motors. Yet another non-standard body design was built by Massey Bros on a batch of Leyland Titans supplied to Southport Corporation in 1937, which included bodies conforming to an earlier style supplied to this operator by the English Electric Co. During the same year Massey Bros. commenced work on their first order for Ipswich Corporation for twelve Ransomes D-type highbridge trolleybuses, and three years later they built a one-off body on another Ransomes, Sims & Jefferies chassis that had been intended as a demonstrator for export to South Africa. Wartime shipping restrictions prevented its delivery and the chassis was diverted to Ipswich Corporation.

The long and the short of it – this Leyland Cub SKP2 of 1936 was ordered by Edwin Box of Dewsbury but due to their takeover by Yorkshire Woollen District Transport Co. Ltd was finished in its livery and given fleet No. 384 (HD 6040). It was Leyland's lightweight small vehicle of the period, in contrast to the monster below.

The three-axle concept was still popular in some quarters, though rear tyre wear could be excessive due to 'scrubbing' on corners. The greater length of the three-axle chassis allowed a body up to 30ft long to be constructed and this in turn obviously gave additional seating capacity. The Thomas family of Llynvi Motors had just taken delivery of their 40-seater Leyland Tiger TS7T when this picture was taken in 1936. George Thomas, on the far right, had driven it down from Oxford to meet the rest of his family outside the National Museum of Wales in Cardiff. Note the former spelling of Llynvi, the later spelling appeared with the letter F replacing the V. (CT)

Southport Corporation No. 53, a Leyland Titan TD5c, was one of a batch of five delivered with clearly recognisable English Electric-designed bodywork in 1937. This must either have been an order placed with Massey to be built to EE design, or, possibly, sub-contracted from the Preston firm as it became increasingly busy with military orders. As Southport is only a few miles from Wigan it is perhaps surprising that Massey Bros. only ever received this one order from the seaside undertaking.

Ipswich Corporation bought 18 locally-built Ransomes, Sims & Jefferies trolleybuses which were then fitted with Massey bodies with delivery spread over almost twelve months during 1937/8. Here we see seven of them lined up at Cobham Road depot, and nearest to the camera is No. 79, (PV 4545).

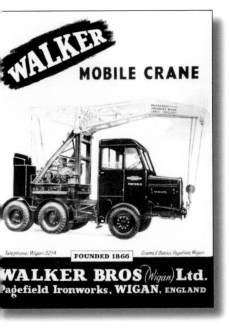

WALKER
MOBILE CRANE

Telephone: Wigan 3214   FOUNDED 1866   Grams & Cables: Pagefield, Wigan

WALKER BROS (Wigan) Ltd.
Pagefield Ironworks, WIGAN, ENGLAND

It is also interesting that around this period, Walker Bros, a well-known Wigan-based engineering company, capable of producing almost anything, gave a contract to Massey Bros for the building of five railcars, which comprised of three for the Trujillo Railway in Peru and two railcar-cabs for the British-run Sao Paulo railway in Brazil. Similar work was undertaken by Northern Counties and later by East Lancashire Coachbuilders.

Alfred Alcock, as designer, was becoming increasingly aware of the growing demand for metal-framed buses but he could not obtain agreement to build them. As just one example of customers moving elsewhere, Salford, staunch Massey supporters from 1927, had first tried metal-framing from the MCW

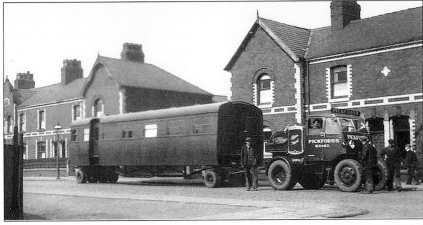

Massey Bros. were contracted by Walker Brothers to build three railcars for the Trujillo Railway in Peru. Here we see two views of a magnificent Pickfords tractor unit built by Foden towing one of the railcars to Walker Brothers for completion and final embellishments. The rather strange frontal appearance of the tractor is explained by the fact that it could be used to pull or push heavy loads as required.

Below we see the impressive finished product. Walker Brothers had their own sidings close to the factory for testing railcars. The ceremony was witnessed by all the dignitaries involved but unfortunately their identities were not recorded for this particular photograph.

Salford No. 6, RJ 7004, was o[ne]
of three Leyland Tiger TS7s bu[ilt]
in 1937. All were withdrawn [in]
1950 when the operator's ne[ed]
for single-deckers was bei[ng]
reduced, and were sold f[or]
further use, but they were t[he]
last Massey vehicles delivered [to]
the operator, Metro-Camm[ell]
and Leyland metal-fram[e]
bodies being preferred.

organisation in 1934. Salford bought further MCW metal-framed bodies, and also examples from Park Royal, Leyland and English Electric between 1937, when they took three single-decker Leylands from Pemberton, and 1939, but never patronised Massey again. Arising from this impasse, he and George Danson, the Works Foreman, decided to leave and to form their own company for the manufacture of such bodywork. They intended to operate in Bolton but had difficulty in finding premises which they could afford. As a result they entered into an agreement with Mr Walter Smith of Blackburn to join him in his business, East Lancashire Coachbuilders Ltd., which had been first registered on 27th October 1934. The company was involved in the manufacture of commercial vehicle bodies and small coaches.

East Lancashire Coachbuilders was reconstituted from 9th May 1938 with the new directors being Walter Smith, Mrs Lilian Smith, Alfred Alcock and George Danson and it was decided to concentrate on the manufacture of bus bodies, including double-deckers, of which Alcock and Danson had experience.

Walter Smith owned Brookhouse Mill on Whalley New Road and this became the base for the company until 1994 when it moved to Whitebirk Industrial Estate. Brookhouse Mill is thought to be the oldest weaving mill in Lancashire and alternate vertical pillars had to be removed in order to manoeuvre the larger vehicles which it was intended to manufacture. Almost inevitably, other personnel from Massey Bros joined Alcock and Danson at East Lancashire Coachbuilders. These included Jack Thomson who became Fitting Shop Foreman, Gerry Cunliffe who became Sheet Metal Shop Foreman and Harold Disley as panel beater.

It was hardly surprising that the early ELCB orders were from operators already familiar with the products of Massey Bros, the first being from Bolton Corporation for ten double-deckers. The outline of these bore a strong resemblance to the Massey design but they were still of composite construction, being built before the design for metal framework had been finalised. The sons of Alfred Alcock and George Danson, George Alcock and Arthur Danson, later joined the company and became directors to succeed their fathers. The story of East Lancashire Coachbuilders up to the year 2000 is told in a book by Harry Postlethwaite, published by Venture Publications Ltd.

The loss of the two key staff members did not affect the Massey Bros enterprise, however, and production continued at full capacity throughout 1938 and 1939. William Massey, the sleeping partner, had three sons who became engaged in the business. Thomas was the eldest and became the foreman painter, Norman became works manager and Arnold the youngest worked on design and was responsible for the metal frame concept when it was eventually introduced. Isaac, the partner who had trained as an accountant, had a daughter Clara, who married Arthur Tyldesley, later to figure prominently in the business.

eigh Corporation number 65, right, shows the
nal pre-war design of single-deck service bus
odies. Similar vehicles but with rear entrances
ere produced for Cumberland Motor Services.
he radiator confirms Massey's records that this
 indeed a Titan double-deck chassis, and without
utovac. Is it by now diesel-engined? The maker's
iew in the yard of one from an earlier batch shows
 dual-doorway layout.
The third photograph shows No. 65 again, this
me waiting at Lower Mosley Street bus station in
lanchester, doubtless on hire to one of the combine
perators who then used this long-distance coach
cation where the Bridgewater Hall now stands.
HSPC lower two)

Between 1934 and 1942, Birkenhead and Bolton Corporations proved to be two of Massey Bros best customers. From 1936 to 1942, Bolton placed 120 Leyland Titans with Massey bodies in service, and the Birkenhead total was 112 during the period 1934 to 1939. Bolton had also purchased five Leyland Tiger single-deckers with Massey bodies in this period, three in 1935 and a further two in 1938. In echoes of Salford's policy, they also took two metal-framed examples from Park Royal in 1938.

The Bolton Leyland Titan TD4c and TD5c models, of which Massey Bros bodied 95, had six-bay structures. There was a strong affinity between the Birkenhead and Bolton batches of 1936, except for the drivers' windscreens. The Birkenhead batch had a sloping screen like the 1934 and 1935 series and resembling the Leyland Titan TD1 and TD2 Leyland body style, whereas the Bolton batch had a more upright screen.

The 1937 Birkenhead and Bolton batches were very similar, both having the more upright windscreen. There were also 25 TD7c, with five-bay bodies, built

Birkenhead Corporation No. 219 was the first of batch of 40 Leyland Titans delivered in 1937; th bus was the sole TD4c and the remainder wer TD5c models. The seating for 54 was finished blue leather which became standard Birkenhea practice from this point on. Three of the vehicle became air raid casualties but were rebodie repaired by Masseys in 1942. (HSPC)

Burnley, Colne and Nelson's No. 152, (HG 6013), Leyland Titan TD5c dating from December 193 was seen standing in a light covering of snow at the Nelson depot shortly after delivery and showing th body styling before the introduction of the curve front to the upper deck. The logo, incorporating th coats of arms of the three authorities, was one of th most distinctive of the municipal embellishment carried by any public service vehicle. (JL)

Number 31 was one of five AE Regents bodied by Massey and supplied to Colcheste Corporation when they place their first order with Masseys 1939. These were fitted with 5 seat highbridge bodies simila in appearance to the vehicle supplied to Chester Corporatio during the same year.

Above: The final pre-war delivery to Birkenhead comprised 40 bodies on Leyland Titan TD5c chassis in 1939. Number 286 is shown in the original three cream bands version of the Birkenhead livery, and flared out panels are now in fashion. (HSPC)

Above right: Resting between duties at Bridgeman Street depot in April 1954 is this Leyland Titan TD5c vehicle showing the front view of the pre-war Massey body styling. Number 232 was part of a batch of 50 similar buses delivered between 1940 and 1942.

In 1938 Cumberland Motor Services took delivery of five Leyland Tiger TS8 half-canopy single-deckers with moquette covered seats that had higher than the usual standard backs giving extra comfort on longer routes. Number 139 is shown outside the Enfield Street coachworks prior to delivery, with outswept panels again in evidence. Sister vehicle No. 142 lasted in service until 1959 and was being used as a static site office in Methley near Leeds as late as the end of 1960.

between 1940 and 1942. In fact, the last 25 TD5c and the TD7c models were built simultaneously, surprisingly so, given the structural differences between the two types. Both varieties featured very rounded lines with D-shaped end windows at the sides of the lower saloons.

The 1939 Bolton batch (some may have been delivered at the end of 1938 as the Doffcocker and Montserrat tram route was abandoned on 31st December 1938 and some new buses would have been required) incorporated the more curved front profile introduced that year but the buses did not have the D-shaped windows at the ends of the lower saloon in the way that the Birkenhead 1939 design did. The last 25 examples of the Bolton order, delivered in 1940/41 were built on the later Leyland Titan TD7C specification and the Massey bodies were to the final pre-war design incorporating five-bay construction.

During the 1930s only small numbers of single-deck vehicles were produced; a notable customer for some of these being – perhaps unsurprisingly – Cumberland Motor Services Ltd. The standard Cumberland single-deck bus body on the TS8 chassis showed a strong affinity to contemporary Ribble design with its half-canopy cab and general proportions at this time.

Seen at Keswick Bus Station about to depart fo Borrowdale and Seatoller was Cumberland Moto Services No. 30, a Leyland TS2 dating from 192 Its original Massey bus body was replaced by thi Massey dual-purpose version in 1939 and it remaine in service until 1949. The official view of No. 94, (RI 5629), left, shows more clearly the glass cantrail ligh and glass louvres over the windows and the slopin roof line, whilst the familiar D-shaped windows ar also prominent. Note that a neat entwined log has replaced the former large bold **CUMBERLANI** lettering on the side panels – clearly this was felt t be more appropriate to a vehicle acting as a coac – even if only in disguise. The deep Cov-Rad radiato conversion was an attempt to modernise the front appearance of the long-outdated chassis.

Until now Massey Bros had not shown any serious interest in building for the luxury coach market, but when three half-canopy bodies were fitted to reconditioned 1929 Leyland Tiger chassis for Cumberland in 1939, replacing the original Massey bodies, two of these were to dual-purpose specification, finished in bus livery and providing 32 bus seats and rear entrances. The third, however, although having a similar body shell, was fitted with front-entrance and 26 coach seats, those on the nearside being single units. It was finished in coach livery. With hindsight, this was hardly a propitious time to enter the luxury coach market, with the outbreak of World War 2 only months away, but, as we noted earlier 'the customer is always right'.

This development of the single-deck design had its counterpart with the double-deck, which generally retained its six-bay construction, now with characteristic D-shaped front and rear side windows in the lower-deck and wide-radius roof contours. Five-bay bodies were, however, supplied to Chester Corporation. Early in 1939 the design was changed to five-bay construction thus improving the overall appearance still further, although those supplied to Bolton and Cumberland during 1939 were of the six-bay layout. By this date the sloping front had given way to a gently curved profile with the curvature taken to the bottom of the windscreen, the lower edge of

An advertising exercise which was doomed to failure, even before the ink had dried, is seen below. The front of the coach is captured quite faithfully but the gentle curvature to the rear is missing – was there a change of heart along the line between concept and completion? Either way, Cumberland's number 31 was destined to remain a solitary example. (STA)

Cumberland No. 31 may have needed a Cov-Rad radiator conversion, and spats to cover the projecting dumb irons of its 1929 built chassis, but no one could fault the interior body appointments. Two-and-one deep leather-trimmed moquette seats with arm rests, radio speakers and a clock, glass antrails for better visibility in the glorious Lake District, curtains to the deep half-drop windows and a discrete measure of chromium trim put this in a top quality league. Note the Massey Bros. gilt transfer on the bulkhead above the chrome fire extinguisher.

Double-deckers always offered a challenge if the two decks were built separately – even in the 'seventies stories of men with brooms marching in military formation whilst supporting the roof are not unknown. Here, though, it is a different proposition for the upper deck is exactly that, not just a roof and cantrail but the full framing and some panelling. Unfortunately, not all the sequence has survived but what the photographer has recorded is sufficient. The roof stands on barrels and is going to be lifted high enough for the lower deck to be driven below it, and then the two sections bolted together. Note the **GEARLESS BUS** lettering on the radiator front grille.

Below, the finished vehicle stands outside Bolton's Town Hall, the deep maroon livery and excellent paint finish being testimony to the quality of the Pemberton workforce. This is another torque convertor Titan, a TD5c, with the identifying sign – the sight glass for the fluid levels on the bulkhead, also carrying the fleet number 175 in the wonderful shaded numerals which nearly all good tramway operators used – and applied to their buses equally lovingly. The distinctive lettering on the radiator is no longer in evidence. (STA)

54

Showing its rear entrance body to good effect is this Leyland Tiger TS8c which was one of two with Massey bodies supplied to Bolton Corporation in the late summer of 1938. There were two more similar vehicles supplied at the same time but with dual-purpose bodies by Park Royal. (STA)

Not one of the best official photographs in the book, but interesting nevertheless. Standing outside the finishing shops and ready for the short delivery journey to its operator Leigh Corporation's No. 71, one of two 1938 Leyland TD5s with lowbridge body and seating for 48 passengers. Both buses have 14 years service before being withdrawn and scrapped in 1952. The whole of Leigh's double-decker fleet consisted of lowbridge buses owing to the low access to the depot which had previously been an engineering factory. Many years later it would become a problem for **SELNEC** and **GMT** but by then Massey Bros. were no more.

The official photographer for some 20 years was Fred W Dew of Wigan and these are three of his images, taken at Enfield Street prior to the delivery of Leyland Titans supplied to Cumberland Motor Services in 1938/9.

These photographs show the evolving Massey body curvature. The top image shows Cumberland Motor Services No. 135 (DAO 50) a lowbridge Leyland Titan TD5 one of a batch of five such vehicles delivered in 1938 with a restrained but not unpleasing appearance.

The lower two photographs show views of No. 144, (DRM 8), one of two TD5s delivered a year later, with the curved treatment applied to front and rear upper-decks together with the end windows on both decks. Cumberland was still an important and regular customer at this time.

56

MR. JOHN ANGUS

Post With Newcastle Firm

We reproduce a portrait of Mr. John Angus, B.Sc., formerly sales manager of Massey Bros., Wigan, who has been appointed sales manager of Northern Coachbuilders, Ltd., Newcastle-on-Tyne. Mr. Angus is well known in

Mr. JOHN ANGUS, B.Sc.

passenger transport circles, and has many friends in both municipal and company undertakings. For a time he was with the English Electric Company at Preston.

The departure of Massey Bros. sales manager John Angus in 1939 had interesting results for Northern Coachbuilders, his new employer. In 1944/5, orders were received for replacement bodies on Leyland chassis for Bolton Corporation and Cumberland. In post-war years a batch of lowbridge NCB bodies on PD1 chassis was built for Cumberland, but no repeat orders ensued. (STA)

which was in the form of a curve, although some of the Bolton examples had a horizontal lower edge to the windscreen. The final pre-war design incorporated front roof panelling that was continued downwards to form the front corner panelling, and so provided one of the most distinctive features of Massey bodies for many years when peacetime standards were re-introduced after the war.

The later 1930s had been particularly successful for Massey Bros, especially with sales to municipalities. It was a time of replacement of many trams by buses, thus increasing the demand for double-deck bodies to the extent that orders for up to 40 at a time were being received from customers whose earlier requirements might have been no more than ten vehicles. Perhaps the ultimate design of Massey Bros pre-war development could be seen in the batch of 40 Leyland Titan TD5c double-deckers supplied to Birkenhead in 1939, typifying the functional half-cab, open rear platform British double-decker in its municipal livery style of three cream bands, in this case with a main colour of pale blue. As with the orders for Bolton and Cumberland, progression continued into early wartime as Massey Bros managed to maintain production at almost normal levels for longer than most other bodybuilders in this period.

It is recorded that the first Massey Bros metal-framed body was completed in June 1939 as Coventry 223, DKV 223 a Daimler COA6 with 56 seats. The chassis was one of a batch of 18, Nos. 212-2 carrying Metro-Cammell bodies and Nos. 224-29, Brush bodies. The single Massey body was bought as an experiment. The Transport Committee minute of 11th July, 1938 reads, "of the tenders received for bodies, the Committee consider that those of the Brush Electrical Engineering Co. Ltd. and Messrs. Metro-Cammell Ltd., amounting to £1,018 and £1,021 per body, are the most advantageous, although, as an experiment, they propose to accept the tender of Messrs. Massey Bros (Wigan) for one body at a price of £890."

It should be borne in mind that buses were still being bought in 1938 and 1939 for a seven year life span. Sixteen of the Daimlers then being ordered by Coventry were for the replacement of buses bought in 1931 and 1932. It was said that the body for No. 223 would last for seven years but in fact it had to be rebuilt in 1946, and the bus was withdrawn in 1953, one of the first of the batch 212-29 to expire. As a matter of interest Coventry's six Brush bodies all had problems by 1945-6, and all were rebuilt between 1946 and 1948, mostly with new pillars and new front bulkheads supplied by Metro-Cammell. The Metro-Cammell bodies were never rebuilt although three required new roofs due to blitz damage, these being made and fitted by Brush in 1941. The first Metro-Cammell body to be withdrawn went in 1953 along with three of the Brush type, though it is thought that these had suffered collision damage. The remainder lasted until 1955 and 1956.

Whilst this is very clearly not a Massey design, records show that this Daimler COA6, No. 233 (DKV 233) is indeed a Massey built vehicle. It was assembled in 1939 from metal sections, as were the other vehicles in the batch for Coventry, but the rest were either Brush or Metro-Cammell products and this example from Wigan was supplied for comparison. It was priced at £890 as against £1,021 for the Birmingham product, but maybe Massey had seriously underestimated the true cost of production. Whatever the actual situation the outcome was clear – Coventry did not pursue the idea and Massey's next metal-framed bus would be for Birkenhead in 1950 as shown on page 86.

Chester No. 32 delivered in 1939 show[s] the curved frontal profile introduce[d] around this time. It is mounted on a[n] AEC Regent II chassis. By the time th[e] next Chester vehicles, including N[o] 39 also on AEC Regent II chassis, wer[e] delivered in June 1940 the frontal profil[e] had changed yet again with increase[d] curvature to the front and heavier corne[r] pillars, a design that was to be used wit[h] little modification for some years in th[e] post-war period – see page 61. (HSPC)

Making a satisfactory tilt test at Enfield Street on a dull July day in 1938, and in the company of unidentified officials, was St Helens trolleybus No. 151 a Ransomes,Simms & Jefferies D4 type, fitted with 50-seat lowbridge body. Note the permanent 'VIA' sign between the destination displays, and, in small lettering on the white band below, the licence number and seating capacity. The houses visible behind the vehicle had also been built by Massey Brothers just a few years previously.

Leigh and Salford were other notable municipal customers placing orders prior to the outbreak of war and the local operator, Wigan Corporation, continued to place regular orders apart from the early post-war period when all-Leyland double-deckers were purchased exclusively. A number of new regular customers became apparent in the mid- to late-'thirties from further afield including Colchester, Great Yarmouth and Kingston upon Hull Corporations who first placed orders in 1939, Colchester and Great Yarmouth also making many repeat purchases in post-war years. Alan Townsin has described the 1930s products of Massey Bros as having 'a characteristic flavour not generally found in bodywork built outside that area of Lancashire' and considers that this was most evident just before the Second World War.

However, not everything in the garden was smelling of roses. The structures of all the 1936-42 bodies supplied to Bolton proved to be rather troublesome. By 1943 some of the 1936 batch on wartime hire to Coventry Corporation (Coventry hired seven vehicles) had to be returned to Bolton with rotting pillars. Some of the bodies moved independently of the chassis while in motion. By 1948/9, Coventry was to experience a repetition of this problem with four wartime Massey bodies, two on Guy Arab I chassis (EKV 300/1), delivered in November 1942, and two on Daimler CWG5 (EKV 821/2) delivered in 1943. Of the five bodies supplied to Cumberland in 1941, numbered 159-63, one of these, No. 162 was destroyed by fire in December 1943 and was rebodied by Northern Coachbuilders in 1944. Of the others, Nos. 159 and 160 were rebuilt by the company in the postwar period whilst Nos. 161 and 163 were rebodied by HV Burlingham in 1950.

In an early form of recycling, the body of No. 161 ended its days as a beach bungalow at St Bees whilst the seats from Nos. 161 and 163, together with those from some of the Massey-bodied Leyland Titan TD4 and TD5 models rebodied in the postwar period, were used to replace wooden seats in wartime Guy Arabs including No. 217, one of the two Massey-bodied Guy Arabs in the Cumberland fleet. The other Massey-bodied Guy Arab No. 216 received the more luxurious moquette-covered seating from the Park Royal-bodied Leyland Titan TD7s built for Southdown and diverted to Cumberland on completion. The watch-words in those dark days were 'make-do-and-mend' and 'waste-not-want-not', sentiments lost on many in today's more affluent society.

When a professional photographer was brought to the body shop at Enfield Street to record this scene it could only have been a sign that something was afoot; the *cause celebre* in this instance was Bolton Corporation No. 119, a Leyland Titan TD5c delivered to the operator in September 1937, and seen here being completely reframed in the lower-deck. In today's compensation culture climate this might be evidence for a claim against the timber supplier – was it indeed just that we wonder?

Britain was already at war when AEC Regent No. 71 of the Hull Corporation Transport fleet was photographed on the edge of Enfield Street prior to delivery in October 1939. It was one of a batch of 20 handsome looking vehicles set off by the distinctive blue and cream livery of this operator.

CHAPTER 4
Wartime

Although bus body-building at Pemberton continued after the outbreak of war on 3rd September 1939, throughout 1940 and into 1941, some manufacturers had already been directed to war effort production, Leyland Motors concentrating on manufacturing tanks, for example. Others, such as Park Royal and Duple, both in London, found themselves building wings and fuselages for Halifax bombers – alongside lines of wartime buses.

Production at Masseys included the batch of Leyland TD5c Titans for Birkenhead (279-318), AEC Regents for Hull (170-89) with delivery to both completed in January 1940, and further Titan TD5c models for Bolton (193-242) completed in November 1941, before the influx of diverted or unfrozen vehicles (see page 67) of which full details can be found in the body list Appendix.

The 1939 contracts continued to be built to peacetime standards, but production gradually diminished because of the reduction in the number of available chassis and material shortages until it came to a halt early in 1942. It is calculated that up to this date Massey had built 1,330 vehicle bodies. In order to maintain the employment of those who had not been called up for military service, the firm reverted to the original business of building and contracting in the form of repairs to and reconstruction of bomb-damaged buildings. Engineering work consisted of assembly of mobile auxiliary fire pumps and, later, building of fire service van bodies on Austin and Ford chassis.

The Ministry of Supply was responsible for control of materials whilst the Ministry of War Transport (MoWT) was now busy planning to guarantee essential movement of war workers. Early steps had actually been counter-productive, when all bus building had been stopped soon after the outbreak of hostilities, with materials and part-completed vehicles 'frozen' by Government directive.

It was quickly realised that people involved in work vital to the war effort needed transport, and that in many cases new provision would be required to cater for the vast munitions effort where, for reasons of local and national security, secret factories were established in remote locations where shell cases and bombs could be filled with the deadly explosive mixtures, away from towns and marauding German bombers.

Because these factories were so remote, and because very large numbers of people were working in them, frequently on shifts around the clock, the movement of several hundred people three times every day became a major task in itself. Operators such as Cumberland and Crosville found themselves unable to cope, and in urgent need of additional vehicles. At the other end of the country, restrictions on travel due to the threat of invasion meant that East Kent and Southdown found themselves with surplus vehicles, and also with orders in build for buses they were not going to need. Park Royal were nearing completion of orders for these two operators when the MoWT stepped in and arranged for the vehicles to be diverted to the two northern companies. They had already been allocated registration numbers and the GCD letters soon identified them to enthusiasts. Crosville took the vehicles just as they came, but Cumberland arranged for Massey Bros to fit their standard destination display, and to repaint them.

Very few details of wartime non-psv producti[on] appear to have survived, a situation common [to] many other coachbuilders in those dark days, a[nd] even fewer photographs have been found. The[se] two fire appliances for the Ministry are paint[ed] in wartime grey and carry the Royal Cypher [of] George VI. Austin P 2959 above, and Fordson 4696 below, are both fitted with wartime hood[ed] headlamps.

Southdown Motor Services had ordered 27 Leylan[d] TD7s with Park Royal bodies for delivery in 19[..] but as explained in the text they were divert[ed] north, Cumberland Motor Services receiving fo[ur] which were repainted into CMS livery at Mass[ey] Brothers at a cost of £47 10 0d. per bus (£47.5[0]) Number 172, with its Southdown registration ma[rk] GCD 691, was photographed at Enfield Street aft[er] receiving its new identity.

swich No. 86 bodied by Masseys in 1940 was a insomes, Sims and Jefferies trolleybus built as a monstrator for a tour of South Africa, but due the outbreak of World War Two was diverted by e MoWT to Ipswich Corporation. It was the last insomes vehicle to enter service with a British erator, was the last trolleybus to be bodied by assey Bros, and was withdrawn and scrapped in ptember 1959.

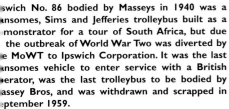

hen Chester's numbers 39-42 on AEC Regent chassis were delivered between June 1940 and ne 1941, not surprisingly the frontal profile atched the Bolton and Birkenhead contracts ing through the works at that time in contrast the previous batch of Chester buses delivered 1939, and illustrated on page 58. Number 39 is en here in post-war days but now has the later yle of destination display compared to that fitted iginally. (HSPC)

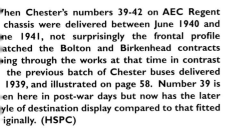

umberland Motor Services No. 161, EAO 701, was ne of five Leyland Titan TD7s supplied in 1941 with assey bodies. They were built entirely to peacetime andards and were delivered in the traditional red d cream livery. By the time this photograph was ken in Carlisle Bus Station, as it was about to epart to Whitehaven, it had been repainted by the erator in wartime grey and white livery. Note the asked headlamps, and the white painted stripes front and rear to aid visibility by others in the ackout. (SLP)

The next move was to release those items, or part-completed vehicles, which had been frozen and thus became 'unfrozen'. Massey bodied a selection of these, as shown. Also made available were vehicles which had been intended to be exported, but which were now considered to be at risk from danger of U-boat attacks to shipping, or likely to be of greater value at home.

A batch of vehicles built to utility specification that was of particular interest formed an allocation of ten trolleybuses for St Helens Corporation in 1942. These were to be the only utility trolleybus bodies constructed by Massey Bros. The Sunbeam chassis had been intended for export to Johannesburg but the outbreak of war precluded their shipping and they were diverted to St Helens. As the export chassis were 8ft wide at a time when the British legal maximum was 7ft 6in special dispensation was granted to allow them to be operated in Great Britain. With full-width cab, low-height and extra width, together with a shallow roof, these vehicles looked most unusual for Massey products.

A number of Daimler COG6 motor bus chassis were similarly affected and one of these was bodied by Massey Bros for Sheffield Corporation, becoming No. 461 in that organisation's fleet, and four AEC Regent chassis were also bodied for this operator at the same time.

Todmorden No. 32, below, was one of four unfroze Leyland TD7s supplied in November 1941. Note th wrong registration – it should have been DWY 394 the error was corrected before the vehicle entere service. Todmorden withdrew its TD7s in 1948, tw years or more before the 1938, 1939 and 1940 TD with Leyland bodies in the fleet. It has never bee established exactly why the TD7s were withdraw so early, but the TD7s were slower than the TD5 due to their heavy flywheels and consequent slo gear changes, making them unsuitable for the hil routes in Todmorden's territory. Significantly, the saw further service with independent operator three of them lasting until the late 'fifties.

Driver and conductress keenly pose for the camera in this early postwar view, with the River Clyde in the background. The vehicle, VS 4214, is a Leyland Titan TD7 showing its lowbridge 'unfrozen' body and was one of two delivered to Greenock Motor Services in February 1942. The Greenock business was merged with Western SMT in 1949.

Posing for the camera prior to delivery, below, on a blea day in April 1942 is Sheffield Corporation's No. A461 (HW. 141) an 'unfrozen' Daimler COG6, in full wartime liver and believed to have been the only such example from th Daimler output. The body will be seen to be of the sam design as that fitted to the four Regents, as seen left.

Sheffield received four unfrozen AEC Regents with Massey bodywork during March 1942 and the transition from pre-war to wartime design is becoming apparent on No. 466 (HWA 146) seen here in the late 1940s. A motley line up behind this bus reveals several other wartime vehicles with a selection of body makers. (RM)

Wartime shipping restrictions prevented 15 Sunbeam chassis being bodied and sent to Johannesburg, and they were diverted to be used in the UK instead. Five went to Nottingham, bodied by Weymann with an 8ft wide version of the standard highbridge wartime utility body, but the balance of ten, supplied to St Helens, were very different. Bodied by Massey they required to be of lowbridge format to pass below a railway bridge and the combination of lowbridge bodywork on an 8ft wide vehicle resulted in the strange appearance seen here. In the upper view No. 158 (DJ 9006) stands in the yard at Pemberton, ready for delivery after its photographs have been taken. The photographer is to be complimented on the finished result, taking into account the drab location and even duller livery. In the lower view the same vehicle is seen in service some years later in the standard red and cream fleet livery. Note that the driver's cab door is located on the nearside, a feature of the St Helens specification. Nottingham's vehicles retained normal offside access.

Massey Bros were also given the job of building six lowbridge bodies on Leyland Titan TD7 chassis. They were allocated by the Ministry of War Transport, one to Cumberland Motor Services, one to Greenock Motor Services and four to Todmorden Joint Omnibus Committee. The latter four were practically free from austerity features, whereas wartime features on the others included the omission of radii to the bottom corners of the windows (actually the omission of window pans, with glazing mounted direct into the framework of the body), the omission of interior lining panels, and simplified seating. Nevertheless, these unfrozen vehicles did not possess the utility features and austerity appearance of the later Ministry specification wartime vehicles.

Belatedly recognising that there would indeed be a need for bus production during the war, a joint committee representing vehicle builders, operators and unions was set up in 1942 to agree standard specifications for bus chassis and bodies, using minimum amounts of materials and labour. Certain manufacturers were authorised to build, initially Guy, later followed by Daimler and Bristol for the chassis. Massey Bros was among those coachbuilders authorised to build highbridge and lowbridge double-deck bodies on new chassis.

Vehicles were allocated to operators by the Ministry of War Transport on the basis of need for the war effort and had to be obtained through the provision of a licence, and the trading-in of a worn-out model for replacement. The story of wartime bus production in Britain is told in the book *The Best of British Buses – Utilities* by Alan Townsin, published by Transport Publishing Company in 1983. Although there was supposedly little flexibility in the basic design of these vehicles, coachbuilders managed to interpret the specification in their own ways – perhaps the fact

Although this vehicle wasn't actually built until 1945 it illustrates perfectly Massey's interpretation of the wartime highbridge utility bus, a Stockpo example photographed in that operator's Heaton Lane depot as though it might have been posed especially for this book. The broadside view show the angular body shape to perfection with the statutory single opening window on each side of each deck, and also illustrates the projection of t bonnet to accommodate the long Gardner 6LW engine, though 5LW units were also fitted in many Arab IIs, of course. Stockport obtained god service from its allocation of 16 Guys and saw no reason to have any rebodied before they were withdrawn in the mid-'sixties.

Newcastle Corporation was supplied with two Guy Arab Mk I models in October 1942. Number 245 (JTN 505) is seen resting between duties. Both vehicles were bought by AA Motor Services of Troon in 1950, No. 245 only being used for spares but sister vehicle No. 246 was used in revenue earning service until becoming their tree-lopper in 1955.

Masseys supplied only one utility vehicle to Rochdale Corporation (above) in 1943, it was a Daimler CWG5 and numbered 187 in their fleet. Further Daimlers were supplied with Massey bodies towards the end of 1945 with a more relaxed specification.

Massey Bros. supplied a number of Scottish operators with utility buses, including Glasgow Corporation who took delivery of two Daimler CWG5s in 1943. This was No. 101 (DGB 448) which had obviously been refurbished, re-glazed and re-painted in normal peacetime livery. It was withdrawn in 1954 and became a towing vehicle shortly after with the dealer Max Speed of Mitcham.

that the man leading the team responsible for the specification was the General Manager of Park Royal Vehicles might just have explained this and it was a subtle way of saying, "yes, all very well but we'll do it our way" Massey wartime bodies were particularly distinctive with the most outstanding features being the deep roof, shape of the offside cab windows and curved lower edge to the windscreen. The well-sloped rear profile of the upper-deck contrasted sharply with the vertical rear ends of some manufacturers but the angled rear dome left no doubt that this was a utility product.

The aim of the specification was to avoid the use of materials that were scarce or required for the war effort, such as aluminium alloys, and to simplify construction by the elimination of compound curves which required skilful panel beating at a time when such skilled labour was in short supply. This was, of course, in the days before glass fibre moulding. Massey Bros retained the polished timber area to the upper portion of the front bulkhead together with polished timber window finishers. Generally, window pans were not allowed, and glazing was mounted direct into the framework of the body. There was an exception to this just down the road from Massey Bros, where Northern Counties was allowed to use metal-framing, and this necessitated the use of window pans. This was partly due to large stocks of window pans being held by that company. The other exception was East Lancashire Coachbuilders where Alfred Alcock not only got away with using metal framing and window pans but manufactured bodies to the pre-war outline including curved rear domes. No explanation has ever been offered as to how he managed this, beyond the possible existence of surplus preformed stock, as at Northern Counties.

The seats in the bodies built to the standard specification were generally to a simplified design and covered in red leathercloth until mid-1943 when varnished wooden slatted seats became the standard. From observations at the time it appears that the unfrozen Leyland Titan TD7s, Guy Arab Is, including the 6LW variants, in the range FD 25451– FD 25950, and the Daimler CWG5s all had leather-covered seats whilst the later bodies up to 1945 had wooden seats. The Leyland Titan TD7 which went to Cumberland as their No. 176 certainly had seats covered in brown leathercloth but to a simplified specification compared to earlier bodies supplied to this operator. The Ministry relaxed the body specification towards the end of 1944 and upholstered seats and additional opening windows began to appear shortly after this.

Wooden seats became the order of the day from mid-1943 and were more comfortable than the picture might suggest. Although this is not a Massey body, the seating design was common to all the utilities and so this is typical of the type. (STA)

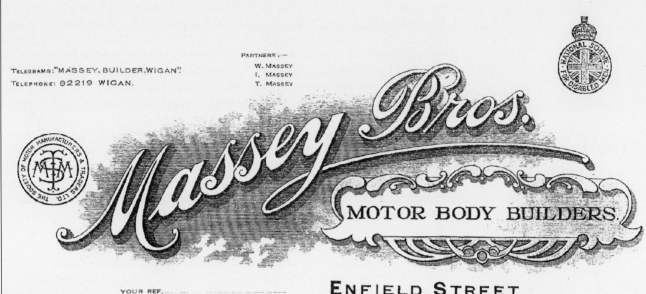

TELEGRAMS: "MASSEY. BUILDER, WIGAN".
TELEPHONE: 82219 WIGAN.

PARTNERS:—
W. MASSEY
I. MASSEY
T. MASSEY

Massey Bros.

MOTOR BODY BUILDERS.

YOUR REF.

OUR REF. IM/GHC.

ENFIELD STREET,
WIGAN.

23rd June. 1943.

WE SPECIALISE IN:

OMNIBUSES

—

TROLLEY BUSES

—

DOUBLE AND SINGLE
DECKERS

—

SALOON COACHES

—

Although we take all precautions
against Fire, we will not hold
ourselves responsible for damage
done by Fire or otherwise to any
Motor or part thereof whilst in
our charge.

The County Borough of Wigan
Motor Taxation Dept.
Town Hall. WIGAN.

Dear Sirs,

As arranged by telephone this afternoon
we enclose you herewith Hackney Form, P.S.V.
Licence, Certificate of Insurance and Cheque
Value £45. 7.3d., in connection with new
Double Deck Omnibus for Messrs Everingham Bros.
Limited, Railway Street, Pocklington. Yorks.

We note that you will arrange immediately
for the Registration Book to be forwarded on
so that transfer can be made without delay, and
also that you will forward the necessary Licence
to Messrs Everingham Bros Ltd, to be in their
possession for 1st July. 1943. as they wish to
run this Bus on that date.

Thanking you in anticipation.

Yours faithfully,
for MASSEY BROTHERS.

The above letterhead clearly shows that, despite the significant volume of war work, Massey
Bros. coachbuilding arm was still operating as a partnership. This situation was to change as
explained on page 78.

ANALYSIS OF WARTIME UTILITY BUS BUILDING AT PEMBERTON

CHASSIS TYPE	1942	1943	1944	1945
GUY ARAB I	17			
GUY ARAB II		33	115	105
DAIMLER CWG5		30		
DAIMLER CWA6		22	1	12

A full list of all known bodies, and, where known,
body numbers, will be found on pages 145 onwards.

The MoS allocation system meant that chassis arrived in batches at Pemberton and, again, the body list Appendix will show how this worked out between Guy and Daimler chassis. By the end of 1945 Massey had bodied 270 of the former and 65 of the latter, 321 being highbridge and 14 lowbridge. As shown, few lowbridge examples were built at Enfield Street, and Massey utility bodies were generally allocated to operators in the north of England and in Scotland.

There was a corresponding specification for wartime single-deck bodies but none were built by Massey Bros. New single-deckers were provided by Bedford with most of the bodies being built by Duple, Mulliner, Roe and Scottish Motor Traction Co Ltd., which, though primarily an operating company, was in those days the Scottish agent for Bedford and became the bodybuilder for many of the OWB models supplied north of the border. The rebodying of single-deckers, where authorised by the Ministry of War Transport, was undertaken by HV Burlingham of Blackpool.

Many bodies of utility specification were supplied to such traditional customers as Birkenhead, Chester and Cumberland Motor Services. However, the wartime allocation system made Massey bodies far more familiar nationwide, taking them into many fleets where they had never been seen before and a list of these will be found on page 72. Sadly, it transpired that once again the timber supplied to Massey Bros had been particularly poor, making the

This **CWA6** Daimler (above) was supplied to the HMD fleet in 1943, being the last of three for the operator. The Stalybridge-based operator was a staunch Daimler supporter and would have doubtless been pleased to have received these instead of Guy Arabs. Number 193 (HMA 157) is seen in post war days.

Another of the municipal fleets combining the interests of several authorities was Burnley, Colne and Nelson and that undertaking's number 21, (HG 157), is seen above right in a dull post-war setting. BCN received 14 Massey bodies during the wartime allocation scheme.

Coventry Corporation No. 321 entered service in July 1943 and is seen 20 years later in Cox Street still looking very presentable. It was renumbered 21 in November 1963, withdrawn a month later, and then sold for further service to a Warwickshire independent. The smart two-tone Hillman Minx about to make a right turn is typical of the period. (AEJ)

This advert was almost certainly produced for the overseas market – specifically the German one – to make the enemy believe that despite the devastating Coventry blitz the Daimler factory there was still in business. It was not, of course.

In contrast, this advertisement, placed by the Ministry o Information, was very definitely aimed at the home marke and clearly showed the very valuable contribution made t the war effort by the UK vehicle manufacturers. (STA both)

Facing page: Photographed in 1947 this Bradford Corporation 1943 Daimler CWG5 was at Hall Ings, resting behind an unidentified balcony top-covered tram bound for Thornbury. The bus was scrapped in 1953. (AEJ)

second overhauls uneconomic. Many became trainers and early candidates for withdrawal. All had gone by early 1952 and relatively few went to new owners. Those that did were promptly rebodied and/or rebuilt to single-deckers.

The Ministry's utility specification was relaxed in November 1944, as previously stated, and early in 1945 Massey bodies began to appear with upholstered seats and additional opening windows. The original specification had been for one half-drop opening window on each side on each deck. However, angled rear domes continued until the wartime standard was withdrawn at the end of 1945.

As soon as possible, some operators updated their utility bodies, with such improvements as upholstered seats and several extra opening windows, or, less commonly in attempts to improve the appearance of the vehicles by fitting rounded rear domes and by varying degrees of rebuilding. Others completely rebuilt existing bodies or re-bodied wartime chassis, some of which went on to give up to 20 or more years of service. The Guy chassis in particular proved to be a type that was simple, easy to maintain and economical with its Gardner engine. It continued to be in strong demand into the 1960s.

Some operators, such as Lancashire United Transport and the West Riding Automobile Company, adopted it as their standard double-deck chassis and others such as Chester Corporation continued to order Massey bodies on Guy chassis. As previously mentioned, it would later be said that Massey Bros seemed to suffer particularly from poor quality timber in wartime, though they were not alone as Brush Coachworks Limited were also mentioned in this context, and on the Ashton-under-Lyne Massey-bodied Guys, the pillars could be detected as loosening at the joints after only six months in service. However, two of these Ashton bodies remained in service for twelve years before rebodying took place. Just down the road from Ashton, Stockport Corporation received 16 Massey-bodied Guys and obtained 18-20 years of service from them with scarcely any outward evidence of major rebuilding having been necessary.

Chester had need for more vehicles to serve the Sealand American airbase which provided home for many of the US bombers used during the conflict. Here one of its Daimlers, No. 45 (FFM 270) is seen after the war in the city's shopping area. This was CWG5, easily recognised by the vertical slats of the radiator.

In 1944 Grimsby Corporation were allocated three Guy Arab II's with Massey utility bodywork, and here looking in need of a wash is No. 79. Fleet numbers 71 and 79 were withdrawn and scrapped in 1963 and 1962 respectively but the third member of the trio, No. 78, remained in service until 1969, making a very respectable quarter century's service for what was intended to be a stop-gap design. (OS)

Independent operator Lancashire United had a major involvement in workers' transport for the war effort, serving coal mines, munitions factories, engineering works, mills and the vast Trafford Park industrial complex near Manchester. This was reflected in the allocation of no less than 76 vehicles into the fleet between 1939 and 1945, including diverted South African exports, unfrozen and utility machines. Four Massey highbridge-bodied Guys were delivered in 1945 and one of the these, No. 312 (FTE 333) is seen on service in 1957. The largest number were bodied by Northern Counties, and no more Massey bodies entered the fleet. The destination TT relates to the fact that the bus is operating instead of a Trackless Trolleybus near to the end of trolleybus operation by sister company SLT – would-be Isle of Man motor cycling aficionados would thus have been disappointed. The significance is that trolleybus fares were cheaper and this bus in charging the lesser rate! (JAS)

Lowestoft, Blackburn and London were operators new to Massey Bros. order book. Whilst the seaside town came back after the war, as will be seen, no more Pemberton products were to enter the other two fleets. Blackburn, like Lancashire United (above), was fully stretched servicing the factories involved in the war effort. London Transport took almost 300 further vehicles, Guy, Daimler and Bristol chassis and a variety of body makes, from 1945 to spring 1946 to cover a perceived shortfall of new buses – the famous RT class. The 20 Massey-bodied Guys were the first to arrive, from May 1945, and G267 (GYL 406) is seen below. Why Lowestoft qualified for wartime vehicles is not clear, but one is seen in the adjoining illustration, whilst a trio of buses in Blackburn's town centre is led by a Massey utility Guy Arab II. (RM lower left; ABC lower right)

Top of the page: Ashton under Lyne was fortunate in that all its wartime allocations were Massey-bodied Guys, four in all, and the last ones were promptly repainted in the full and very smart dark blue, red and white livery shown here. Dangers from marauding aircraft were considered to be over when the last ones were delivered in 1945. Most operators received a mixed selection, often of chassis and body makes new to their fleets.

Above, left and right: Some Massey Bros. utility buses were painted a dark red, almost red oxide colour, and Stockport's 216 (JA 7716) is seen in Manchester's Parker Street bus station in this condition. In contrast number 212 from the same batch of seven vehicles is seen in early post-war operating in its home town after a full repaint into the Corporation's smart red and white livery. Stockport was another operator which chose not to return to Pemberton after the wartime allocations which clearly served it well. Alongside No. 212 stands part of the answer – a locally-built Crossley with both chassis and body built within the Borough. Support home industry and keep local people employed! (HSPC)

CHAPTER 5
Postwar developments to 1950

With the end of hostilities, first in Europe and then in Japan, people in Britain looked forward to a return to normality, with peace and prosperity, but they would have a long wait. The cost of the war, both in human and monetary terms, had brought the country to its knees and now the burden of wartime loans became apparent as they were required to be repaid. Added to all this was a change of Government, with very different aspirations from its predecessor. Laudable as some of those aspirations were, the bottom line was always the same – whilst there is no money available, little can be done. Austerity continued to be the key word, and even tighter restrictions than had applied during the war years became necessary. When bread was rationed that was seen as the last straw.

The effects were soon felt in the transport industry as raw materials continued to be in desperately short supply, especially so with aluminium and steel, whilst seasoned timber was virtually non-existent. Timber needed to be cut and left to dry out, otherwise it would rot very quickly. And, of course, that is exactly what happened, and why so many of the early post-war bodies were no better, or were worse, than their wartime counterparts. Bus bodies using unseasoned timber were doomed from the day they were built. Generally, rationing and allocations were the order of the day throughout the country, and red tape abounded.

Allocations of buses by the Ministry of Supply had brought many new 'customers' to Massey's doors, as they had to other bodybuilders. It would be interesting to see who would come back now that they had some measure of choice. Perhaps the greatest beneficiary of the situation was Guy Motors. It had been brought back from near oblivion in the late 1930s, and its wartime chassis had made it many friends throughout the industry. With Leyland building only double-deckers, and looking for export business, Guy would be able to capitalise on its wartime Arab masterpiece, gaining considerable business from those new friends.

In the half-decade 1935-39 Massey had bodied no Guy chassis; in the corresponding period from 1946-50 70 Guys passed through the Pemberton works. Operators supplied with utility bodies on Guy or Daimler chassis but not previously Massey customers included

Aberdeen, Accrington, Ashton-under-Lyne, Baker (Warsop), Barrow in Furness, Blackburn, Bradford, Brown (Gaerlochhead), Central SMT, Clyde Coast, Derby, Doncaster, Dundee, Edinburgh, Everingham (Pocklington), Glasgow, Graham (Paisley), Grimsby, Harper (Heath Hayes), Lanarkshire, Lancashire United, Lancaster, Laurie (Hamilton), London Transport, Newbury & District, Newcastle on Tyne, Northern General, Nottingham, Rawtenstall, Red & White, Rochdale, SHMD, Scottish Motor Traction, Severn (Stainforth), South Shields, Stockport, Truman (Shirebrook), Walsall, West Hartlepool, West Mon, Western SMT, Yorkshire Traction, Yorkshire Woollen, Young (Paisley)

Not everyone would return of course; local operator Lancashire United had been allocated four highbridge Massey utilities on Guy chassis, but although they took large numbers of the post-war Wolverhampton chassis until 1967 they never took another Massey body. Some you win, some you lose.

The post-war orders would continue the general previous pattern of coming from Municipalities and Independent operators, with South Wales being well represented as before. Tilling Group orders were non-existent, as were any from the other major group, BET. A revision of shareholdings during 1942 following a restructuring of these two giants had resulted in some operators 'changing sides', two prime examples being Crosville to the Tilling Group and

Two views of Rochdale Corporation No. 21, one of ten Daimler CWD6 models delivered at the end of 1945 and showing the immediate post-war styling employed by Massey. The first photograph shows No. 21 when new and homeward bound on the 17 service from Manchester to Rochdale jointly operated with Manchester Corporation. The second picture shows the same vehicle some years later awaiting passengers in Rochdale town centre. The blue and cream livery, with its swoops, contrasted with the red and cream of Manchester's vehicles, which by this time were being supplied in its post-war livery without streamline swoops. (STA left; EO below)

North Western to BET. It would be the movement of Cumberland from family-owned to joining the Tilling stable that would affect Massey Bros. though, for, at a stroke, they lost one of their oldest, most loyal and very significant customers, as we shall see.

Notwithstanding the many difficulties with staff and material shortages, Massey Bros was one of the first bodybuilders to return to peacetime standards, and superior bodies on Daimler CW chassis were delivered to Newcastle and Rochdale Corporations before the end of 1945. Daimler and Guy had, of course, kept the industry going with their wartime chassis, and Massey had bodied some 65 of the former and 270 of the latter between 1942 and 1945. These first post-war bodies were characterised by the provision of window pans giving radiused lower corners to the windows and outswept lower side panels, which contrasted greatly with the austerity appearance that had been imposed on manufacturers.

Government policy was, understandably, focused on the massive debt and our inability to import raw materials through our inability to pay for them. Accordingly, exports were given absolute priority and such scarce resources as were available were allocated, through Government directives, to those overseas orders which would bring in desperately needed currency.

It also became vital to maximise output, and at nearby Leyland Motors, as one example, all bus output was concentrated on standard double-deck designs, either 53-seat lowbridge or 56-seat highbridge, front engine and rear entrance. Livery and choice of seat trim was about as far as many operators could influence the finished product. Whilst this was fine for keeping production levels high at Leyland it did open the door for other bodybuilders, provided they could obtain chassis and materials to build bodywork. It is interesting to recall that between 1939, when it ceased peacetime bus building, and 1950 Leyland built no single-decker bodies whatsoever, returning to this market only when it introduced its underfloor-engined chassis, of which more later.

The dimensions to which buses and coaches could be built were, at this time, unchanged from pre-war days. All vehicles were restricted to an overall width of 7ft 6in, and whilst 2-axled single-deckers could be 27ft 6in long, double-deckers were limited to 26ft. Vehicles with three axles, of whatever body configuration, were limited to 30ft. The industry was now pressing for change and bodybuilders would soon be faced with operators wanting to take advantage when the regulations were relaxed in 1946, initially allowing the width to be increased to 8ft where the route had been approved for such vehicles by the appropriate Traffic Commissioners. By 1948 all vehicles could be built to the new width, but a small minority of operators continued to take 7ft 6in vehicles where narrow streets were a particular problem. Warrington and Jersey were two widely separated examples, though the Warrington vehicles were bodied by ELCB.

Massey Bros. records do not indicate which operators were first in taking 8ft-wide vehicles, but looking through the many photographs it will soon become apparent where the change has taken place.

During the final two months of 1945 Massey's bodyshop turned out 16 vehicles on Daimler CWD chassis, ten for Rochdale and six for Newcastle, as previously mentioned. The Newcastle contract was completed by April 1946, and other customers taking bodies on that same chassis during the spring of that year included West Hartlepool, Sunderland, Chesterfield and the Scottish independent Sutherland of Peterhead.

Peacetime chassis supply began with the Guy Arab III single-deck examples, and the first AEC Regal chassis, both being completed by June, with two for Chester being first post-war AECs out of the factory. By Christmas some 68 bodies had been built in that first full year of peacetime production. Birkenhead had the honour of taking the first Leyland double-deckers, twelve of the new PD1 model being completed and delivered before the year end.

In December 1946 Mr CT Humpidge, general manager and engineer of Rochdale Corporation, designed a body for fitting to a 1938 Leyland Titan TD5c chassis of which the original Cravens unit had been severely damaged during an accident. Mr Humpidge's idea was primarily to reduce the number of platform accidents and secondly to eliminate draughts and dust, making the vehicle warmer and more comfortable, particularly on limited-stop services. The wider-than-normal central entrance was protected by double air-operated doors, which could be operated by the driver or conductor. A warning light was fitted in front of the driver indicating whether the doors were opened or closed. No further examples of this type were built, however.

An interesting design change at this period was the shape of the lower deck end windows, which at first were semi-circular. By 1948 the rounded shape had changed to incorporate a larger radius at the top as in the 1939 outline, of which examples had gone to Cumberland Motor Services and Bolton. The early post-war highbridge body possessed a more upright front profile, and the front corner pillars were more slender than in the final pre-war design.

The immediate post-war highbridge design was something of an interim one and was soon superseded by the more traditional Massey curved-front styling. Examples of this traditional design were delivered to Birkenhead in late 1946 and to Chester in 1947. Neither of these long-standing Massey customers received the interim design.

In complete contrast to the first post-war highbridge bodies, a new lowbridge design was introduced in 1947, with examples being supplied to Cumberland Motor Services, Southend Corporation and several independent operators. This was notable for the extreme degree of curvature and

The body on this vehicle was originally attributed South Wales coachbuilder DJ Davies. As can b here JC 8427 was definitely Massey bodied, and outside the Pemberton Works awaiting deliv Roberts (Purple Motors) of Bethesda in Februar It was finally withdrawn in 1966 and went to Coaches of Dunstable where it lasted for three before being scrapped.

The Rochdale Corporation Leyland Titan for whic the General Manager Mr Humpidge designe the forward entrance and staircase arrangemer was duly completed in December 1946 ar photographed on a typically gloomy winter day. The vehicle is also seen a few years later Rochdale town centre, surrounded by vehicles fro the home and neighbouring fleets. The upper vie shows the post-war body outline very clearly.

nderland Corporation No. 18 was one of four Massey bodies
Daimler CWD6 chassis delivered in 1946. They all gave
elve years service before being withdrawn and sold to Wessex
aches of Bristol who converted this particular bus to a towing
hicle three years later, in 1961.

Number 45 (EF 7529) in the West Hartlepool fleet was one of three Daimler
CWD6 examples delivered in February 1946 with similar body styling to the
vehicle in the previous photograph. Operators in the north east seemed very
keen on displaying adverts at the front of their vehicles with *Shop at Binns*
probably being the most famous. (RLK)

ove left: The Tees-Side Railless Traction Board
as based at South Bank, near Middlesbrough, and
ught this Leyland Titan PD1A in 1947. It is seen
ior to delivery at the Summersales Colliery, just
wn the road from the Massey premises where
wly bodied vehicles were taken to be weighed
d often, as here, photographed.

ove right: Greenshields was a small independent
erator from the picturesque village of Salsburgh,
' miles east of Glasgow. They purchased this 55-
at lowbridge-bodied Guy Arab II in 1946 and it
came No. 6 in their fleet. Photographed before
livery, it shows the pronounced front upper-deck
ke to good effect. In 1960 Greenshields were
ken over by Golden Eagle Coaches, also based in
lsburgh.

rake to the front which made these bodies even more distinctive than their
highbridge counterparts. The roof of the lowbridge body was much deeper than
the usual Massey deep and well-radiused design. This certainly avoided the
flat-topped appearance found on some lowbridge outlines, although visibility
was less satisfactory from the passengers' point of view. In both lowbridge
and highbridge post-war designs the distinctive polished woodwork of the front
bulkhead gave way to white paint, and on Leyland chassis, the curved lower
edge of the windscreen was replaced by a straight edge. This was due to the
Leyland dash which could not be cut because of the instrument panel. These
variations, however, all managed to retain the distinctive Massey appearance.

The early post-war single-deck designs were no less distinctive and
characteristically 'Massey'. Appearing in 1946 they featured the D-shaped
window to the first bay, a well-raked windscreen and a half-canopy which was
unusual on a service bus, though common in coach design at the time. A later
version incorporated a full-width front canopy. Orders for single-deckers were
less numerous than those for double-deckers, largely for the reasons already

Stockton Corporation ordered their first Massey bodies in 1947, and in a three year period to the end of 1949 a total of 43 were delivered on various chassis. The two photographs on the left and below left, are of vehicles from the initial order for Daimler CWD6 models showing the more upright frontal design used during the immediate post-war period. Numbers 45 and 43 were photographed the early 'fifties. (RLK, below left)

Massey-bodied Bristols were something of a rarity. Below is Stockton-on-Tees No. 10, a Bristol K6G built in 1947. Note the change in angle of the front panel spoiling the line and giving the front of the body an awkward and old-fashioned appearance. (RLK)

mentioned, but nevertheless a wide range of operators was supplied including Cumberland Motor Services along with Birkenhead, Chester and Newcastle Corporations, and some small independents.

During this period, Massey-bodied double-deckers gained popularity in the north-east of England, with substantial orders coming from Newcastle, Stockton and Sunderland Corporations. A surprising order during this period was for 20 Guy Arab III single-deck dual-purpose buses for Walter Alexander & Sons Ltd and eight similar vehicles with bus bodies for Newcastle upon Tyne Corporation. There were many independents entering Massey Bros order book for the first time and two interesting orders for double-deck bodies on Bristol K6G chassis were completed in July 1947, four for Stockton-on-Tees and three for Merthyr Tydfil.

Perhaps the most prosperous time of Massey Bros history was this post-war period from 1946 to 1950 when the company still standardised on composite (timber-framed) construction. Early post-war bodies invariably proved troublesome due largely to the use of unseasoned timber in the framework as discussed earlier, and many bodies required varying degrees of repair and rebuilding at a relatively early age. Massey Bros products were no exception, and it may have been this factor, together with the general trend of the industry, which influenced the directors to look towards metal-framed construction as good timber became ever more difficult to obtain. All ten lowbridge-

Pictured in July 1946 below and on the opposite page outside the finishing shop at Enfield Street with the engine running ready to embark on the long journey northwards, was Walter Alexander (Fife) Limited No. G38, a Guy Arab III which was one of 20 similar vehicles supplied in the late 1940s Alexander's bodyshops were busy rebuilding their own wartime double-deckers, and also building new Leyland PD1s under sub-contract to Leyland Motors at this time.

Stockton Corporation placed orders for Massey bodies on four different chassis makes during the immediate post-war period. This particular vehicle was one of eight supplied on Guy Arab chassis (two on Mk II and six on Mk III). Number 10, (GUP 558), a Mk III model, awaits departure from Enfield Street to the north east on a dull February day in 1947. The Massey body transfer is just visible.

Chester Corporation purchased two AEC Regals in 1946, both with 32-seat front entrance, half canopy bodies. Number 65 (FFM 661) was spotted in the town centre in the early 'fifties and ultimately gave II years service before being withdrawn and scrapped. Sister vehicle No. 64 lasted until 1963. (HSPC)

As mentioned in the text the Guy Arab III single deckers supplied to Newcastle Corporation were the first post-war chassis received by Massey Bros. Former Newcastle No. 56 later joined the fleet of M Charlton & Sons Ltd, of Newburgh in the county of Northumberland. Charltons operated several stage carriage services in the Tyne Valley. In 1961 their services passed to Mid Tyne Transport who continued to trade as Charltons and to Tyne Valley Coaches in 1967. On passing to Charltons it was given fleet No. 27 and is pictured at Haltwhistle. (RCD)

bodied Leyland Titan PD1s supplied to Cumberland in 1948 were extensively rebuilt by the company in 1955 and 1956 in advance of the rebuilding which took place on the Northern Coachbuilders bodies supplied at the same time.

This was the last order placed by Cumberland Motor Services due to the BTC/Tilling Group policy on vehicle purchasing. As part of the government's moves toward nationalisation of the transport industry, *the Transport Act 1947* resulted in the formation of the British Transport Commission (BTC). The railway companies were nationalised from 1st January 1948 with the result that their significant stake in the Tilling and many BET bus companies passed into public ownership from that date. Tilling sold its remaining holdings to the BTC at the beginning of 1949, as did the Scottish Motor Traction group.

In 1948 the Massey brothers resolved to form the business into a limited company and the Certificate of Incorporation is shown on the facing page. The initial directors were, unsurprisingly, the three brothers but sadly William and Isaac died within a few years. As a result, Arthur Tyldesley, Isaac's son-in-law, who was born in Wigan in 1908 and who had been working in the electricity supply industry, initially in Wigan and then in Salford, as an electrical engineer, joined the company in 1950 as managing director. The surviving brother, Thomas (often referred to as Uncle Tom) died in 1954 and Arthur Tyldesley then became chairman of the company, assisted by George Chapman as company secretary. Although William was a silent partner in the firm, his three sons were all employed by Massey Bros. Arnold worked on the shop floor and died in the early 'sixties. Thomas became paint shop foreman but retired before the NCME takeover and died in 1975. Norman became joint managing director with Arthur Tyldesley and they both went to NCME on a consultancy basis. Arthur retired soon after to Ambleside but Norman did not retire until 1974 and died in 1983.

Leyland Tiger PS1s were thin on the ground wh[en] this one was supplied to the north Staffordshi[re] independent Mainwaring, in September 19[..]. Number 21 was the second of two, and is weari[ng] the dark red livery which was changed to blue a[nd] cream two years later. There had been five PS[1s] going through at this time, with an earlier five [–] the first post-war Leyland single-deckers – going [to] Cumberland in March of that year.

Colchester Corporation No. 54 was one of four AEC Regent II models with classic late 'forties body styling delivered in the spring of 1947. One was withdrawn in 1964 whilst the others, including this one, lasted another two years, until 1966.

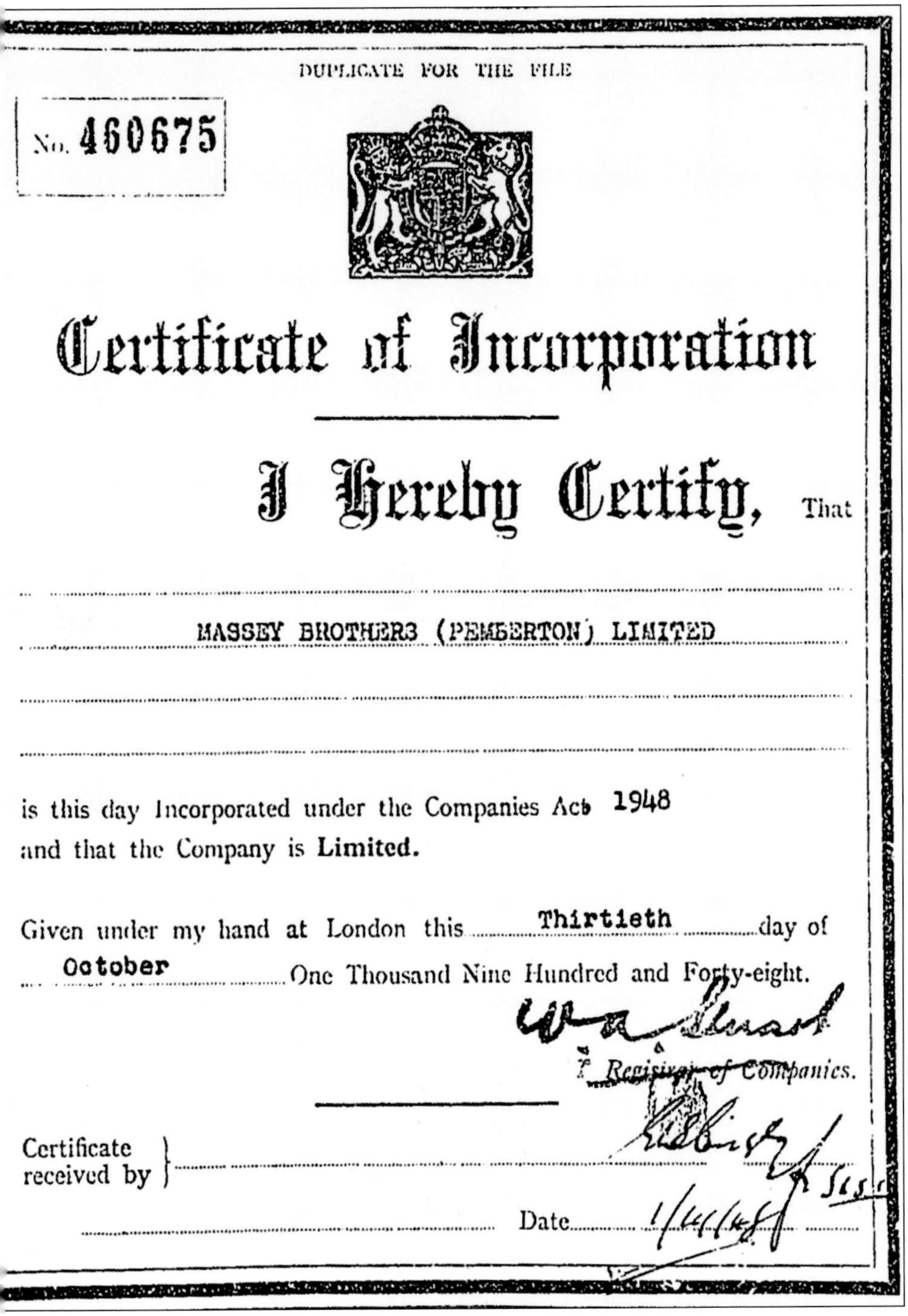

DUPLICATE FOR THE FILE

No. 460675

Certificate of Incorporation

I Hereby Certify, That

MASSEY BROTHERS (PEMBERTON) LIMITED

is this day Incorporated under the Companies Act **1948** and that the Company is **Limited.**

Given under my hand at London this **Thirtieth** day of **October** One Thousand Nine Hundred and Forty-eight.

Registrar of Companies.

Certificate received by }

Date 1/4/48

Link broken as Norman retires

The last link between a well-known Pemberton family and the old-established coach-building firm of Massey Brothers, Enfield Street, was broken last Friday.

For Mr. Norman Massey, the only remaining member of the family still in the firm, retired at the age of 65.

Mr. Massey, of West Mount, Orrell, has completed 50 years service with Massey Brothers. The firm was founded by his father and two of his uncles. For several generations, many Pemberton people have found employment in the firm's Enfield Street workshops.

Since Mr. Massey started work, the methods of production have changed greatly. In his early days he worked on all kinds of vehicle bodies, including the old fashioned trams used by Salford Corporation. Today the firm produces the bodywork and luxury finish of modern buses.

Although Massey Brothers was taken over by the Northern Counties firm about six years ago, Mr. Massey stayed on as works manager. A widower, Mr. Massey will now have more time to enjoy his hobbies of music and gardening.

Mr. Massey.

When Norman Massey retired in 1974 the local newspaper gave him a suitable send off as seen above. (STA)

As stated opposite, in 1948 the partners of Massey Bros. formed a company which was trade as Massey Brothers (Pemberton) Limited. (The original papers referred to the company as 'Massey Bros. (Pemberton) Limited' but it would seem that such abbreviations did not find favour with the bureaucrats at Companies House!). The following year they had a sale agreement drawn up and sold the business to the new company for £35,000. The initial directors were William, Isaac and Thomas Massey and the share capital was set £70,000. William and Isaac died in 1949 and 1950 respectively and were subsequently replaced by Clara Tyldesley (nee Massey, daughter of Isaac) and her husband Arthur.

In 1955 the share capital was written down by 50%, quite possibly in a move which reflected the difficult trading conditions of the previous few years, (see production chart on page 144) and following from this the legal bar on paying dividends (including to the family members as shareholders) whilst the balance sheet was showing losses.

Although the company was no longer trading in its own right, it was not until 1997 that was finally wound up.

Showing its well proportioned body and D-shaped windows to good effect was Chester Corporation's No. 60 (HFM 170), one of three Daimler CVA6 types, here passing the town centre's famous Rows on route 25 in the early 'fifties. *Andrews Liver Salts* graced the sides of many buses in those days and every decent sized town boasted a branch of the *Maypole* combine.

Another vehicle with bodywork similar to the above, apart from a chan to the bottom curve of the lower-deck end windows, which are n straight. Great Yarmouth Corporation's No. 53 (EX 5933) was one of t Leyland Titan PD1As delivered in 1948. It is seen on the sea-front ne Wellington Pier. Note that at this time Great Yarmouth were still usi their original two-letter registration marks.

West Monmouthshire Omnibus Board bought this lowbridge bodied AEC Regent III in 1948. The two photographs on the right show the vehicle at Summersales Colliery down the road from Massey's works, where, as mentioned previously, vehicles were weighed before certification and delivery to the customer.

Notwithstanding all the checks and inspection routines is displaying the wrong registration number (GWO 442) while being weighed. However, the error was later rectified and the necessary correction made (GWO 422), as shown in the picture below when the bus was photographed on home territory in service on its way back to Blackwood depot.

It was numbered 17 in this mainly Leyland fleet and gave 17 years service before being withdrawn and eventually sold for scrap in 1966. (STA below)

These two Leylands were from the last batch of vehicles bodied by Massey Bros. for Cumberland Motor Services, ending an association which had lasted 25 years. The views at the bodybuilders show Leyland PD1 number 245, (GAO 783) above, and 246 (GAO 784) left, just before entering service in March 1948. An example in service from the same batch is No. 219, (GAO 757) seen in Workington bus station and waiting to depart for Harrington. (RM, below)

Pictured at the 1948 Commercial Motor Show in London is Chester Corporation's No. 72, a Foden PVD6, 'price, complete as shown £4,131', as stated in the catalogue. This vehicle was the first of a batch of eight with typical Massey body styling of that period. A further two had bodies of similar styling built by the firm of D J Davies based in south Wales. (PT)

Massey Brothers only ever bodied one Crossley after WWII, this bus becoming a firm favourite with many enthusiasts. It was numbered 55 in the Colchester fleet and dates from November 1948. The long droopy wings spoil the appearance of an otherwise pleasing design. It is seen here on the number 6 service in the early 1960s. (LM)

Burnley Colne and Nelson Joint Transport Committee, to give the full title, bought six Leyland Tiger PS1 examples in 1948. Number 16 is shown in a pre-delivery shot with the Burnley driver Mr Bert Heaps in the cab; his son Cliff is a volunteer for the Leyland Preservation Society.

A rather restrained (by Massey standards) highbridge body wa introduced in the post-war period and seemed something of compromise but was nevertheless attractive. LVK88 was one o 28 AEC Regent III 9612E chassis supplied in 1948/9 to Newcastl Corporation and is seen after repainting from the blue and crear livery as delivered into the later yellow version seen here. Most o the batch lasted until 1962/3. (RCD)

Between duties in the Queensgate depot yard is a Leyland Tiger PS1 from the same batch as the vehicle above. The whole batch was rebuilt by BCN in 1958 and No. 19 shown here was the last one, being withdrawn in 1965. (JL)

Milton Bus Service of Stoke-on-Trent purchased two of these Leylan PS1s in 1947 this one being No. 10 (NRF 950). Milton's were take over by Potteries Motor Traction four years later when they wer both renumbered S319 (10) and S320 (11) remaining in service unt 1960. Compare the different door types on this and the Burnley PS

Stopped to pose for the camera while on delivery to Birkenhead Corporation were two Guy Arab Mk IIIs, numbers 148 and 146, part of a batch of fifteen such vehicles that entered service in March and April of 1949. Note the almost defiant placing of the coat of arms as near as could be to the filler cap, and the polished trim to catch the inevitable drips from refuelling. The offside indicator is unusual, though not unique, and the whole appearance marks attention to detail and pride which would, hopefully, be reflected in those who operate and those who ride in these fine vehicles.

Top left: Twenty five Leyland Titan PD2/3s were delivered to Stockton Corporation in 1949 and number 63 (KPT 768) is seen suitably adorned for the local Festival Week in 1951.

Top right and middle left: The first of a batch of 30 Daimler CVG6 models for Birkenhead Corporation were delivered between August 1949 and March 1950. Number 172 (ACM 630) poses in the August sunshine at the much-photographed Summersales Colliery location with Norman Massey standing alongside in the lower view. These buses gave an average of 15 years service before withdrawal in the mid-'sixties.

Below: A splendid shot of Phillips of Hollywell's Foden PVD6 (FDM 724) as it wends its way through its hometown near to the Dee estuary in north east Wales en route to the local Courtaulds factory in March 1967. The Foden bonnet blended very well with the Massey body curves.

CHAPTER 6
Changing times in the '50s

The first post-war metal-framed body was produced in 1950. It was of highbridge pattern and became No. 201 (ABG 301) in the fleet of Birkenhead Corporation, one of a batch of fifteen on Guy Arab 6LW chassis. The others of the batch were of the then-conventional composite construction. The metal-framed example omitted the then-current D-shaped end windows in the lower saloon and the outswept lower panels traditionally associated with Massey bodies. Good interior finish and appointment were always characteristics of the make. Even the wartime bodies retained the attractively grained interior window fillets and bulkhead framework. The metal-framed designs maintained the tradition, together with that of attractive external appearance. Indeed, in some ways, the later metal-framed designs were reminiscent of the handsome outlines of 1939. Metal-framed bodies rapidly became the standard, and Massey Bros produced few composite bodies after 1952 and none after 1954. The company built up a good reputation among operators for solid and reliable construction of its metal-framed bodies.

With the advent of metal-framed construction, the lowbridge design was changed to incorporate a less sharply-raked front profile with a shallower roof line. This design was to continue to the end of production.

Following the post-war bus boom, in 1951/2 body production at Enfield Street amounted only to a total of 23 new bodies for this period. However, this figure was augmented by the refurbishment of 20 Birkenhead Corporation TD5c double-deckers from a 1939 batch. A special single-decker was built for Barton Transport, the famous independent operator in the East Midlands, which was designated as a Barton BTS1 and given a dual-purpose body. Chester Corporation decided to rebody four wartime utility Guy Arab II double-deckers.

Birkenhead Corporation's No. 201, (ABG 301), had the distinction of being the first Massey all-metal bodied production double-decker, and was also fitted with a sliding cab-door. The Guy Arab III is seen at Summersales Colliery prior to delivery in October 1950. The change from D-shaped windows has improved the appearance of the bodyside and this must be classed as one of the best traditional Massey designs. Note how the Gardner 6LW engine causes the radiator to project forward beyond the cab front. This would not have been possible until the permissible overall length was increased to 27ft 6in – wartime vehicles with this engine had needed a special MoWT dispensation.

AEC chassis were back in favour during 1951 when Southend Corporation purchased six Regent III models of the 6811A designation with lowbridge bodywork. They had the smaller 7.7-litre engine, crash gearboxes and vacuum brakes, but were considered adequate for the short and relatively flat routes in operation before route co-ordination in 1955. The top and centre pictures show No. 262 at Summersales Colliery for weighing prior to delivery; note the old destination layout.

The lower photograph shows No. 258 in service with the new destination display to accommodate the many permutations that existed once the route co-ordination agreement with Eastern National was in force.

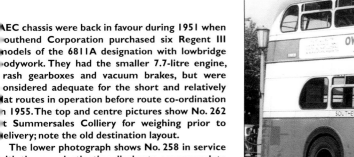

Complete with trade plates is Bury Corporation No. 73, one of four 1938 TS8c chassis rebuilt to TD5 designation and this time with double-deck bodies. It is standing at the pit-head complex of Summersales Colliery. The original four Tigers had been supplied with Burlingham single-deck bodywork but Bury were unable to sell them in this form and in late 1951 decided to have them rebodied. They were all withdrawn in 1958 and passed to Tiger (dealer) of Salsburgh who sold three of them to Paton Brothers of Renfrew and the other to Dunoon Motor Services. Number 53 in the Paton fleet was spotted a few years later at an unidentified location.

Barton Transport No. 651 was one of a number of rebuilds undertaken by this independent during the post-war period, and in this instance designated BTS1. The chassis on this vehicle was previously a Leyland PS1 from 1948 (No. 541) with a Duple body but it was rebuilt in 1951 with a new 30ft chassis frame and sent to Massey Bros. for a new dual-purpose body which was photographed in October 1951 prior to delivery. It was withdrawn in 1966 and sold to a church youth club. In June 1972 it became a mobile caravan, but in 1973 was back in service with Gosport Buses of Glasgow and was last seen in Ayr in 1979. Pictured below is the rear of 651 also taken when new at Pemberton. Despite the extent of the reconstruction it retained its original registration number throughout its life.

Pictured above at Bank Qua
Warrington, in the early 'sixties wa
Naylor's of Stockton Heath Gu
Arab III (NMB 314), with its 55-se
lowbridge body dating from 1951.

Lowestoft Corporation had previously purchase
its bodywork from nearby Eastern Coach Work
just a good stone's throw from their own depe
in the seaside town. When ECW were preclude
from supplying non-Tilling Group fleets the loc
Corporation turned back to Massey – the differenc
in distance between the two suppliers could hard
have been greater! Number 28, (LBJ 743), was on
of two AEC Regent IIIs about to make the lor
delivery journey to East Anglia in January 1951.

Whieldon's (Green Bus) of Rugeley in Staffordshire bought many Fodens over the years including this 37-seat Foden PVSC6 coach (XRE 979) delivered in August 1952, and Massey's last coach body. Number 25 in the Whieldon fleet was caught on camera at Lamberhead Green near to Massey's works, often used in the 'fifties and 'sixties for pre-delivery shots. It was to remain in service until December 1964 when it was withdrawn and scrapped.

Below: Having just started its long journey to south Wales, Llynfi Motors No. 59 (KTX 631) a Leyland Tiger PS2/3 with dual-purpose bodywork, pauses in Lodge Lane on the western perimeter of Haydock Park Racecourse in April 1951 for a photographic session.

Pre-delivery views near Haydock Park Racecourse in M[?] 1952 of a Foden PVD6 for James Smith of Barrhead, pa[?] of the Scottish Co-operative Wholesale Society since 194[?] The vehicle survived until 1963 when it was withdrawn a[?] scrapped. It is clear from these two pages, and reference [?] the body list, that Massey and Foden were no strangers [?] each other.

As seen earlier Phillips of Holywell, a town near the Riv[?] Dee estuary in north east Wales, purchased this Foden PVI[?] (FDM 724) in 1949, and here it is pictured below outsi[?] the Foden works in Sandbach before delivery. The front e[?] arrangement of the Foden was particularly neat, as can [?] seen. The vehicle went into 'preservation' in January 197[?] with Hollis of nearby Queensferry, and thence to BaMMO[?] in December 1980 where it is currently stored pendin[?] eventual restoration. (PT)

owbotham of Harriseahead near
toke-on-Trent purchased this Foden
VD6 in 1952 and it is shown prior to
elivery in June of that year. Potteries
otor Traction acquired the fleet of
owbotham's in 1959 giving it fleet
umber H812. The second photograph
ows it after the takeover in PMT
very inside one of its new owner's
epots. (PT)

Massey Bros receiving the order for two of these (46, (FFM 278) and 55, (FFM 299). It is interesting to note that the other two, 53 and 54, (FFM 297/8), rebodied by D J Davies of Merthyr Tydfil gave only a further nine years' service, whereas the Massey examples continued for another seventeen years. Yet another interesting vehicle was the full-fronted Foden coach built for Green Bus of Rugeley seen on page 91.

It was around this time that Southend Corporation decided to replace their trolleybus fleet and London Transport were replacing their non-standard wartime deliveries with new RTs. As a result a large number of Daimler CWs appeared on the second-hand market. Southend Corporation inspected 18 of these vehicles at the premises of second-hand bus dealer North's of Leeds. Thirteen were found to be suitable for rebodying by Massey Bros which they undertook between February and June 1954. These vehicles were the first in the Southend fleet to be fitted from new with the revised style destination display in readiness for their new co-ordinated services. The Corporation, still five vehicles short, ordered a batch of five Leyland Titan PD2/20s that Massey Bros duly completed in September.

The smart HP Sauce van body referred to in t[ ] adjacent text.

Shortly after delivery of these buses, Massey Bros received a highly interesting 'one-off' order from another source in the town of Southend, which was for the building of a mobile police station on a Vanmaster trailer.

Moorfields of Pemberton, only a short distance from Enfield Street, sub-contracted Massey Bros to build three 5-ton HP Sauce vans on Austin chassis. These were to be used at the HP Birmingham depot, the order being completed in 1956. Unfortunately, no colour photographs exist of these vehicles.

Meanwhile Morecambe & Heysham, Exeter and Maidstone Corporations placed their first orders for double-deck bodies. At this time there was a desire within the industry to reduce vehicle weight in order to lower fuel consumption (mainly due to sharp increases in fuel duty in 1951/2, followed by the Suez Crisis in 1956 ,making fuel supplies a bit worrisome), so lightweight bodies became the order of the day. The reduction in weight was generally achieved by simplified construction and spartan interior finish. Massey Bros, and

In 1951 Caerphilly UDC ordered a Leyland PS2/5 with bodywork from Bruce Coachworks of Cardiff but that organisation closed down before the order could be handled and the body order was switched to Massey Brothers. Number 1, looking very smart, was photographed in June 1952 and continued in service until 1969 when it became a training/towing vehicle and was renumbered 51. It is worth reflecting that at the time this bus was being delivered to Caerphilly, Ribble vehicles passing through Wigan would have included examples of Leyland's Royal Tiger underfloor-engined buses and coaches. This was the last-but-one front-engined single-deck bus Massey built for the home market.

Southend Corporation's wartime lowbridge Daimler CWA6's were worked hard, and six were rebodied by Massey in 1952. This is No. 231, BHJ 805, nearing completion in the Massey bodyshop. This was one of a batch of six to be rebodied (sister vehicle 806 is visible behind) and this particular vehicle had clocked up 691,596 miles when finally withdrawn in 1965, a testimony to the rugged wartime Daimler chassis. Note that Southend have had the radiators chromium plated to enhance the appearance, in keeping with the rest of its very smart fleet.

The traditional appurtenances of the bodybuilding shop – wooden ladders, planks and trestles – would be unlikely to be approved for use in today's more safety conscious environment. Barrels, milk crates and oil drums were regularly used to support items from temporary benches, as in the foreground, to complete chassis or even single-deck buses in build.

Below is a view of one the former London Transport wartime Daimlers mentioned on the facing page, after being rebodied and ready for its trip back down south. Note the revised destination layout referred to in the text on the facing page.

indeed some other coachbuilders resisted the temptation and continued to produce well-proportioned and well-finished bodies. As part of this move, Park Royal Vehicles replaced their well-proportioned attractive and well-finished body style with what was often regarded as the ugliest double-decker of the time. Arising from this a number of operators, who had previously standardised on Park Royal bodies, looked elsewhere. Southampton commenced using East Lancashire Coachbuilders, whilst Barrow-in-Furness and the previously mentioned Morecambe & Heysham turned to Massey Bros Ipswich Corporation placed orders with both Massey Bros and ELCB. Production of single-deck bodies on underfloor-

engined chassis got under way in the early 1950s but these represented only a small proportion of the total Massey output. During 1953 and 1954, two forty-seater buses were supplied to the Wankie Colliery in Southern Rhodesia (now Zimbabwe). A total of eight Foden FD6/12s, each seating 53, was supplied to the Mozambique Railways.

In 1954 Massey Bros. received an order for t building of eight 53-seat bus bodies on specia adapted Foden FG6/12 commercial chassis for t Lourenco Marques section of the Mozambiq Railways. Two are seen in build, above, whilst completed example is shown below about to hoisted aboard the ship before its long sea voya on one of Clan Lines' vessels.

SOUTHERN RHODESIA

WANKIE AREA

Operating Conditions —Worst in Country

—SO FODENS ARE THE CHOICE

Jack Henderson, cab builder to Messrs. Hubert Davies & Co. Ltd., our agents for the Rhodesias.

The famous Wankie Collieries operate seventy vehicles and mobile plant under the worst conditions in the Colony. In the fleet are the ten Fodens shown above, plus two more Fodens since added and another Foden is on the way. Mr. Phil Broster called at Wankie in the course of his latest overseas tour and since then Mr. W. B. Priestley, Road Transport Manager at Wankie, has been kind enough to add the following information.

His department has a European staff of ten, fifty African drivers and 130 African loading boys. The best drivers are recruited from the loading boys, starting right from scratch and the African instructor obtains an easy 75 per cent. pass on heavy vehicles.

All vehicles are serviced and, because of dust, oil is changed every 500 miles. Tyre mileage is about a third of that obtained in Britain.

All drivers are on spring bonus and spring breakage has dropped by 80 per cent. since this was instituted.

* *

Mr. Priestley has supplied a list of the routes served by his buses—too lengthy to print—but it is interesting to note that most routes take in Piccadilly Circus, e.g. Route No. 9—Garage, Barber's Shop, Gordon's Store, Post Office, Piccadilly Circus, Club, Gold Course, New Town, Lower Colliery Road, Garage.

* *

It cannot be imagined that the Piccadilly Circus of Wankie tolerates lounge liz-

ards but snakes can be troublesome and Mr. Priestley reports a request from one of his drivers that we should put a wire gauze window over the ventilator holes in front of the cab, adding:

"The last Foden that was delivered (a 7½ ton Side Tipper) was coming from some development work in the bush when a snake popped its head through the ventilator on the inside of the cab, looked around and popped back again. Lockheed Hydraulics and Foden Booster came into operation immediately, and a hurried exit was made by Driver and crew. The ventilator holes were stuffed with cementbags and the vehicle driven back to the Garage, where the crew demanded removal of the snake. Mr. Barratt (my Fore-

man) and myself made an examination of the engine, radiator cowling, etc., blasted everything we could with water and compressed air, but no snake appeared; the crew were insistent that the snake was still there, and flatly refused to go out again.

Whilst we were arguing as to whether the snake was there or not, it appeared on the windscreen ledge inside the cab; there was a hurried stampede of boys, and the snake was attacked and despatched with sundry jack handles and sweeping brushes."

Request noted Mr. Priestley, and if the window fails to do the trick we will fly out one of our most talented snake charmers. By the way, we are curious about the type of snake. Could it be a vindscreen viper?

During 1953/4 Masseys also built two 31-seat bus bodies on Foden PVSC6 chassis for the Wankie Colliery in southern Rhodesia – now Zimbabwe – one of which is seen prior to delivery at Foden's works and described in the article above. The item will be seen to record a bonus paid to the drivers – a spring bonus – which resulted in an 80% reduction in broken springs. In between dodging potholes and avoiding snakes, their drivers appeared to have a fairly normal sort of occupation for bus and lorry drivers. (PT)

Two regular attenders at rallies over the years have been former Chester Corporation's Guy Arab IV number 1, (RFM 641), dating from 1953, seen here in Manchester's Heaton Park for the annual Trans-Lancs Rally, and former Birkenhead Corporation number 242, (BG 8557), an Arab II dating from 1944 and one of 15 rebodied by Massey in 1953, and seen far from home at the annual London to Brighton run at the beginning of May, around 1970. (JAS both)

Shown just prior to delivery in March 1953 was this Daimler CVD6 (GBW 336) which was one of four ordered by Smith of Upper Heyford in Oxfordshire. Apparently these were the only buses to be spray painted by Massey Brothers.

One of three stylish AEC Regent IIIs supplied to Colchester Corporation in 1953. This is number 10 (WPU 732) shown before delivery. All gave invaluable service before being withdrawn in October 1971. Comparison of this vehicle and the Heyfordian Daimler above clearly show the increase in width to 8ft of the Colchester vehicle's bodywork.

A forward-entrance lowbridge double-decker, evolved for Baxter's Bus Services Ltd of Airdrie, became another design available from 1960 and was based on four bays with a single sliding door. Four bodies to this design were constructed for Baxter's, mounted on Leyland Titan PD2/37 chassis. The requirement was for lowbridge bodies and the design involved the use of a special staircase which featured two sections to its upper portion, one serving the front of the upper saloon and the other the remainder. Baxter's took four between 1960 and 1961 and this illustrates again Massey Bros readiness to provide what the customer required.

Three highbridge versions were ordered by Chester Corporation on Guy Arab IV chassis complete with Johannesburg-style bonnets/radiators. These were Chester Corporation's first 8ft wide and 30ft long vehicles.

At the same time Caerphilly UDC ordered two 44-seat bodies on Leyland PSU1/13 chassis (OTG 517/8). The next example was a single body, again on a Leyland Royal Tiger chassis, delivered to Barrow-in-Furness Corporation the following year. This bore some resemblance to the early 1950s Leyland body (Leyland body-building ceased in 1954) and was unusual in being fitted with dual-purpose seating – it was registered BEO 397.

The highbridge body was also slightly re-styled in 1954, the most visual change being the upper deck front windows, which now appeared with only a small radius to the upper-corner. Again, what might have been considered to be a more modern four-bay design was offered but most customers preferred the original five-bay construction. A distinctive feature of the four-bay design was the additional short window adjacent to the rear platform, balanced by a corresponding window or panel on the offside. A forward-entrance was offered on the highbridge 30ft body from 1958, employing five-bay construction, again with a single sliding door. The final permutation was the forward-entrance highbridge 27ft body introduced in 1960, using four-bay construction and with the option of a single sliding door or a four-section jack-knife door.

This advert drew attention to the windows, but soon double-sliding units would become more popular. The Barrow vehicle in which they were mounted appears overleaf. (STA)

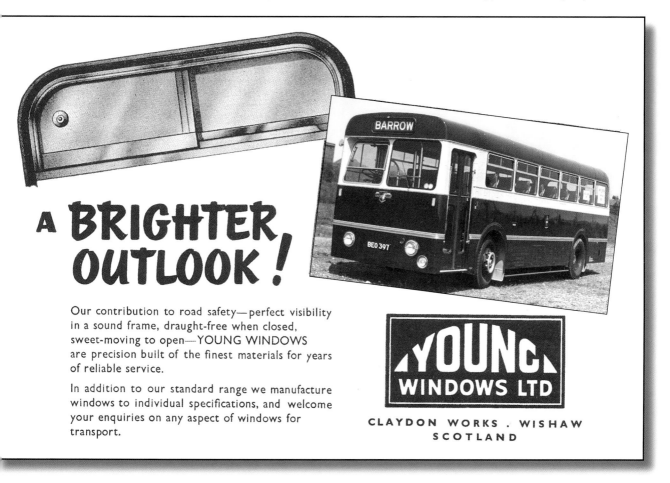

A **BRIGHTER OUTLOOK!**

Our contribution to road safety—perfect visibility in a sound frame, draught-free when closed, sweet-moving to open—YOUNG WINDOWS are precision built of the finest materials for years of reliable service.

In addition to our standard range we manufacture windows to individual specifications, and welcome your enquiries on any aspect of windows for transport.

YOUNG WINDOWS LTD

CLAYDON WORKS . WISHAW
SCOTLAND

Small batches of single-deckers were supplied to Birkenhead, Chester, Exeter and Ipswich Corporations and to Jersey Motor Transport in the 1960s. Those for Jersey were on special Leyland Tiger Cub chassis built to the dimensions of 27ft 6in long and 7ft 6in wide, to comply with the maximum permitted size in Jersey at that time. They were readily identifiable by the reduced overhang behind the rear wheels. It is interesting to note that in reporting their arrival, the local press in Jersey referred to these 40-seaters as "large capacity vehicles". Another innovation for Jersey reported at the same time was the use of continuous bell-press equipment.

These single-deckers were, however, to a later box-like design in which few established Massey characteristics were apparent. Four of these were supplied to Caerphilly UDC in 1963/4 and had seating for 55 which was a large capacity for single-deckers at that time. Dual-door versions of the same design were also built for Caerphilly and Chester Corporation in 1966. The three Chester vehicles were 40-seaters and had bays of differing widths in order to accommodate the centre door. Just a short distance away from Pemberton, a first-time order was received from J Fishwick & Sons of Leyland who ordered two 45-seater Leyland Tiger Cub PSUC1/12s.

Photographed outside the Massey workshops i 1956 was Baxter's of Airdrie No. 34, EVJ 807, th very last front-engined single-decker to be bodie at Pemberton, complete with trade plates an ready for the long northbound journey. This AE Regal I dating from 1947 and originally new to Jone of Burley Gate near Hereford passed to Hadwi of Ulverston before being bought by Baxter an rebodied by Massey Brothers. It survived into SO ownership and was eventually withdrawn in 1965.

Barrow Corporation had not ordered an new single-deckers since 1933, when, i the early 'fifties, several were purchase one of which was this Leyland Royal Tige PSU1/13, number 52 (BEO 397) with dua purpose seating for 43 passengers, use mainly for private hire. The vehicle was use in an advertisement for 'brighter window as seen on the previous page.

Caerphilly UDC purchased two Leylan Royal Tiger PSU1/13s in 1954, and show here is No. 7 before delivery. Note the fl driver's windscreen compared to the Roy Tiger of Barrow Corporation in the adjace illustration.

One of the new buses being unloaded this morning.   Photo : Lynn

New-type buses for J.M.T.

The J.M.T. Company took delivery this morning of two new-type buses, the first of five ordered. The remaining three are expected within a fortnight.

With a Leyland Motors chassis and Massey-built bodies, they seat 40 passengers and an additional number standing. A feature of them is the provision of a cash counter near the driver, at which passengers will pay fares when the buses are being operated by one man.

When this "one man" system is operated, an illuminated sign reading "pay as you enter" will be on display in front of the bus. At the moment, however, J.M.T. official plan to have both, drivers and conductors, aboard.

Passengers should welcome the bell-push, which takes the form of a continuous strip running along the length of the roof. It can be used at any point in the bus.

The J.M.T. hopes that these large-capacity vehicles will help them move passengers more quickly during the summer rush.

Jersey Motor Transport No. 623 being unloaded from MV Statenlan at New North Quay in St Helier on 31st May, 1962. This bus was later lengthened to 30ft, in 1967, giving five more passenger seats.

Numbered **DD10** in the fleet of **W Gash & Sons** of Newark, Nottinghamshire, was this Daimler CVG6, seen before delivery in July 1954 and then soon afterwards in service. The Gash fleet, in two shades of green, was always well turned out and the rear platform doors and Daimler nearside mudguard arrangement help to produce an extremely handsome vehicle. (HSP left and below both)

Famous entertainers of the period including pianist Sempreni are advertised at the entrance to Great Yarmouth's Wellington Pier, no doubt ready to entertain the crowds who will be coming to escape the rain coming in on the left of our picture. Meanwhile a Corporation Leyland Titan PD2/22 from a 1957 batch awaits passengers taking shelter elsewhere. (STA)

Southend Corporation No. 279, a Leyland Titan PD2/12 with lowbridge 65-seat bodywork complete with 'new-look' front. It was one of a batch of twelve supplied in 1955/6.

Below, left and right: Massey Brothers became firm favourites with Maidstone Corporation after the initial deliveries in 1956. These two photographs show number 1 (WKP 71) which was the first in a batch of six Leyland Titan PD2/20s noteworthy for having the revised front which did away with the traditional radiator, as also seen on the Yarmouth and Southend vehicles on this page.

Above left: Maidstone number 9 with its distinctive registration plate – 999 AKT – in its home town contrasts with fellow 413 seen above right in the Lancashire seaside town of Morecambe. During the mid-'seventies Lancaster City Council needed a speedy replacement for some older vehicles and bought several second-hand vehicles including four Leyland Titan PD2/30's from Maidstone Corporation. Former number 13 (413 GKT) was spotted at the Battery in Morecambe in 1975 having gained a neat renumbering exercise making it into 413 and was cannibalised for spares later that year. All four vehicles retained Maidstone's livery throughout their short lives with Lancaster.

Exeter Corporation's first order placed with Massey Bros. was for a batch of five Guy Arab IVs, placed in 1956. Number 51 is seen passing Grey Cars attractive Beadle Commer ROD 756. The newly appointed manager at Exeter had previously been at Chester.

Wigan number 7, above, was one of three Leyland Titan PD2/30 models with platform doors, delivered in 1958. On the right, number 62 is the forward-entrance successor version to the above, one of four Titan PD3/2 examples delivered a year later. Both views were taken on the Lamberhead Industrial Estate almost adjacent to the Massey works.

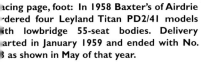

Facing page, foot: In 1958 Baxter's of Airdrie ordered four Leyland Titan PD2/41 models with lowbridge 55-seat bodies. Delivery started in January 1959 and ended with No. 8 as shown in May of that year.

Below: Moore's of Kelvedon in Essex placed their first order with Massey in 1959. Seen here is the first of two Guy Arab IV examples with lowbridge bodywork shortly after delivery.

Turners of Brown Edge, a village between Leek and Stoke-on-Trent, took delivery of this Leyland PD2/30 in December 1957 with open rear platform bodywork and numbered it 11 in the fleet. When number 12 arrived in June 1959 it was a Titan PD3/1 and featured a forward entrance with sliding door, as seen below. After sale by Turners it saw further service in the north east with three further owners and was finally scrapped in 1979.

is pristine Daimler, DCS 616 of the A1 Group (Hunter) in yrshire, was originally built for them as a single-deck 35-seat ach by Irvine of Salsburgh on the Daimler CVD6SD chassis. It as rebuilt by Massey in 1958 with a double-deck body as seen re whilst en route to Ardrossan in the 'sixties. It is in the pically smart condition of vehicles in this fleet. (RD)

Southend Corporation No. 315 a Leyland Titan PD3/6 from 1958 seen on Driver Training duties waiting outside the main depot in September 1974. (BB)

assey Bros. had provided the body on this Guy Arab in 1948 for Rees & Williams of Tycroes in south Wales d were called upon to rebody it ten years later. It was otographed before being delivered to R&W for the cond time, with trade plates accompanying the original gistration mark of ETH 104.

oore's of Kelvedon were taken over by Eastern National 1963. This view shows No. 2015 (20 PVX) in the livery of e latter company and is one of two Guy Arab IVs dating om 1959. (See also page 105)

CHAPTER 7
The final years – 1960-1967

The introduction of the rear-engined Leyland Atlantean in the later 1950s was not universally welcomed in the industry, many operators preferring to wait and see how the new concept actually worked out in service. Accordingly there was a continuing demand for the well-tried and tested front-engined Leyland, AEC, Daimler, and Guy models, and Massey's order book reflected this. Operators taking these traditional models included many long-standing customers of the Pemberton output, in particular the Municipalities which had provided so much regular business.

During the final years Barrow, Bedwas & Machen, Birkenhead, Caerphilly, Chester, Colchester, Exeter, Great Yarmouth, Lowestoft, Lytham, Maidstone, Morecambe & Heysham, Southend, West Mon and Wigan double-deck vehicles continued the long municipal tradition, though some of these were customers new to Massey as the output charts in the appendices will show. There was also still a small amount of rebodying taking place, a routine which was easy to accomplish on traditional chassis but which would be much less so on the new rear-engined designs coming into fashion. Burton on Trent had three Guy Arab IIIs rebodied in 1960, whilst Moores of Kelvedon had an Arab I and two Arab IIs rebodied around the same time.

The industry was changing, however, and the creation of large groupings in the chassis manufacturing side with AEC having earlier taken over Maudslay and Crossley, and included in the ACV empire the bodybuilding plants at Park Royal, Crossley and Roe were tending to push out the smaller manufacturers. The Transport Holding Company, owners of the Tilling Group including the Bristol chassis and Eastern Coach Works bodybuilders, represented a market closed to Masseys. Similarly, almost no BET business came to Pemberton, save where an independent had been taken over and outstanding orders were delivered to the new owner.

This changing scene was favouring the bigger manufacturers when large orders were placed, in quantities which Massey could not have accommodated – and probably not have financed even if it had had the space to build the vehicles. Thus the pattern of regular small orders in manageable batches was ideally suited to the Company, its factory, its workforce, and, no doubt, the ethos of the method of doing business with, and obtaining orders from, its customers. When this began to change the Massey family began to question where the future lay for their Company.

Below: The press and council officials of Morecambe & Heysham Corporation view their three new buses outside the town hall in March 1960. The vehicles in camera are highbridge Leyland Titans model PD2/37 with front entrance and seating for 64 passengers. Their fleet numbers are 87-89.

Number 87 seen again, below left, in the brighter livery opposite Central Pier, Morecambe in July 1971. These three were the first Leyland double-deck chassis to be purchased by the Corporation. (RD)

Below right: Some vehicles were converted to open toppers and number 34, now named Bashful is seen in Heysham village. (RD)

Styles in . . . . .

THE unconventional 56-seat double-deck bus seen here is to go into service shortly with Baxter's Bus Services Ltd., of Airdrie, Scotland. The unconventional features lie in the body design by Massey Brothers (Pemberton) Ltd. The chassis is a Leyland Titan.

The design provides more circulating space at the foot of the stairs than is usual with front entrance buses, in which the conductor often finds himself in the way of passengers boarding and alighting. In this bus there is a space between the driver's compartment and the Y-shaped staircase where the conductor can stand, obstructing neither the passengers' or the driver's view of the wide front entrance, which has an air-pressure operated sliding door with a low window in it for the driver to see the kerb.

. . . . . Stairs

Situated immediately opposite the entrance, the staircase has two branches—the left one leading to the front row of seats in the upper saloon and the other to the gangway running along the sides of the remaining seats.

Two of these buses have been built for Baxter's, and three of similar design for Morecambe and Heysham Municipality. The Morecambe buses differ in being high bridge models, with a central gangway in the upper deck, and seats for 64 passengers.

Between 1949 and 1956 Barrow-
Furness Corporation purchased o
Park Royal double-deck bodies,
total of 60 being taken into servi
all on Leyland Titan PD2 chassis, t
of which were rebodied by Roe
1959/60. In 1961 a further ten PD
were purchased but these were fitt
with forward-entrance bodies
Massey Brothers. These were initia
numbered 1-10 but were renumber
in 1970 to 101-110 and remained
service until 1981. At the handin
over ceremony on the facing pa
Mr Arthur Tyldesley, then Managi
Director of Masseys, is sho
2nd from the right and Mr Albe
Burrows, then Barrow's Gene
Manager, is on the far right. The vi
below demonstrates very clea
the wide doorway and separation
passengers for the upper and low
decks. It also shows that unl
Baxters, Barrow gave no thought
to where the conductor might sta
(STA both)

110

xing business with pleasure – when the Jersey single-deckers were delivered Arthur Tyldesley and his family were able to take the opportunity to go
ng and enjoy some of the sights on the island, and are captured here enjoying a ride in a more relaxed mode of transport. Below, the handover of
Barrow vehicles was recorded for posterity as the Councillors and members of the Transport Committee inspected the vehicles. Municipal pride
s always high on such occasions and the manufacturer would be secretly hoping that his workforce's efforts would find favour! Clearly everybody is
y pleased with these new double-deckers and doubtless there will be a suitable buffet – or better – to follow. (STA below)

Wigan Corporation took 17 of the Leyland Titan PD3 vehicles between 1959 and early 1962, their fleet numbers being scattered haphazardly as was Wigan's practice, and number 58 is seen here in service bound for Ashton in Makerfield. The boundary changes of 1974 saw Wigan absorbed into Greater Manchester and, accordingly, its bus fleet passed into the Greater Manchester fleet. Like most of the GM constituents Wigan had been fiercely proud and had maintained its vehicles to a high standard in its distinctive and well-cared maroon and white livery. In what may be construed as a small gesture of defiance, the final vehicle to be painted in the colours was taken for a portrait to be made for posterity outside the gates of Haigh Hall on Wigan Lane, the scene of many such pictures in happier times for both Massey and Northern Counties bodied brand new vehicles. The legal lettering has not yet been applied, but the fleet number 3230 confirms that it is now a Greater Manchester vehicle. (STA below)

ees & Williams were based in Tycroes, a village near
mmanford in south Wales. They took several Massey-
odied buses over a period of some 14 years and the vehicle
ictured (YTH 815) was the last one purchased. It is a Guy
rab IV with lowbridge body fitted with platform doors and
e distinctive if perhaps not very attractive 'Johannesburg'
ont. It is seen in the lower view resting between journeys
 the Company's busy service 16, Llandilo to Ammanford,
nilst in the larger view above it is now in the service of
Varstones, in Staffordshire. (DC)

Photographed in the arctic winter conditions of 1962/63 was Morecambe's number 91, one of two Titan PD2A/27 models delivered some months earli in April 1962. Whilst the lady strides purposefully towards the bus, standing at Happy Mount Park terminus, the other passengers are no doubt hopi the driver will soon close the doors and shut out the cold! Morecambe Bay and the hills of the Lake District form the chilly backdrop. (STA both)

Two smart looking Daimlers from the Burton-upon-Trent fleet. Number 85 on the left is a CCG5 dating from 1964 while nearest the camera is No. 80, a CSG5 delivered in 1962. (LM)

Photographed soon after delivery outside the depot in May 1961, right, was Jersey Motor Transport's No. 622. This was another of the first batch of Leyland Tiger Cub PSUC1/5s and clearly shows the narrow outline of these buses.

1962 Wigan Corporation purchased this Leyland PSUC1/11 Tiger Cub for one-man duties. Number 21 was seen in Wallgate, having just passed under one of the bridges carrying the West Coast main railway line.

Massey-bodied buses were popular in East Anglia and Lowesto[ft] Corporation was no exception to this trend, having purchased sma[ll] numbers from 1945 in the periods when the products of local build[er] Eastern Coach Works were not available on the general market. Th[e] contrast in delivery mileage could hardly have been greater! Her[e] number 7, one of a pair of AEC Regent Vs, is seen near the Wiga[n] factory in late December 1962 before crossing the country to th[e] Norfolk coast and England's most easterly town, and just escaping th[e] big freeze of 1962/3 which began over Christmas.

Below left and right: Exeter City Transport took delivery of 25 Leylan[d] Titan PD2A/30 buses between 1961 and 1965 in batches of five. Thes[e] two vehicles are from 1963, No. 89 is shown on the left in the Exete[r] livery while on the right is No. 85 seen later and sporting the livery [of] The Devon General Omnibus and Touring Co. (RD above right)

Below: Forward entrance Massey bodies came to the Fylde Coast in 1964 when Lytham St Annes Corporation purchased three examples on Leyland PD2A/27 chassis and numbered them 68-70. One of the trio is shown in St Annes on 29th June 1974 after the undertaking had passed to Fylde Borough Council during local government boundary changes. (RD)

Below: This 1964 lowbridge AEC Regent V was spotted on the length[y] Bedwas to Newport service. It was formerly Bedwas & Machen No.[?] and was seen running as No. 92 for the then newly formed Rhymne[y] Valley District Council. (RD)

Photographed at Seacombe Ferry in June 1968 is Birkenhead's number 92, one of four Leyland Leopard PSUs with seating for 42 passengers. They had replaced the ageing Leyland Tiger PS1s in 1964 and were originally supplied with rear destination boxes, but these were removed in 1971. (AEJ)

The twelve PD3/6 double-deckers delivered to Southend Corporation in 1965 were something of a surprise in having *Northbridge* 70-seat bodies. This chassis suspension had first needed to be modified, however, to allow them to pass beneath the High Street railway bridge. Number 333, the first of the batch, is seen before delivery. The registration plates were later moved to just below the driver's cab as seen below.

Spotted on hire to London Transport was number 343, one of the last of the batch, and indeed the last Massey-bodied vehicles delivered to Southend. The Corporation were set to order another similar batch with Massey bodies in 1967 but following the takeover by Northern Counties the order was switched to East Lancashire Coachbuilders in Blackburn. (AEJ)

Although there were by then many Leyland Atlantean, Daimler Fleetline and Bristol VR rear-engined buses on the roads carrying a variety of bodywork from the then existing rivals, Massey Bros first double-decker body on a rear-engined chassis did not appear until 1964. This was on a Daimler Fleetline chassis (model CRG6LX) for J Brown of Dreghorn, a member of the Ayrshire Co-operative, A1 Service of Ardrossan, and it was painted in their distinctive livery and registered AAG 312B. It was destined to be the one and only Fleetline chassis bodied by the Company.

Like the new single-deck design it was of square, angular appearance, possessing little in common with any previous Massey design. Nevertheless it was well-proportioned and stood out from some of the more ungainly-looking

Facing page: Masseys' first venture into front entrance/rear-engined double-deck bodies came in 1964 when James Brown of Dreghorn, part of the A1 group of Ardrossan, bought this Daimler Fleetline CRG6LX-30 seen above before delivery. The low height of the vehicle is clearly evident in the lower view which also shows a former London Transport RT on the left of the picture. The lowbridge design appears better balanced to the eye than the rather gaunt highbridge version as seen below on this page. (LM)

rear-engined buses then being produced by some other bodybuilders. The trade press reported at the time that the interior appointment was to Massey's usual high standard. Extensive use was made of Formica panelling, and Easco fluorescent lighting along with 'Peters' air-operated doors contributed to the high-quality specification. Similar bodies were later supplied on Atlantean chassis to Colchester and Maidstone Corporations and to a number of independent operators. It is noteworthy, however, that none was supplied to such traditional Massey customers as Chester, Southend and the South Wales municipalities.

In 1965 the first orders for bodies on Leyland Atlantean chassis were put through the factory, comprising eight for Maidstone with bodywork of similar style to the unique Fleetline of two years earlier. Two further batches, in 1967 and 1968, brought Maidstone's order to 20 vehicles, just two-thirds of the total Atlantean output before ownership of the company changed. The other ten Atlanteans were supplied to Colchester, three in 1967 and seven in 1968.

Thus, in 1966 the final frontal design appeared on the traditional double-deck body for front-engined chassis. The characteristic Massey curved frontal profile, originally introduced in 1939, was replaced with a straight, more upright front which still looked neat and well-proportioned. The lower deck panels were straight instead of curving at the bottom, thus facilitating the interchange of body parts with those of the new Atlantean design. This design was available in five-bay form when specified with rear entrance and four-bay arrangements when a front-entrance was required. It bore a clear resemblance to the NCME product and sliding or jack-knife doors could be specified.

Maidstone Corporation ordered their first rear-engined buses in 1965. These were eight Leyland Atlantean PDR1/1 models and number 27 is shown prior to delivery. Further batches, this time for twelve similar vehicles, were ordered a year later. Maidstone chose Atlanteans as its trolleybus replacements.

However, the previous, more rounded, design remained available alongside the revised model, resulting in many permutations from which the customer could choose from this comparatively small supplier.

In amongst all this double-decker activity a small number of single-deckers were still being built and, in fact, the last new Massey design was another

Colchester Corporation's number 42, one of a batch of six Leyland Titan PD2A/30s dating from 1966 and thus contemporary with the Maidstone Atlantean on the previous page. An unidentified example of Colchester's own Atlanteans is seen behind.

single-decker. It departed from the box-like style with its BET-type double curvature windscreens, front panel with curved corners, and peaked domes, front and rear. Two-piece jack-knife doors were fitted at front and centre, and the whole concept presented a much improved appearance. In 1966, five 41-seaters on Leyland Leopard chassis were delivered to Exeter Corporation and in 1968 four 40-seaters on AEC Reliance chassis went to Ipswich Corporation, both batches featuring a more rounded design. The very last single-decker, a Leyland Tiger Cub, was ordered by Chester Corporation, and had the previous box-like features.

The change of Government in 1964 had brought in a Labour administration and its Transport supremo – Barbara Castle – was pledged to improve public transport. This was to be accomplished by the formation of Passenger Transport Authorities in the main urban conglomerates, with the intention of also reducing congestion in the cities by encouraging better use of the buses.

One major effect of this new and laudable policy was the need to replace large numbers of old and sometimes obsolete vehicles with new, smart, comfortable and attractive machines. To assist in achieving this a grant – Bus Grant – was available to operators purchasing new vehicles which conformed to a specification which included the ability to operated by one person. Initially 25% of the cost this was later increased to 50% when the Tory Government came to power. At a stroke Massey's worst fears were realised and on their own doorstep the amalgamation of the various local authorities in Manchester and Liverpool meant that in future very large orders would be placed for completely standardised vehicles within the new organisations.

The time had come to call it a day and a buyer was sought, and quickly found, and the takeover of Massey Bros by the Northern Counties Motor & Engineering Company Limited took place in March 1967.

Northern Counties of Wigan Lane, Wigan, was a well-respected bus body builder which had been established in 1919, at about the time that Massey Bros started their body building activities nearby. Unlike Massey Bros. there was the will, and financial backing, to cope with the potentially very large future orders; what was

On 1st April 1974, under Local Government reorganisation, the Rhymney Valley District Council was formed in the new Welsh county of Gwent. It absorbed the administrative areas of Caerphilly, Gelligaer and Bedwas & Machen and with them their bus fleets. LNY 536D was one of two Leyland Titan PD2/37s with lowbridge bodywork supplied to Caerphilly in 1966 and is seen above shortly after the formation of the new Council. It is now in preservation. (RD)

Burton Corporation No. 96 (GFA 96D) was delivered new in December 1966 and was photographed on the Burton station overbridge in January 1977. Burton became the administrative centre for East Staffordshire in the boundary changes of 1974 and the picture shows the newer livery under their new name. (AEJ)

Looking like this vehicle is in operation [on] a country service when in fact it is maki[ng] a pre-delivery photographic expediti[on] to Pemberton's Lamberhead Industr[ial] Estate is Exeter City Transport's No. [8,] a Leyland Leopard which was one [of] five delivered in October 1966. Loc[al] landmark Highfield Church can be seen [to] the right background.

Number 3 in the fleet of the Leyla[nd] independent operator J Fishwick & Son[s,] a Massey-bodied 45-seat Leyland Tig[er] Cub PSUC1/12 dating from 1966, is se[en] leaving Preston for Chorley in Septemb[er] 1972. The photograph below shows [it] some years later in the fleet of Willia[ms] Motors of Llangollen devoid of the Leyla[nd] badge. (RD left)

lacking, however, was space to expand in that Company's Wigan Lane premises. Taking over Massey Bros. factory, workforce and customer base made perfect sense. Norman Massey was retained by Northern Counties as a foreman until he retired in 1974, while Arthur Tyldesley was retained as a consultant for 18 months, after which he retired to Ambleside in the Lake District.

Even after the takeover, bodies to the Massey Bros design continued to be built for some time in the Enfield Street Works. The last double-deckers comprised small batches of Leyland Atlanteans for Colchester and Maidstone Corporations, a solitary Atlantean for A1 of Ardrossan, and some front-entrance Leyland Titan PD2s for Wigan. These orders were punctuated with the building of the last lowbridge body, to the order of Bedwas & Machen Urban District Council, on a Leyland Titan PD3/4 chassis (PAX 466F), of 30ft length and five-bay construction. This historic vehicle turned out to be the final traditional lowbridge body to be built in Britain and was subsequently sold for preservation. By this time all the vehicles in the fleets of Colchester and Maidstone had reached a state of standardisation, unique to them, in that all their then current vehicles were bodied by Massey Bros. Another interesting fact was that Massey Bros had at some time or another supplied bodies to each of the East Anglian municipal undertakings.

It is also worth noting that Newport Corporation were about to place an order for five bodies on Leyland Atlantean chassis but because Massey Bros could not meet the

Massey Bros. had the distinction [of] building the very last lowbridge (si[de] gangwayed) double-decker, and it [is] seen here. (RM)

hen Wigan took two Leyland Panther Cubs in 1967
ssey supplied the 43-seat dual-door bodywork, as seen
re on number 20 in the town centre not long after the
s entered service. Following withdrawal in 1980 it was
d to an operator on the island of Malta and after finally
ing withdrawn from active service it was repatriated
d is now being restored in preservation in the UK.

delivery date the order was given to the Scottish bodybuilder Alexanders. Between September and November 1968, 13 bodies were built by Massey Bros for Birkenhead Corporation on Leyland Atlantean chassis but these were numbered in the NCME body series and carried that builder's plates.

The final orders, comprising six double-deckers on Guy Arab V front–engined chassis were built by Northern Counties for Chester Corporation with Massey-style lower saloons and NCME-style upper saloons, between March and October 1969 (XFM 42-44G, DFM 345-7H). The final three represented the last Guy Arab chassis to be built for service in Britain and also the final batch of traditional British front-engined double-deckers.

High standards of interior finish were always associated with the products of Massey Bros Such details as polished timber interior fillets and fittings, leather cloth covered lining panels and diffused interior lighting come to mind, and the use of screws instead of rivets. In later years when, as previously mentioned, some of their competitors sacrificed standards of interior finish in the then fashionable quest for weight saving, Massey Bros continued to produce well-finished vehicles incorporating extensive use of laminated plastics as a finishing material. Of particular note were the gold anodised

aidstone Corporation Leyland Atlantean number 45,
KM 145G, clearly demonstrates the great difference in
ody styling adopted when rear engined chassis came to
e dealt with.

Birkenhead Corporation No. 142 is seen at Spi Cross roads, Bebington, in the early 'seventi This was one of the second batch with the new style of bodywork, the familiar curved front a roof profile giving way to a more upright fron appearance.

Rhymney Valley District Council's formatic was described on page 122 and here we see t newer design of front entrance bodywork former Caerphilly number 38, photograph in Caerphilly town centre on the long route from Cardiff to Tredegar. Author Michael Yelt has produced histories of Bedwas & Machen a Gelligaer in Venture's *Prestige Series*. (RD)

Number 47 in the Colchester fleet makes its w down St John's Street on the number 2 servi from Ipswich Road to Severalls. It was one ten Atlantean PDR1/1 models delivered to t operator in 1967/8. The box-line structure is far cry from Massey's earlier well-rounded a much-loved designs.

This Leyland Atlantean PDR1/1 was nine years old when photographed at the top, water tower-dominated end, of Colchester's High Street in March 1977. Across the road are two 'household names', men's tailors and outfitters, Hepworth and Dunn & Co., which have since disappeared from the British retail scene. (SD)

This fine vehicle, KSD 661F, was a Leyland Atlantean with Massey bodywork new to A Hunter, part of A1 group in Ardrossan. It worked hard for twelve years but wasn't recertified in 1980 and was replaced. Behind it is EAG 981D of the 1966 batch of distinctive Alexander-bodied Daimler Fleetlines, and the buses are seen at Saltcoats Station in the late 'sixties. (LMR)

aluminium window finishers which were unique to Massey bodies. It is believed that Massey Bros built over 2,600 bodies during their 49 years of service to the transport industry.

As has been explained, most of Massey Bros customers had been independents, and small or medium-sized municipal operators, but some larger company fleets acquired Massey bodies through takeovers. In 1961 the Scottish independent J Laurie & Co of Hamilton was taken over by Central SMT, a member of the Scottish Bus Group. Included in Laurie's 35 vehicle fleet were two Massey bodies, one on a Guy Arab chassis and one on a Leyland Titan PD3. The following year, Baxter's Bus Service Ltd of Airdrie was taken over by another large SBG subsidiary company, Scottish Omnibuses Ltd. Among the total of 53 vehicles were 21 with Massey bodies, including the forward-entrance double-deckers mentioned previously.

The famous Essex independent operator, Moore Brothers Ltd of Kelvedon, with a fleet of 39 vehicles was believed to be the oldest continuous business of its kind in the country, with a history going back to 1815. It was taken over in 1963 by the Eastern National Omnibus Co. Included in the fleet were nine Massey-bodied double-deckers. In addition, two 30ft-long Guy Arabs with Massey lowbridge bodies were on order at the time of takeover. These two were delivered direct to Eastern National with Tilling T-type destination indicators, making them the first new deliveries from Massey Bros to a BTC Group Company since the Leyland Titan PD1s for Cumberland Motor Services in 1948.

With the advent of the Passenger Transport Executives as operators in 1969, Massey Bros' largest customer, Birkenhead Corporation Transport, was swallowed up by the Merseyside PTE and so Massey bodies went on to carry the various liveries of that operator. Later, in 1974, the company's own local operator, Wigan Corporation Transport, was lost to Greater Manchester PTE. Here again, several Wigan Massey-bodied vehicles went into the PTE livery of orange and white. One of these, a front-entrance Leyland Titan PD2, registered AEK 1B, went on to outlive the PTE as an operator by becoming a driver training vehicle with company successor Greater Manchester Buses South Ltd.

Former Wigan Leyland PD2 AE now part of the GM Buses tra fleet, makes a circuit of the Hyde skid pan area for the photogra though sadly the oil-and-water was no longer in use. (JAS)

Another takeover of Massey-bodied buses came on 1st April 1971 and involved the purchase by the Devon General Omnibus & Touring Co Ltd of the business and fleet of Exeter Corporation Transport Department. In a total fleet of 65 vehicles no less than 40 were Massey-bodied, 35 being double-deck and five single-deck. They were initially operated in the Exeter livery of green and cream but later received the National Bus Company poppy red.

At the time of the takeover by Northern Counties there was still a considerable demand for new buses. At this period, Northern Counties' annual production was about 200 bodies, Massey Bros having averaged between 50 and 60 a year. Initially, both factories continued in use, with Northern Counties using the Enfield Street premises for finishing and painting, the partly completed vehicles being driven there from Wigan Lane. Northern Counties gradually developed the Massey site with a succession of ever-larger buildings around the periphery. Finally, an impressive new single-span building was erected on the major part of the site in 1983. The Wigan Lane premises were vacated after sale to the North West Health Authority and production was then continued at the modernised Enfield Street works. In May 1995, Northern Counties was purchased for £10 million by the Henlys Group, then owner of Plaxton. The Northern Counties name was dropped in 1999 and vehicles were badged as Plaxton.

In 2001 Henlys became part of a joint venture with the Mayflower Group, owner of the chassis manufacturer Dennis and the Scottish bodybuilder Alexander. The joint venture was known as TransBus, and vehicles were badged using the TransBus name. After the failure of the Mayflower Group in 2004, TransBus was sold to a private group of investors and became Alexander Dennis. The former Northern Counties facility was closed by Alexander Dennis in January 2005. The history of Northern Counties is recounted by Bob Rowe in his excellent book published in 2006 by Venture Publications.

A number of Massey-bodied buses have been restored and preserved; a few even remain in revenue earning service, a testament to their solid construction. As an ex-bus driver from the south-east of England recently remarked 'they were the only buses in Kent that didn't rattle'.

At the time of writing (August 2011) the Enfield Street premises are in use as part of an industrial estate, but many people in that area still remember Massey-bodied buses journeying down Enfield Street and onward to their many destinations, taking one of Lancashire's high class products to all corners of the country.

One of the three Chester Corporation dual-entrance Leyland Tiger Cub PSUC1/11s seen here on 30 July 1977. Number 52 dates from 1966 and clearly shows the large destination displays favoured by this operator. Notice also the flap for the 'Pay as You Enter' sign, open in this instance but closed when a conductor was being carried.

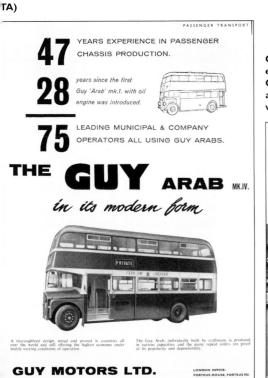

PASSENGER TRANSPORT

47

YEARS EXPERIENCE IN PASSENGER CHASSIS PRODUCTION.

28

years since the first Guy 'Arab' mk.1. with oil engine was introduced.

75

LEADING MUNICIPAL & COMPANY OPERATORS ALL USING GUY ARABS.

THE **GUY** ARAB MK.IV.

in its modern form

A thoroughbred design, tested and proved in countries all over the world and still offering the highest economy under widely varying conditions of operation.

The Guy Arab, individually built by craftsmen, is produced in various capacities, and the many repeat orders are proof of its popularity and dependability.

GUY MOTORS LTD.

WOLVERHAMPTON *Phone*: 31241

LONDON OFFICE:
PORTEUS HOUSE, PORTEUS RD.
PADDINGTON, LONDON, W.2.
Phone: Paddington 4492

Guy were pleased to be able to announce that they were supplying Arabs with forward entrance bodywork, and one – in later livery - is seen right, outside Chester Town Hall. One of Crosville's infamous Seddon single-deckers is seen behind in the days when chassis and engine were still together – before the latter were removed after the Seddons were withdrawn, to replace the units in Leyland Nationals.

127

IN LATER LIFE

Above: Bury had its single-deckers rebuilt because they were unable to sell them after the arrival on the scene of the new underfloor-engined vehicles. The rebuilds were withdrawn in 1958 and passed to a dealer in Salsburgh who quickly sold three of them to Paton Brothers of Renfrew and the other to Dunoon Motor Services. EN 7704 and BG 9229 (formerly with Birkenhead, of course) are seen in service with their Renfrew owner during the early 'sixties. (IGMS upper right)

Above, left and right: With the formation of the Merseyside PTE some transfer of vehicles from constituent operators took place. BBG 119C a 1965 Leyland PD2/40 formerly No. 119 in the Birkenhead fleet became 63 in the St Helens district fleet and received the attractive St Helens red and cream livery. It was seen near the town centre in March 1976. On the right is another PD2/40, seen about the same time but in the centre of Liverpool which was formerly Birkenhead No. 83 now in Merseyside PTE livery and numbered L459. (RD centre left)

Stevenson's of Uttoxeter had just acquired Maidstone's number 45, and renumbered it to their number 34 when it was photographed at Tutbury level crossing in south Staffordshire in June 1979, looking smart in its new coat of paint. It was by now some eleven years old. (AEJ)

MASSEY VEHICLES IN COLOUR

...wich No. 86 bodied by Massey's ...1940 was a Ransomes, Sims and ...feries trolleybus and is seen at ...ndon Road turning circle on a ...ecial working during 1952. This ...hicle was built as a demonstrator ...r a tour of South Africa but due ...the outbreak of World War ...o was instead purchased by ...swich Corporation. It was the ...t Ransomes vehicle to enter ...rvice with a British operator and ...s withdrawn and scrapped in ...ptember 1959. (WJW)

...ockton Corporation placed ...ders for a total of 43 Massey-...died double-deckers in the ...mediate post-war period. ...imber 48 was one of a batch ...25 Leyland Titan PD2/3s ...th typical body for that ...riod and delivered in the final ...ree months of 1949. It was ...otographed in Stockton High ...reet in September 1963. (GL)

The logo shown at the top of the first page of this book was one of two official Massey Bros. transfers and had not changed in nearly fifty years. It was placed mainly on the nearside front panel and sometimes the offside; it even appeared inside the vehicle. Its colour was changed when it clashed with certain liveries. The Author would value information sent via the Publishers concerning the use of the second, seen alongside, as to when and where it was used.

Photographed in Hamilton in 19??
this AEC Regent III was origina???
one of two such vehicles purchas??
by Sutherland of Peterhead ???
1949. They were transferred in??
the Alexander (Northern) fleet ???
1962 and NRC22 (FAV 827) h??
been in preservation since 19??
(GA)

Burwell & District lowbridge Daimler CVD6 (JVE 447), complete with platform doors, supplied in June 1951 and shown here on a local service in 1965. Note the front rake applied to lowbridge buses by Massey Bros. in the late 'forties/early 'fifties period.; note also the not uncommon knocked backed lower radiator shell where the vehicle has 'grounded'. This bus gave 19 years service before being withdrawn in May 1970 and lay derelict until being scrapped in 1990. (GL)

In 1951 Caerphilly UDC ordered a Leyland PS2/5 with Bruce bodywork but Bruce Coachworks of Cardiff closed down and the body order was switched to Massey Bros. Number 1, photographed in June 1952 before delivery, continued in service until 1969 when it became a training/towing vehicle and was renumbered 51. It was later rescued for preservation and the finished result can be seen below whilst the accuracy of the finished result is clearly impressive. (HWC below)

Looking smart in its owner's livery, Rothesay Motor Services, is this Guy Arab II which was one of four wartime chassis re-bodied with 58-seat highbridge bodywork. The original bodies had been Park Royal wartime utility models. (IGMS)

Southend Corporation's number 29 was a Leyland Titan PD2/12 with 55-seat lowbridge bodywork. It was one of a batch of twelve supplied in 1955, and is seen before delivery.

The evocative line up below shows similar bodywork on Southend rebodied wartime Daimlers, together with a smart AEC Regent, and the unmistakable upright front of one of Metro-Cammell's Orions. (IGMS)

Birkenhead Corporation's intake for 1956 was 15 Guy Arab IVs, five with East Lancs, bodywork, the remaining ten by Massey including No. 378 shown here prior to being exhibited at the Commercial Motor Show and having different interior finishes from the others. These were also the first vehicles in the fleet to be fitted with flashing direction indicators.

Exeter Corporation became a new Massey customer following the appointment of W Austin as general manager. He had previously held the manager's post at Chester, where he had been a regular customer for Massey products. Not only that, but he introduced the Devon city to Guy buses, also a Chester choice. This is 54 (UFJ 294), one of the first batch, ready for delivery in 1957. Sister vehicle 52 from the same batch survives in preservation.

Colchester Corporation No. 18 wa[s] one of four AEC Regent Vs built i[n] 1957 and seen before delivery to th[e] operator.

Photographed around the same tim[e] in July 1957 was Caerphilly UDC's N[o.] 24, a Leyland Titan PD2/40 with 5[5]-seat lowbridge body.

Showing the prominent colour scheme of McGill of Barrhead is this Leyland Titan PD2/30 (NHS 764) completed in March 1959.

Laurie of Hamilton number 69, a Leyland Titan PD3/2 operating under the name of Chieftain, showing the forward entrance and photographed in the glorious summer of 1959.

About to embark on the long journey to Essex in July 1959 was this Moore of Kelvedon lowbridge Guy Arab IV.

Bedwas & Machen UDC No. (originally No. 5) is an AEC Regent dating from 1961 and is seen in the operator's attractive livery about to embark on a PSV Circle tour.

Originally No. 21 in the West Monmouthshire Board fleet and now preserved is this Leyland Titan PD2/40 dating from 1961. (JAS)

est Monmouth No. 13 (UWO 688) was originally a eyland Titan PD2/41 'special' with Willowbrook single-deck dy built for the Bargoed Hill route in 1959 but was rebuilt 1966 (when the route changed) with this Massey Bros. wbridge double-deck body. It was spotted in Wetteren, elgium in August 2004.

his forward entrance PD3A/2, below, was delivered to Vigan in 1961 and now resides in the Museum of Transport Manchester. A handsome vehicle in an attractive livery.

137

Turning out of St Helier's Weighbridge bus station in 1969 was Jersey Motor Transport's No. 611, one of five Leyland Tiger Cub PSUC1/5s bought in 1961 This bus still survives today as a travelling home in the Ipswich area. (JK)

Pictured running below the imposi Gorey Castle in May 1973 is JMT N 622, another of the Leyland Tig Cubs, this time in the blue and whi livery introduced in 1971. (JK)

...ught between journeys on a *...ally Transport* enthusiasts' day ...Blackpool, and standing outside ...e Lancastrian Transport Museum ...ere it now resides, was ex-...tham St Annes number 70, one ...three Leyland Titan PD2A/27 ...es dating from 1964. (JAS)

...olchester Corporation's No. 37 ...s one of three Leyland Titans ...signated **PD2A/30Spl** denoting ...at it was 7ft 6in wide. The ...uivalent 8ft 0in wide standard ...rsion (PD2/31) had by then been ...scontinued. It is shown before ...livery in 1964.

Passing through Irvine on the 5 August 1970 was this Daim[ler] Fleetline CRG6LX dat[ing] from 1964 in the ownership [of] Brown's of Dreghorn part of [A.1] (Ardrossan). (JK)

Southend Corporation order[ed] twelve Leyland Titan PD3 highbridge double-deckers [in] 1965. This batch probably h[ad] the most varied of caree[rs] at Southend being hired o[ut] to Colchester Corporati[on] London Transport and City [of] Cardiff though this one w[as] photographed on home groun[d].

nnor & Graham of
ington, near Hull,
erated this ex-Maidstone
rporation Atlantean
m 1978 until 1982 when
vas withdrawn and used
spares.

idstone Corporation
land Atlantean No. 41
E 341E) is seen in Mill
eet on 19th June 1976,
d the very upright design
es an impression of
ater height. (ST)

This shows the rear nearside of Ipswich Corporation AEC Reliance No. 69 showing the unusual dual door layout with centre exit, which these buses introduced to the town, and are still evident on several buses remaining from the 1990s. The doors were not necessarily popular with maintenance staff but this door layout was perpetuated on all full sized buses, saloons and double-deckers purchased until the mid 1990s. The bus appears to be on layover with two East Lancs Regents, and a Roe Atlantean sometime in 1980. (OP)

Ipswich No. 70 from the same batch as the above vehicle, but showing the front nearside, is seen in the view alongside. (OP)

On the long interurban route from its home town, jointly-operated with St Helens Corporation, Ribble and Lancashire United, Wigan's Leyland PD2/37 No. 46 with forward-entrance bodywork, arrives at South Castle Street in Liverpool's city centre on 30th May 1968, when only two months old. The Metro-Cammell 'Orion' design of Liverpool's AEC Regent V No. A213 of 1957 may look more up-to-date yet compares unfavourably in styling, livery and interior finish. (TJ)

The last buses built solely by Massey were Leyland Atlantean PDR1/1's for Birkenhe[...] Corporation in 1968. This is No. 156 (LCM 156[...] photographed shortly after delivery operat[...] on the Woodside to Heswall route. (TJ)

Colchester Corporation's No. 49 from the last batch of Atlanteans displays the operator's later livery scheme and its Massey bodywork.

In 1969 Chester Corporation took delivery of six forward entrance Guy Arab V double-deckers with Massey style lower saloons and NCME style upper saloons following a takeover by the latter company. Number 42 shown here is now preserved. (JAS)

PREAMBLE
to the Massey Bros. body list

The earlier part of the list that follows on pages 145-160 is a compilation by the Author, from various sources, of all identifiable Massey bodies built up to mid-1926. From the evidence of newspaper adverts there were many cars, vans and small lorry bodies constructed during their initial bodybuilding venture which remain untraceable. Owing to the scant information from the period this section is inevitably incomplete.

The second part, covering body Contract numbers 565 to 1750 is based on the work of the late Arthur Ellis who was allowed to copy information from Massey's records in 1958. This is followed by another compilation, by David Gray, of the bodies built between 1946 and 1949. During that period Massey appear to have issued 264 Contract numbers but only 262 new 'bus' bodies (plus two rebuilds) have been identified.

The final part, from body Contract number 1996, is based on the work of another researcher through Massey's records – by then at Northern Counties – whose identity has been mislaid but to whom we nevertheless owe our thanks. It is somewhat unfortunate that the two researchers' efforts did not join up.

The body Contract numbers of virtually all the double-deck buses from 2140 onwards were checked on the individual vehicles by Martin Ingle – stamped in their hidden-away place in the wooden framing for the emergency exit door. Starting with 2675, 'body' numbers were proudly displayed on the Massey identification plate and all of these were likewise checked.

Arthur Ellis's notes show that Massey 'body numbers' were actually, in Massey parlance, 'Contract numbers'. From the numbering perspective, each individual body was regarded as a separate contract with its own individual Contract number. References to these numbers were inevitably shortened to 'C numbers' or for example 'C/1234' and it would seem that this has led to the mistaken belief that Massey's 'body numbers' had a C prefix.

Massey's records sometimes only contained minimal det eg '5 double-deck bus bodies on Leyland chassis'. Because of it has not proved possible to attribute specific Contract numb to individual vehicles for several batches. These are annota with a * in the list. The identities of many of the earlier vehi have been deduced by a 'best fit' process but some have det all attempts to identify them and the Author would welco any further clues.

On a more specific point, there were minor anoma within Massey's records of Contract numbers 641-69. Art Ellis noted that there were ten vehicles (only) recorded aga Contract numbers 641-51' – this appears to have been cau by the omission of a body from a batch for Cumberland the absence of another (rebody) for Cumberland is inexplica These two vehicles have merely been listed without attempt to infer their Contract numbers. Following on, two vehi were omitted from somewhere within the run of Contr numbers to 669. The next 16 recorded vehicles are conseque listed below in the sequence in which they apparently appea in the original records with 667/8 arbitrarily nominated as unrecorded bodies. With 30 bodies to fit in the range 641-69 quoted Contract number/vehicle relationships are somew uncertain.

FOOTNOTE
Amongst many interesting vehicles built at Pemberton read may find Body Contract numbers 735/40-2 rather unus – these bodies were supplied with a detachable rigid cen section in the bus roof and easily-swapped seats to enable th to be quickly converted from service buses to long-dista 'sunshine-roofed' coaches. There is an article taken from *Motor Transport* magazine describing the design of such vehic see page 31.

The chart below shows the annual output and it will be noted that the low point in1951 coincides with the writing down of capital as explained on page 79.

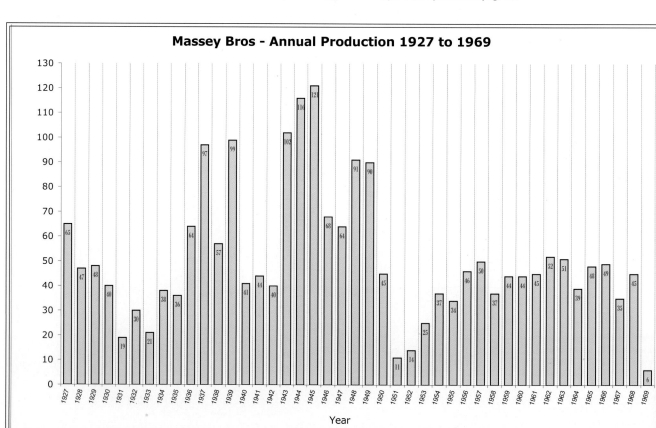

Left table:

BNUM	CONFIG	REGN	CHASSIS MAKE	NUMBER	YEAR	OPERATOR	NOTE
	Lorry	BN3249	Ford Model T	?	10/19	Pennington, Golbome	
	Ch??	CP1156	AEC	14297	-/19	Owner unknown (Halifax)	
	Van	EK1610	Ford Model T	?	3/20	Massey Bros, Pemberton	
	Ch??	EK1688	Tilling-Stevens ??	?	4/20	Goulding Ltd., Wigan 1	
	Ch??	EK1689	Tilling-Stevens ??	?	4/20	Goulding Ltd., Wigan 2	
	Ch??	EK1690	Tilling-Stevens ??	?	4/20	Goulding Ltd., Wigan 3	
	Lorry	EK2210	Albion	?	4/20	Pye, Heswall	
	B32R	EK2227	Tilling-Stevens	?	5/20	Wigan 4	
	B32R	EK74	Tilling-Stevens	?	5/20	Wigan 5	
	B32R	EK2287	Tilling-Stevens	?	6/20	Wigan 6	
	B32R	EK2288	Tilling-Stevens	?	6/20	Wigan 7	
	B32R	???	Tilling-Stevens	?	6/20	Wigan 8	
	B32R	EK2497	Tilling-Stevens	?	7/20	Wigan 9	
	B29	EK2299	Tilling-Stevens	?	7/20	Lambsfield Motors, Skerton	
	B??D	T9054	Daimler 22hp	1783	7/20	Thomas (Llynfi), Maesteg	
	B28R	CK3384	Leyd	?	12/20	Hodgson & Barnes, Preston	1
	Ch29	LH9972	Daimler B	B3102	-/20	Johnson (Royal Blue), Rhyl	1
	Lorry	EK133	Maudslay 4-ton	?	-/20	Crompton & Sons Ltd., Wigan	
	Ch20	???	Lancia	?	-/20	Lancaster, Pemberton	
	Ch20	???	Fiat	?	-/20	Lancaster, Pemberton	2
	B32R	DM1799	Leyd 36M	10672	-/20	Brookes Brothers, Rhyl, 30	2
	Van	NC741	Ford Model T	?	-/20	Wilkinson & Sons Ltd., Manchester	2
	Ch14	WR9500	Karrier WDS	?	5/21	Bennett, Askern	
	B24D	EH2684	Daimler Y ???	1818	5/21	Cooke Robinson, Hanley 4	
	Ch??	EK2185	Daimler Y ???	?	6/21	Moorfield, Pemberton	
	62seat	Tram	English Electric	?	6/21	Wigan 81	
	62seat	Tram	English Electric	?	6/21	Wigan 82	
	62seat	Tram	English Electric	?	7/21	Wigan 83	
	-16-	CC4	Ford Model T	?	7/21	Pritchard, Llanrug	
	62seat	Tram	English Electric	?	8/21	Wigan 84	
	62seat	Tram	English Electric	?	9/21	Wigan 85	
	62seat	Tram	English Electric	?	10/21	Wigan 86	
	B32R	CC851	Karrier K3	5010	11/21	Tocia, Aberdaron	
	Van	EK????	Daimler Y ??? Van	?	12/21	Wigan 87	
	B??	CU914	Ford Model T	?	12/21	Moorfield, Pemberton	
	62seat	Tram	English Electric	?	-/21	Owner unknown (South Shields)	1
	62seat	Tram	English Electric	?	1/22	Wigan 89	
	62seat	Tram	English Electric	?	2/22	Wigan 90	
	B20F	NT2033	Guy A	2075	2/22	Davies, Worthen, Salop	
	B20	CW3253	Vulcan 25hp	1674	11/22	Cumberland 21	
	B20	CW3259	Vulcan 25hp	1958	12/22	Cumberland 5	
	Lorry	IJ??	Daimler	?	-/22	Ards Motor Transport, Newtownards	
	B32R	DJ384	Daimler B	B2704	-/22	St Helens & District Motor Services 1	
	B26R	DJ539	Daimler Y	5965	-/22	St Helens & District Motor Services 3	
	B30F	IJ42.xx	Ford Model TT	?	-/22	Norton & Co, Kilkeel	
	B14F	???	Ford Model TT	?	-/22	Roberts, Hanley	
	B14F	???	Ford Model TT	?	-/22	Kenyon, Grindleford	
	B20R	TC2126	Fiat	88017	1/23	Freeman, Chorley	
	B32	AO6651	Daimler Y	?	1/23	Cumberland 16	
	B32	AO6899	Daimler Y	?	1/23	Cumberland 15	
	B32	AO6901	Daimler Y	?	1/23	Cumberland 25	
	B14	WY6897	Fiat	92293	3/23	Barrett & Thornton, Otley	
	Ch15	MN2521	Traffic	?	4/23	Gawne, Douglas IoM	
	Ch19	MN2522	Traffic Truck	7060	4/23	Berridge & Co., Douglas IoM	1
	B20	AO6652	Daimler Y	?	4/23	Cumberland 38	
	B18	EK3194	Berliet	?	5/23	Cumberland 38	
	B18	EK3196	Berliet	?	5/23	Cumberland 39	
	B20	AO8870	Guy 2-ton	?	5/23	Wilson Bros, Whitehaven	
	B14	TC4824	Albion PE24	?	7/23	Freeman, Chorley	
	B20F	???	Fiat	4000A	8/23	Albion Motors	
	B18	WT137	Fiat	95589	8/23	Harrogate Carriage Co.	
	B18	WT550	Guy BA	2141	9/23	Aston, Jump	3
	B32	AO9264	Daimler Y	?	10/23	Cumberland 43	
	B32	AO9265	Daimler Y	?	10/23	Cumberland 44	
	B14	NY4206	Fiat	66490	10/23	Thomas (Llynfi), Maesteg	
	B32	AO9040	Daimler Y	?	10/23	Cumberland 11	1

Right table:

BNUM	CONFIG	REGN	CHASSIS MAKE	NUMBER	YEAR	OPERATOR	NOTE
	B32	AO8911	Daimler Y	63904 ?	10/23	Cumberland 12	1
	B14	TC5831	Ford Model TT	3900444	11/23	Corless & Son, Charnock Richard	
	B26D	CB2035	Daimler Y	3279	12/23	Sanderson Bros, Glasgow	1
	B26	TC6120	Leyd S3	19649	1/24	Ellison, Eccleston	
	B32	WT1652	Leyd S5 (rebuild)	?	1/24	Hartley Brothers & Rhodes, Kippax	
	B32R	CK3551	Leyd RAF (G6)	20142	2/24	Hodgson & Barnes, Preston	
	B32	CB4494	Leyd RAF (G6)	20157	3/24	Lancs Ind. (Pendle Motors), Blackburn L1	
	B20F	EK3529	Thornycroft BT	10243	3/24	Wigan 1	
	B32	EK3495	Leyd RAF (G6)	20158	4/24	Lancs Ind. (Pendle Motors), Blackburn L2?	
	B28	WT3569	Leyd RAF (G7)	20187	4/24	Aston, Jump	
	Ch20	SM4387	Guy	1170	4/24	Robertson, Lockerbie	
	B30R	TC7502	Leyd RAF (G6)	20172	4/24	Orr, Little Lever	
	B32R	TC8433	Leyd RAF (G6)	20205	4/24	Lambsfield Motors, Skerton	
	B32	RM304	Daimler (S4)	5935	6/24	Cumberland 17	
	B28	CW5365	Leyd RAF (S4)	20202	7/24	Croisdale, Burnley	
	B32	RM305	Daimler Y	6424	8/24	Cumberland 23	
	B32	RM306	Daimler Y	6934	8/24	Cumberland 57	
	B32	RM307	Daimler Y	5362	8/24	Cumberland 58	
	B20F	OS1237	Berliet	14394	8/24	Brook (The Pilot), Stranraer	1
	B32F	NU4334	Leyd RAF (G6)	20204	9/24	Chapman, Belper	
	B??	TC9653	Leyd RAF (S4)	23263	10/24	Calder Motor Co., Gt.Harwood	
	B20	NY6910	Leyd RAF (GH7)	23399	11/24	Owner unknown	
	B??F	???	Daimler	4360	11/24	Thomas (Llynfi), Maesteg	
	B??F	EK3622	Berliet	?	-/24	Archer Robinson OR Blue Bus both	4
	B??D	LS1358	AEC	?	-/24	Bridlington	
	Ch32	CB2085	Dennis	13417	1/25	Brook & Amos (The Pilot), Galashiels	1
	B32	TD600	Leyd RAF (GH7)	23424	2/25	Lancaster, Pemberton	
	B32	TD1778	Leyd C7	35407	4/25	Owner unknown	
	B35R	RM1040	Daimler Y	4207	4/25	Ellison, Eccleston	1
	B35	RM1041	Daimler Y	5425	4/25	Cumberland 20	
	B35	RM1042	Daimler Y	6318	4/25	Cumberland 21	
	B35	RM1043	Daimler Y	4170	5/25	Cumberland 28	
	Ch15	MN3808	Denby	?	5/25	Cumberland 38	
	B32	TD2598	Leyd C9	35623	6/25	McMullin (The Huntsman), Douglas IoM	
	B35	RM1044	Daimler Y	5366	6/25	Stanier, Newchapel	1
	B35F	RM1045	Daimler Y	5856	6/25	Cumberland 60	
	B30R	RM1519	AEC Renown 411	411027	6/25	Cumberland 61	
	B30F	RM1520	AEC Renown 411	411026	7/25	Westmorland Motor Services 14	
	B30R	RM1521	AEC Renown 411	411030	7/25	Westmorland Motor Services 15	
	B26R	BX5912	AEC 202	?	7/25	Westmorland Motor Services 16	
	B31	RM1522	Thornycroft A1	5835	7/25	Thomas & Sons (MMT), Tir-y-dail	
	B31	RM1523	Daimler Y	6075	8/25	Cumberland 62	
	B20F	EK4243	Daimler Y	11917	8/25	Cumberland 63	
	B32	RM1970	Daimler Y	5387?	9/25	Wigan 3	
	B29R	RM1971	Daimler Y	5733	11/25	Cumberland 64	
	B32	RM2049	AEC Renown 411	411101	11/25	Cumberland 65	
	B20	CB5814	AEC Renown 413	413024	12/25	Cumberland 67	
	Lorry	OS1358	Berliet	?	-/25	Unknown, Liverpool	5
	B??F	???	Tilling-Stevens ?B9A?	?	1/26	Tilling-Stevens, Maidstone	6
	B32	CB5909	AEC Renown 413	413025	2/26	Lancs Ind. (Pendle Motors), Blackburn 33	
	B32	CB5922	AEC Renown 413	413027	2/26	Lancs Ind. (Pendle Motors), Blackburn 34	
	B30	CB5968	AEC Renown 413	413026	3/26	Lancs Ind. (Pendle Motors), Blackburn 35	
	B20	CK3720	Guy O	8460	3/26	Hodgson & Barnes, Preston	
	B20R	CK3723	Guy O	8457	3/26	Hodgson & Barnes, Preston	
	B30R	CB6065	AEC Renown 413	413029	4/26	Lancs Ind. (Pendle Motors), Blackburn 36	
	B31R	CB6066	AEC Renown 413	413028	4/26	Lancs Ind. (Pendle Motors), Blackburn 37	
	B25F	RM2818	Daimler Y	4452	7/26	Cumberland 40	
	B34	RM2817	Daimler Y	4559	7/26	Cumberland 71	
	B25F	CP4900	Albion PJ26	5015A	8/26	Holdsworth t/a Hebble 17	
565	B34	CB6343	AEC Ramilles 507	507065	7/26	Lancs Ind. (Pendle Motors), Blackburn 39	7
566	B34	CB6344	AEC Ramilles 507	507066	7/26	Lancs Ind. (Pendle Motors), Blackburn 40	
567	Lorry	???	Karrier K2	?	3/26	Karrier Motors, Huddersfield	
568	Ch15	MN4477	Reo Speedwagon	?	6/26	Corfelt & Ekins (Majestic), Douglas IoM	
569	Ch15	MN4539	Traffic	BA2367	6/26	McMullin (The Huntsman), Douglas IoM 2	
570	C20	???	Guy BA	?	6/26	East Lancs, Blackburn 10	8
571	C14	???	Guy 1-ton	?	6/26	Inman (Cecil), Morecambe 3	
572	B28	???	Thornycroft J	?	7/26	Lancashire & Westmorland, Lancaster	
573	B14	???	Ford 1-ton	?	7/26	Norton & Co, Kilkeel	
574	Ch14	BN9075	Chevrolet 1-ton	?	7/26	Pennington, Bolton	
575	B26F	CP4897	Albion PK26	5012E	7/26	Holdsworth t/a Hebble 14	
576	???	???	Ford 1-ton	?	8/26	Spence & Johnstone, Belfast	
577	B26F	CP4960	Albion PK26	5013E	8/26	Holdsworth t/a Hebble 16	
578	C22	BN9422	Leyd C9	36449	8/26	Lees, Radcliffe	1

BNUM	CONFIG	CHASSIS MAKE	REGN	NUMBER	YEAR	OPERATOR	NOTE
579	B20	Maudslay ML2	HH3345	3988	9/26	Farrer & Faulder, Carlisle	
580	Ch14	Guy JA	CB6582	JA12198	8/26	East Lancs., Blackburn	
581	B26	Daimler CK	CP2589	4360	–/26	Thomas (Llynfi), Maesteg	1
582	B14	Chevrolet LN	WK2140	16600	5/27	Rugby Autocar Co., Coventry	
583	B30	AEC Grenville 506	DR1027	506099	10/26	Pullen, Plymouth ? on loan ? AEC Southall demo	
584	C17	Berliet	???	?	–/26	Sharrock, Goose Green, Wigan	
585	B25F	Daimler Y	AO6901	?	1/27	Cumberland 25	1
586	B25F	Daimler Y	AO7198	6124	1/27	Cumberland 26	1
587	B28D	AEC Ramillies 507	MN4903	507081	4/27	Meageen (Manxland), Douglas IoM 1	9
588	B28D	AEC Ramillies 507	MN4909	507087	4/27	Meageen (Manxland), Douglas IoM 4	9
589	B28D	AEC Ramillies 507	MN4902	507083	4/27	Meageen (Manxland), Douglas IoM 6	9
590	L52R	Guy FCX	RM4364	FCX22481	9/27	Cumberland 74	
591	Lorry	Chevrolet	???	?	–/27	Martlew, Orrell	
592	Ch16	Dennis 30-cwt	???	?	3/27	Greenwood (Cosy Coach), Morecambe	
593	Van	Thornycroft A1	???	?	2/27	Shaw (Brewers), Leigh	
594	B28F	ADC 416A	MN4928	416011	5/27	Meageen (Manxland), Douglas IoM 8	
595	B28F	ADC 416A	MN4929	416013	5/27	Meageen (Manxland), Douglas IoM 3	
596	B28F	ADC 416A	MN4930	416014	5/27	Meageen (Manxland), Douglas IoM 5	
597	B28F	ADC 416A	MN4910	416010	4/27	Meageen (Manxland), Douglas IoM 2	
598	B28F	ADC 416A	MN4927	416012	5/27	Meageen (Manxland), Douglas IoM 7	
599	Amb.	Austin 20 Ambulance	???	?	–/27	Wigan Union	
600	B14	Morris Z5	???	?	–/27	Penman (Dealer), Dumfries - operator unknown	
601	B32F	Albion PM28	CP5695	7008D	5/27	Holdsworth t/a Hebble 23	
602	Ch16	Crossley	???	?	–/27	Howarth (Parth Motors), Platt Bridge	
603	Ch14	Lancia	???	?	–/27	Rishton, Accrington	
604	B30	Thornycroft LB	EK4849	13470	5/27	Wigan 19	
605	B30	Thornycroft UB	EK4850	14494	5/27	Wigan 20	
606	C26	Guy B	CB7240	B22168	5/27	East Lancs., Blackburn	
607	Ch20	Star LL	CK3882	?	5/27	Hodgson JG, Preston	
608	B26R	Leyd Lioness PLC1	RM3872	45817	6/27	Workington Motor Service Co.	
609	Ch26	Karrier CL6	WM818	380——	6/27	Skewen Garage (Blue Bird), Skewen 5	10
610	B26R	Crossley	WM5032	10672	6/27	McMullin (The Huntsman), Douglas IoM 3	
611*	Ch26	Leyd 36hp	BN4189	50	5/27	Lees, Radcliffe	1
612	C20	Vulcan 3XB	KA8288	3411	5/27	Collingwood, Liverpool 12	
613	B20	Morris	TE105	?	–/27	Sharrock, Halsall 4	
614	Ch15	Vulcan	MN4905	?	4/27	Rigby (The Swan), Douglas IoM	
615	B26	Vulcan	ED4629	51853	5/27	Ashton, Warrington	
616	B14	Dennis 30-cwt	TU5627	15351	5/27	Whetnall, Barnton	
617	Ch14	Chevrolet	WM669	?	–/27	Smith J.W., Moston	
618	Ch14	Chevrolet LM	???	?	–/27	Fox (Pride o' the Dales), Bridlington	
619	B28R	Leyd Lion PLSC1	MN5106	45954	7/27	Manxland, IoM 26	10
620	B31R	Leyd Lion PLSC1	RM4107	45953	7/27	Cumberland 3	
621	B31R	Leyd Lion PLSC1	RM4109	45957	7/27	Cumberland 4	
622	B31R	Leyd Lion PLSC1	RM4106	45956	7/27	Cumberland 6	
623	B28R	Leyd Lion PLSC1	MN5105	45955	7/27	Manxland, IoM 27	10
624	B32D	Karrier WL6	BA6735	42034	–/27	Salford 25	
625	B32D	Karrier WL6	BA6736	42035	–/27	Salford 26	
626	B32D	Karrier WL6	BA6737	42036	–/27	Salford 27	
627	B32D	Karrier WL6	BA6738	42039	–/27	Salford 28	
628	B32D	Karrier WL6	BA6739	42040	–/27	Salford 29	
629	B32D	Karrier WL6	BA6740	42041	–/27	Salford 30	
630	B32D	Karrier WL6	BA6741	42037	–/27	Salford 31	
631	B32D	Karrier WL6	BA6742	42038	–/27	Salford 32	
632	B32D	Karrier WL6	BA6743	42042	–/27	Salford 33	
633	B32D	Karrier WL6	BA6744	42043	–/27	Salford 34	
634	B32D	Karrier WL6	BA6745	42045	–/27	Salford 35	
635	B32D	Karrier WL6	BA6746	42044	–/27	Salford 36	
636	Ch14	Dennis	???	?	–/27	Croft, Yeadon	
637	B26	Karrier CL4	PY7275	?	7/27	Bridlington & Scarborough Daily Service 10	10
638	B32F	Albion PM28	CP5968	7016G	8/27	Holdsworth t/a Hebble 29	
639	B32F	Albion PM28	CP5969	7016J	8/27	Holdsworth t/a Hebble 30	
640	B31R	Leyd Lion PLSC1	RM4108	46042	10/27	Cumberland 1	
641*	B31R	Leyd Lion PLSC1	RM4110	46038	10/27	Cumberland 33	
642*	B31R	Leyd Lion PLSC1	RM4366	46041	10/27	Cumberland 34	
643*	B31R	Leyd Lion PLSC1	RM4367	46040	10/27	Cumberland 35	
644*	B31R	Leyd Lion PLSC1	RM4368	46039	1/28	Cumberland 39	
*	B32	Leyd G7	AO9102	12468	12/27	Cumberland 41	1
645*	B14	Chevrolet 25-cwt	ED4769	5172	–/27	Naylor, Stockton Heath	
646*	B32	Tilling-Stevens	TE2661	?	2/28	Dallas, Leyland	18
647*	B32	Leyd Lion PLSC3	TE2143	46257	11/27	Yarrow Motor Co (Ellison), Eccleston	1
648*	B30F	Leyd S5	B8575	5288	11/27		

BNUM	CONFIG	CHASSIS MAKE	REGN	NUMBER	YEAR	OPERATOR	NOTE
650*	B32F	Albion PM28	CP6242	7022H	1/28	Holdsworth t/a Hebble 35	
651*	B32F	Albion PM28	CP6243	7021J	1/28	Holdsworth t/a Hebble 36	
652*	Ch24	Leyd Lioness PLC1	RM4722	46421	4/28	Workington Motor Service Co.	1
653*	Ch24	Leyd Lioness PLC1	RM4723	46422	3/28	Workington Motor Service Co.	1
654*	C20	Guy 2-ton	AO8870	?	3/28	Wilson Bros, Whitehaven	
655*	C16	Guy CW	RM4783	CW8839	4/28	Wilson Bros, Whitehaven	
656*	C32F	Albion PM28	CP6546	7023J	4/28	Holdsworth t/a Hebble 50	18
657*	C26	Leyd RAF	FR8957	?	–/28	Roberts, Blackpool	1
658*	C26	Dennis G	???	?	3/28	Gough, Mountain Ash	11
659*	Ch20	Dennis G	CK3967	70136	3/28	Lockett & Lonsdale, Preston	11
660*	B35F	Leyd Lion G	VT7916	46669	4/28	Brown, Tunstall 14	
661*	Lorry	Dennis	???	?	–/28	Windy Arbour, Wigan 1	1
662*	C26	Tilling-Stevens B10B	???	?	–/28	Garlick, Burrell & Edwards, Liverpool	
663*	B26	Guy	SM4387	1170	4/28	Dickson, Dumfries	12
664*	C32F	Leyd A13	BN4190	10656	4/28	Lees, Radcliffe	1
665*	C32	Tilling-Stevens B10A	KD2204	5544	6/28	Garlick, Burrell & Edwards, Liverpool	
666*	C26	Tilling-Stevens B10A	???	?	–/28	Garlick, Burrell & Edwards, Liverpool	
667*	C32	Albion PNA26	DK5027	5056I	5/28	Chadwick Barlow & Co., Rochdale	
668*	C26	Leyd Lion PLSC3	VH1438	47208	5/28	Hanson, Milnsbridge 4	
669*	C32	Leyd Lion PLSC3	FR9106	5554	5/28	Standerwick, Blackpool	18
670	C26D	Tilling-Stevens B10B	UA4304	5150	6/28	Barr, Leeds 30	14
671	C26D	Dennis	TE3332	45933	3/28	Marsden, Mossley	
672	C29	Dennis	TE4521	47246	6/28	Woodward, Atherton	
673	B32F	Leyd Lioness LC1	TE4254	46724	5/28	Manxland, IoM 11	
674	B28R	Leyd Lion PLSC3	MN5490	46557	5/28	Manxland, IoM 21	
675	B28R	Leyd Lion PLSC3	MN5491	46562	5/28	Manxland, IoM 31	
676	B28R	Leyd Lion PLSC3	MN5493	46565	5/28	Manxland, IoM 32	
677	B28R	Leyd Lion PLSC3	MN5492	70252	5/28	Manxland, IoM 33	
678	C20	Dennis G	CK4033	46341	5/28	Progress, Chorley	
679	B32F	Leyd Lion PLSC3	CK4034	46340	5/28	Ribble 566	
680	B31R	Leyd Lion PLSC3	RM5194	46558	5/28	Ribble 567	
681	B31R	Leyd Lion PLSC3	RM5193	46561	8/28	Cumberland 86	
682	B28R	Leyd Lion PLSC3	MN5584	46722	7/28	Cumberland 65	
683	B28R	Leyd Lion PLSC3	RA6007	5064L	6/28	Manxland, IoM 34	
684	Ch15	Austro Daimler	CP6760	7029A	5/28	Rigby (The Swan), Douglas IoM	9
685	B25F	Albion PJ26	CP6761	7029B	5/28	Heeley, New Tupton	
686	B32F	Albion PM28	CP6864	7035B	7/28	Holdsworth t/a Hebble 38	
687	B32F	Albion PM28	UA4877	5596	7/28	Holdsworth t/a Hebble 39	
688	B32F	Tilling-Stevens B10B2	TB5925	12272	7/28	Holdsworth t/a Hebble 47	14
689	B28	Leyd G5 or G7 ?	???	?	8/28	Barr, Leeds ?31?	14
690	C26	Chevrolet	???	?	–/28	Yarrow Motor Co (Ellison), Eccleston	14
691	B14	Chevrolet	???	?	–/28	Barr, Leeds	13
692	C32F	Lancia-Barton 3 axle	VO256	?	12/28	Naylor, Stockton Heath 3	
693	C26R	Daimler CJK22	FR2242	CJK22	2/29	Barton, Beeston 107	1
694	C18	Guy	???	?	–/29	Brown, Tunstall 5	
695	C24	Guy	???	?	–/29	Merseyside, Liverpool 12	
696						Direct Coal (Pride of the Chase Coaches), Stafford	
697						Direct Coal (Pride of the Chase Coaches), Stafford	
698	B32	Pagefield	4B1007	?	3/29	Yarrow Motor Co (Ellison), Eccleston	
699	C32	Tilling-Stevens B10A2	CB8715	6387	3/29	Cronshaw, Blackburn 16	14
700	C23	Guy	TB4263	1068	–/29	Moorfield, Pemberton	1
701	B32	AEC 509	VT3122	509151	6/29	Brown, Tunstall 5	
702	B32	Tilling-Stevens B10A2	DK5552	10731	3/29	Holt Brothers (Yelloway), Rochdale 24	14
703	B32F	Gilford 166 OT	DK5553	60604	3/29	Holt Brothers (Yelloway), Rochdale	15
704	B29R	Leyd Tiger TS2	RM5635	60121	5/29	Cumberland 7	
705	B29R	Leyd Tiger TS2	RM5636	60573	5/29	Cumberland 14	
706	B29R	Leyd Tiger TS2	RM6015	60575	5/29	Cumberland 15	
707	B29R	Leyd Tiger TS2	RM6016	60576	5/29	Cumberland 16	
708	B29R	Leyd Tiger TS2	RM6017	90094	5/29	Cumberland 30	
709	H28/24R	Dennis HS (Prototype)	RM6018	60391	–/29	Cumberland 31	
710	B35R	Leyd Tiger TS1	PG6564	60602	6/29	Dennis Brothers, Guildford (demonstrator)	16
711	B35R	Leyd Tiger TS1	TE8290	9177	7/29	Green (Freeman), Chorley 15	
712	B20	Guy	TE8291	763063	4/29	Green (Freeman), Chorley 16	
713	C32	Leyd Tiger TS2	TE8830	?	7/29	Green (Freeman), Chorley 12	
714	B32F	Ford Model AA	TE7631	10731	6/29	Progress Motors, Chorley	
715	B14F	Chevrolet 30-cwt	RM5944	?	6/29	Cumberland 12	
716	B16F	Chevrolet 30-cwt	???	6425	5/29	Ratcliffe, Egremont	
717	B32F	Chevrolet 30-cwt	EM2302	55668	7/29	Merseyside, Liverpool 60	18
718	C16	Tilling-Stevens B10A2	TE8789	6432	7/29	Bell (Tower Motors), Morecambe	
719	B32F	Tilling-Stevens B10A2	EM2301	6432	5/29	Merseyside, Liverpool 59	18
720	B32F	Tilling-Stevens B10A2	EM2300	6427	5/29	Merseyside, Liverpool 58	18
721	B32R	AEC Reliance 660	HD3903	660121	5/29	Box, Dewsbury	

Left table:

BNUM	CONFIG	CHASSIS MAKE	REGN	NUMBER	YEAR	OPERATOR	NOTE
723*	B26	Tilling-Stevens B10A2	DK5820	?	5/29	Holt Brothers (Yelloway), Rochdale 25	14
724*	B26	Tilling-Stevens B10A2	DK5821	?	5/29	Holt Brothers (Yelloway), Rochdale 22	14
725*	B26	Tilling-Stevens B10A2	DK5822	?	6/29	Holt Brothers (Yelloway), Rochdale 23	14
726	H52R	Tilling-Stevens TS17A	TE9052	6105	7/29	Widnes 25	18
727	B31F	Albion PMA28	CP7708	7053A	7/29	Hebble 76	
728	B31F	Albion PMA28	CP7709	7053E	7/29	Hebble 77	
729	B31F	Albion PMA28	CP7710	7053B	8/29	Hebble 78	
730	C26	Star Flyer VB4	LG1854	1005	6/29	Bowyer, Northwich	
731	Lorry	Ford Model AA	???	?	7/29	Williamson, Preesall	
732	C20	Ford 30-cwt	EK7151	?	–/29	Walls, Wigan	
733	H36/29D	???	???	?	–/29	Wakley, Northop	
734	B32F	Guy	EM2422	6002	12/29	Merseyside, Liverpool 101	18
735	DP26F	Tilling-Stevens B10A	KD9402	6621	3/30	Nor-West, Liverpool 26	18
736	Van	Manchester	???	?	–/29	Colliery Explosives, Wigan	
737	B32F	Tilling-Stevens B10A2	KD8224	6610	10/29	Nor-West, Liverpool 21	18
738	B32F	Tilling-Stevens B10A2	KD8225	6590	11/29	Nor-West, Liverpool 22	18
739	B32F	Tilling-Stevens B10A2	KD8235	6654	11/29	Nor-West, Liverpool 23	18
740*	DP26F	Tilling-Stevens B10A2	EM2415	6653	12/29	Merseyside, Liverpool 70	18
741*	B32F/	Tilling-Stevens B10A2	EM2416	6655	12/29	Merseyside, Liverpool 75	18
742*	DP26F	Tilling-Stevens B10A2	???	?	–/30	Garlick, Burrell & Edwards, Liverpool	
743	B32F	Tilling-Stevens B10A2	EM2421	6612	1/30	Merseyside, Liverpool 78	18
744	B32F	Tilling-Stevens B10A2	EM2420	6489	12/29	Merseyside, Liverpool 76	18
745	B32F	Tilling-Stevens B10A2	KD8241	6497	12/29	Nor-West, Liverpool 24	18
746	L27/24R	Leyd Titan TD1	RM6623	71222	3/30	Cumberland 105	
747	L27/24R	Leyd Titan TD1	RM6621	71220	3/30	Cumberland 103	
748	L27/24R	Leyd Titan TD1	RM6622	71221	3/30	Cumberland 104	
749	L27/24R	Leyd Titan TD1	RM6624	71223	3/30	Cumberland 106	
750	L27/24R	Leyd Titan TD1	RM6625	71225	4/30	Cumberland 107	
751	L27/24R	Leyd Titan TD1	RM6626	71224	4/30	Cumberland 108	
752	L27/24R	Leyd Titan TD1	RM6627	71226	5/30	Cumberland 109	
753	L27/24R	Leyd Titan TD1	RM6628	71227	5/30	Cumberland 110	
754	H65D	AEC Renown 664	ED5880	664001	4/30	Warrington 39	
755	H65D	AEC Renown 664	ED5881	664002	4/30	Warrington 40	
756	C26F	Tilling-Stevens B10A2	KD9401	6499	4/30	Merseyside, Liverpool 25	18
757	L27/24R	Leyd Titan TD1	EN4500	71273	4/30	Bury 20	
758	L27/24R	Leyd Titan TD1	EN4501	71229	4/30	Bury 21	
759	L27/24R	Leyd Titan TD1	EN4502	71272	5/30	Bury 22	
760	L27/24R	Leyd Titan TD1	EN4503	71274	5/30	Bury 23	
761	C14	Chevrolet U	TF1335	65097	4/30	Fox, Morecambe	
762*	C14	Crossley	AU2622	?	5/30	Morecambe Motors (Silver Grey)	19
763*	C14	Crossley	MN6595	62912	5/30	McMullin (The Huntsman), Douglas IoM	1
764	C20	Chevrolet LQ	TF1311	?	5/30	Simpson, Wigan	1
765	C26F	BAT Cruiser	EK7510	B643	4/30	Merseyside, Liverpool 37	
766	C26F	Bristol B	KD9410	B644	5/30	Merseyside, Liverpool 38	
767	C26	Bristol B	KD9411	18355	5/30	Sharrock, Goose Green, Wigan	
768	B32R	Thornycroft A6	EK7568	60992	6/30	Cumberland 111	
769	B32R	Leyd Tiger TS2	RM6629	60994	6/30	Cumberland 112	
770	B32R	Leyd Tiger TS2	RM6630	60993	6/30	Cumberland 113	
771	B32R	Leyd Tiger TS2	RM6631	60995	6/30	Cumberland 114	
772	B32R	Leyd Tiger TS2	RM6632	60907	11/30	Cumberland 47 (demo from AEC Southall)	20
773	L22/28R	Dennis HV	EA4622	95002	7/30	West Bromwich 36	
774	L22/28R	Dennis HV	EA4623	95003	7/30	West Bromwich 37	
775	L22/28R	Dennis HV	EA4624	95004	7/30	West Bromwich 38	
776	H24/24R	Dennis HV	BR8293	95005	7/30	Sunderland 23	
777	H24/24R	Dennis HV	BR8294	95006	8/30	Sunderland 24	
778	H24/24R	Dennis HV	BR8295	95007	8/30	Sunderland 25	
779	H30/26R	Leyd Titan TD1	ED6140	71572	10/30	Warrington 41	
780	H30/26R	Leyd Titan TD1	ED6141	71573	9/30	Warrington 42	
781	H30/26R	Leyd Titan TD1	ED6142	71574	9/30	Warrington 43	
782	L24/24R	AEC Regent	RM8032	6611008	11/30	Green, Haverfordwest	
783	B35F	Leyd Tiger TS3	DE8019	?	3/31	Wigan 55	
784	L24/24R	Leyd Titan TD1	EK8088	71988	3/31	Wigan 56	
785	L24/24R	Leyd Titan TD1	EK8089	71989	3/31	Wigan 68	
786	L24/24R	Leyd Titan TD1	EK8108	71994	3/31	Wigan 69	
787	L24/24R	Leyd Titan TD1	EK8109	71998	3/31	Wigan 70	
788	L24/24R	Leyd Titan TD1	EK8110	72000	4/31	Wigan 71	
789	L24/24R	Leyd Titan TD1	EK8111	71999	3/31	Wigan 72	
790	L24/24R	Leyd Titan TD1	EK8112	72001	3/31	Wigan 73	
791	L24/24R	Leyd Titan TD1	EK8113	72006	4/31	Wigan 74	
792	L24/24R	Leyd Titan TD1	EK8114	?	4/31	Wigan 75	

Right table:

BNUM	CONFIG	CHASSIS MAKE	REGN	NUMBER	YEAR	OPERATOR	NOTE
793	L24/24R	Leyd Titan TD1	EK8115	72007	4/31	Wigan 75	
794	L27/24R	Daimler CH6	BG205	9041	5/31	Birkenhead 157	
795	L27/24R	Daimler CH6	BG206	9042	5/31	Birkenhead 158	
796	H30/26R	Leyd Titan TD1	ED6463	72087	5/31	Warrington 44	
797	H30/26R	Leyd Titan TD1	ED6464	72088	6/31	Warrington 45	
798	H30/26R	Leyd Titan TD1	ED6465	72089	6/31	Warrington 46	
799	B32D	Leyd Lion LT3	TF6361	51744	9/31	Leigh 42	
800	B32D	Leyd Lion LT3	TF6362	51745	9/31	Leigh 43	
801	B32D	Leyd Lion LT3	TF6363	51746	9/31	Leigh 44	
802						No record - thought to have been cancelled	NR
803	L27/24R	Leyd Titan TD1	BG472	72330	1/32	Birkenhead 159	
804	L27/24R	Leyd Titan TD1	BG473	72331	1/32	Birkenhead 160	
805	L27/24R	Leyd Titan TD1	BG474	72332	1/32	Birkenhead 161	
806	L27/24R	Leyd Titan TD1	BG475	72333	1/32	Birkenhead 162	
807	L27/24R	Leyd Titan TD1	BG476	72334	1/32	Birkenhead 163	
808	C32R	AEC Regal	BG613	6621179	3/32	MacDonald & Co. (Maxways), Birkenhead	
809	C32R	AEC Regal	BG614	6621180	3/32	MacDonald & Co. (Maxways), Birkenhead	
810	C32R	AEC Regal	BG615	6621181	6/32	MacDonald & Co. (Maxways), Birkenhead	
811	C32R	AEC Regal	BG616	6621182	–/32	MacDonald & Co. (Maxways), Birkenhead	
812	C32R	AEC Regal	BG617	6621183	6/32	MacDonald & Co. (Maxways), Birkenhead	
813	C32R	AEC Regal	BG618	6621184	3/32	MacDonald & Co. (Maxways), Birkenhead	
814	C32R	AEC Regal	HD4674	6621200	3/32	Box, Dewsbury	
815*	B31F	Leyd Lion PLSC1	RM2225	45059	4/32	Cumberland 29	
816*	B31F	Leyd Lion PLSC1	RM2226	45060	4/32	Cumberland 32	
817	B31F	Leyd Lion PLSC1	RM2227	45061	4/32	Cumberland 68	
818*	B31F	Leyd Lion PLSC1	RM2228	45062	4/32	Cumberland 69	
819*	B31F	Leyd Lion PLSC1	RM2229	45063	4/32	Cumberland 70	
820	L26/26R	Daimler CH6	BG746	9100	5/32	Birkenhead 171	
821	L26/26R	Daimler CH6	BG747	9101	5/32	Birkenhead 172	
822	L26/26R	Daimler CH6	BG748	9102	5/32	Birkenhead 173	
823	L26/26R	Daimler CH6	BG749	9103	5/32	Birkenhead 174	
824	L26/26R	Daimler CH6	BG750	9099	5/32	Birkenhead 175	
825	C31F	Albion Valkyrie PW65	R86337	160111	5/32	Heeley, New Tupton 1	
826*	B35F	Leyd Lion LT5	DE8816	1397	6/32	Green, Haverfordwest	
827*	B35F	Leyd Lion LT5	DE8865	1435	6/32	Green, Haverfordwest	
828	B34F	AEC Regal	VT8024	6621349	6/32	Brown, Tunstall 17	
829*	B31F	Leyd Lion LT5	DE8942	1604	7/32	Green, Haverfordwest	
830	Lorry	Bedford 2-ton	???	?	6/32	Conroy Brothers, Wigan	
831	Lorry	Austin 12/6	???	?	–/32	Williams, Wigan	
832	Van	Leyd Cub	FV68	60149	3/33	Colliery Explosives, Wigan	1
833	B35F	Leyd Tiger TS2	BG1500	2716	5/33	Thomas (Llynfi), Maesteg	
834	L27/24R	Leyd Titan TD2	BG1501	2717	5/33	Birkenhead 176	
835	L27/24R	Leyd Titan TD2	BG1503	2718	5/33	Birkenhead 177	
836	L27/24R	Leyd Titan TD2	BG1504	2719	5/33	Birkenhead 178	
837	L27/24R	Leyd Titan TD2	BG1505	2720	5/33	Birkenhead 179	
838	L27/24R	Leyd Titan TD2	BG1506	2721	5/33	Birkenhead 180	
839	L27/24R	Leyd Titan TD2	BG1507	2722	5/33	Birkenhead 181	
840	L27/24R	Leyd Titan TD2	BG1508	2723	5/33	Birkenhead 182	
841	L27/24R	Leyd Titan TD2	EK9310	2724	5/33	Birkenhead 183	
842	L27/24R	Leyd Titan TD2	EK9311	2737	6/33	Birkenhead 184	
843*	B32R	Leyd Tiger TS4	EK9312	2738	6/33	Wigan 16	
844*	B32R	Leyd Tiger TS4	JC1343	2739	6/33	Wigan 18	
845*	B32R	Leyd Tiger TS4	VT6537	2973	7/33	Evans (Seiont Motors), Caernarvon	
846	B32F	Leyd Lion LT2	TJ3451	51618	–/33	Thomas (Llynfi), Maesteg	1
847	L24/24R	Leyd Titan TD3	TJ3451	3571	12/33	Leigh 47	
848	L24/24R	Leyd Titan TD3	TJ3452	3572	12/33	Leigh 48	
849	Lorry	Bedford 30-cwt	???	?	–/33	Conroy Brothers, Wigan	
850	Lorry	Bedford 2-ton	???	?	–/33	Conroy Brothers, Wigan	
851	Lorry	Dennis 40/5-cwt	???	?	–/33	Peak & Company, Wigan	
852	Van	Dodge 15-cwt	???	?	–/33	Colliery Explosives, Wigan	
853*	B31R	Leyd Lion PLSC3	RM5058	47228	4/34	Cumberland 25	1
854*	B31R	Leyd Lion PLSC3	RM5165	46564	5/34	Cumberland 8	1
855*	B31R	Leyd Lion PLSC3	RM5166	46563	4/34	Cumberland 13	1
856*	B31R	Leyd Lion PLSC3	RM5167	46556	5/34	Cumberland 24	1
857*	B31R	Leyd Lion PLSC3	RM5168	47209	4/34	Cumberland 28	1
858*	B31R	Leyd Lion PLSC3	RM5565	46726	4/34	Cumberland 89	1
859*	B31R	Leyd Lion PLSC3	RM5537	46725	4/34	Cumberland 58	1
860*	B32R	Leyd Lion PLSC3	RM5635	60120	4/34	Cumberland 7	1
861	B32R	Leyd Tiger TS2	AAO574	4506	8/34	Cumberland 38	1
862	B31R	Leyd Lion LT5A	AAO575	4507	8/34	Cumberland 40	1
863	B31R	Leyd Lion LT5A	AAO576	4508	8/34	Cumberland 41	1
864	B32R	Leyd Lion LT5A	AAO577	4509	8/34	Cumberland 49	1
865	B32R	Leyd Lion LT5A	AAO491	4502	6/34	Cumberland 56	1
866	L26/26R	Leyd Titan TD3	AAO491	4502	6/34	Cumberland 56	1
867	L26/26R	Leyd Titan TD3	AAO492	4503	6/34	Cumberland 59	1

BNUM	CONFIG	REGN	CHASSIS MAKE	NUMBER	YEAR	OPERATOR	NOTE
868	L26/26R	AAO493	Leyd Titan TD3	4504	6/34	Cumberland 60	
869	L26/26R	AAO494	Leyd Titan TD3	4505	6/34	Cumberland 61	
870	L24/24R	TJ5736	Crossley Mancunian	91785	5/34	Leigh 49	
871*	H26/22R	RJ3006	Leyd Titan TD3	4698	9/34	Salford 24	
872*	H26/22R	RJ3007	Leyd Titan TD3	4699	9/34	Salford 26	
873*	H26/22R	RJ3008	Leyd Titan TD3	4700	9/34	Salford 28	
874*	H26/22R	RJ3009	Leyd Titan TD3	4701	9/34	Salford 30	
875*	H26/22R	RJ3010	Leyd Titan TD3	4702	9/34	Salford 32	
876	Van	???	Dodge 2-ton	?	-/34	Colliery Explosives, Wigan	
877*	H26/22R	RJ3011	Crossley Mancunian	91787	8/34	Salford 36	
878*	H26/22R	RJ3012	Crossley Mancunian	91788	8/34	Salford 113	
879	B35R	TG8179	Leyd Tiger TS6c	4842	7/34	Willmore Motors, Neath 7	
880*	H28/24R	BG2657	Leyd Titan TD3c	5041	10/34	Birkenhead 192	
881*	H28/24R	BG2658	Leyd Titan TD3c	5044	10/34	Birkenhead 193	
882*	H28/24R	BG2659	Leyd Titan TD3c	5045	10/34	Birkenhead 194	
883*	H28/24R	BG2660	Leyd Titan TD3c	5046	10/34	Birkenhead 195	
884*	H28/24R	BG2661	Leyd Titan TD3c	5051	10/34	Birkenhead 196	
885*	H28/24R	BG2662	Leyd Titan TD3c	5052	10/34	Birkenhead 197	
886	H30/24R	FM8936	Leyd Titan TD3	5190	11/34	Chester 25	
887*	B32R	TJ8706	Leyd Lion LT5A	5847	3/35	Widnes 34	
888*	B32R	TJ8707	Leyd Lion LT5A	5848	3/35	Widnes 35	
889*	B32R	TJ8708	Leyd Lion LT5A	5849	3/35	Widnes 36	
890*	L24/24R	TJ7524	Leyd Titan TD3c	5436	12/34	Leigh 50	
891*	L24/24R	TJ7525	Leyd Titan TD3c	5435	12/34	Leigh 51	
892*	L24/24R	TJ7526	Leyd Titan TD3c	5438	12/34	Leigh 52	
893*	L24/24R	TJ7527	Leyd Titan TD3c	5440	12/34	Leigh 53	
894*	L24/24R	TJ7528	Leyd Titan TD3c	5439	1/35	Leigh 54	
895*	L24/24R	TJ7529	Leyd Titan TD3c	5437	12/34	Leigh 55	
896*	H26/22R	RJ3536	Leyd Titan TD4	5855	-/35	Salford 34	
897*	H26/22R	RJ3537	Leyd Titan TD4	5856	-/35	Salford 35	
898*	H26/22R	RJ3538	Leyd Titan TD4	5857	-/35	Salford 43	
899*	H26/22R	RJ3539	Leyd Titan TD4	5858	-/35	Salford 45	
900*	H26/22R	RJ3540	Leyd Titan TD4	5859	-/35	Salford 46	
901	H34/29D	TJ9010	Leyd/GEC TB10	4588	2/35	Leyland Motors Limited	
902*	L24/26R	DJ6453	Leyd TB4	5759	5/35	St Helens 127	
903*	L24/26R	DJ6454	Leyd TB4	5761	5/35	St Helens 128	
904*	L24/26R	DJ6455	Leyd TB4	5764	5/35	St Helens 129	
905*	L24/26R	DJ6456	Leyd TB4	5765	5/35	St Helens 130	
906*	L24/26R	DJ6457	Leyd TB4	5763	5/35	St Helens 131	
907*	L24/26R	DJ6458	Leyd TB4	5762	5/35	St Helens 132	
908*	L24/26R	DJ6459	Leyd TB4	5760	5/35	St Helens 133	
909*	L24/26R	DJ6460	Leyd TB4	5768	5/35	St Helens 134	
910*	L24/26R	DJ6461	Leyd TB4	5769	6/35	St Helens 135	
911*	L24/26R	DJ6462	Leyd TB4	5767	6/35	St Helens 136	
912*	L24/26R	DJ6463	Leyd TB4	5766	6/35	Birkenhead 198	
913	H30/24R	BG3423	Leyd Titan TD4c	7363	6/35	Birkenhead 198	
914	H30/24R	BG3424	Leyd Titan TD4c	7364	6/35	Birkenhead 199	
915	H30/24R	BG3425	Leyd Titan TD4c	7366	7/35	Birkenhead 200	
916	H30/24R	BG3426	Leyd Titan TD4c	7367	7/35	Birkenhead 201	
917	H30/24R	BG3427	Leyd Titan TD4c	7369	7/35	Birkenhead 202	
918	L27/26R	RM6627	Leyd Titan TD1	71226	5/35	Cumberland 109	
919	L24/24R	ATC643	Leyd Titan TD4c	7855	10/35	Leigh 56	
920	L24/24R	ATC644	Leyd Titan TD4c	7856	10/35	Leigh 57	
921	B30R	WH6851	Leyd Tiger TS7c	7869	10/35	Bolton 97	
922	B30R	WH6852	Leyd Tiger TS7c	7870	11/35	Bolton 98	
923	B30R	WH6853	Leyd Tiger TS7c	7871	11/35	Bolton 99	
924	Amb.	???	Morris Ambulance	?	-/35	Leigh Joint Hospitals Board	
925*	B32R	ATD681	Leyd Lion LT7	8923	12/35	Widnes 37	
926*	B32R	ATD682	Leyd Lion LT7	8924	12/35	Widnes 38	
927*	B32R	ATD683	Leyd Lion LT7	8925	12/35	Widnes 39	
928	L24/26R	DJ6863	Ransomes, S & J D	2445	4/36	St Helens 137	
929	L24/26R	DJ6864	Ransomes, S & J D	2446	4/36	St Helens 138	
930	L24/26R	DJ6865	Ransomes, S & J D	2447	4/36	St Helens 139	
931	L24/26R	DJ6866	Ransomes, S & J D	2448	4/36	St Helens 140	
932	L24/26R	DJ6867	Ransomes, S & J D	2449	4/36	St Helens 141	
933	L27/26R	BAO772	Leyd Titan TD4	10015	4/36	Cumberland 115	
934	L27/26R	BAO773	Leyd Titan TD4	10016	5/36	Cumberland 116	
935	L27/26R	BAO774	Leyd Titan TD4	10017	5/36	Cumberland 117	
936	L27/26R	BAO775	Leyd Titan TD4	10018	4/36	Cumberland 118	
937	L27/26R	BAO776	Leyd Titan TD4	10019	5/36	Cumberland 119	
938	L27/26R	BAO777	Leyd Titan TD4	10020	5/36	Cumberland 120	
939	L27/26R	BAO762	AEC Regent	O6613770	3/36	Cumberland 12	
940	L27/26R	BAO763	AEC Regent	O6613771	3/36	Cumberland 47	
941	H30/24R	BG4381	Leyd Titan TD4c	10133	6/36	Birkenhead 208	
942	H30/24R	BG4382	Leyd Titan TD4c	10134	6/36	Birkenhead 209	

BNUM	CONFIG	REGN	CHASSIS MAKE	NUMBER	YEAR	OPERATOR	NOTE
943	H30/24R	BG4383	Leyd Titan TD4c	10135	6/36	Birkenhead 210	
944	H30/24R	BG4384	Leyd Titan TD4c	10136	6/36	Birkenhead 211	
945	H30/24R	BG4385	Leyd Titan TD4c	10137	6/36	Birkenhead 212	
946	H30/24R	BG4386	Leyd Titan TD4c	10138	6/36	Birkenhead 213	
947	H30/24R	BG4387	Leyd Titan TD4c	10139	6/36	Birkenhead 214	
948	H30/24R	BG4388	Leyd Titan TD4c	10140	6/36	Birkenhead 215	
949	H30/24R	BG4389	Leyd Titan TD4c	10141	6/36	Birkenhead 216	
950	H30/24R	BG4390	Leyd Titan TD4c	10142	6/36	Birkenhead 217	
951	H28/24R	AFM517	Leyd Titan TD4c	10226	5/36	Chester 26	
952	H28/24R	AFM518	Leyd Titan TD4c	10227	5/36	Chester 27	
953	H28/24R	AFM519	Leyd Titan TD4c	10228	5/36	Chester 28	
954	C20F	HD6040	Leyd Cub SKP2	5894	7/36	Yorkshire Woollen, 384	21
955	B39R	ACY104	Leyd Tiger TS7T	9822	11/36	Thomas (Llynfi), Maesteg	
956	B32R	VN9434	Leyd TB3	10774	12/36	Tees-Side 9	
957	B32R	VN9435	Leyd TB3	10775	12/36	Tees-Side 10	
958	B32R	VN9436	Leyd TB3	10778	12/36	Tees-Side 11	
959	B32R	VN9437	Leyd TB3	10777	12/36	Tees-Side 12	
960	H30/24R	VN9438	Leyd TB3	10776	12/36	Tees-Side 13	
961	H30/24R	BG4391	Leyd Titan TD4c	10654	6/36	Birkenhead 218	
962	H26/22R	RJ6601	Leyd Titan TD4c	11024	-/36	Salford 44	
963	H26/22R	RJ6602	Leyd Titan TD4c	11025	-/36	Salford 47	
964	H26/22R	RJ6603	Leyd Titan TD4c	11026	-/36	Salford 48	
965	H26/22R	RJ6604	Leyd Titan TD4c	11034	-/36	Salford 131	
966	H26/22R	RJ6605	Leyd Titan TD4c	10606	10/36	Salford 132	
967	L26/26R	WH7806	Leyd Titan TD4c	10607	9/36	Bolton 30	
968	L26/26R	WH7807	Leyd Titan TD4c	10608	9/36	Bolton 31	
969	L26/26R	WH7808	Leyd Titan TD4c	10609	8/36	Bolton 32	
970	L26/26R	WH7809	Leyd Titan TD4c	10610	8/36	Bolton 33	
971	L26/26R	WH7810	Leyd Titan TD4c	10611	9/36	Bolton 34	
972	L26/26R	WH7811	Leyd Titan TD4c	10612	8/36	Bolton 35	
973	L26/26R	WH7812	Leyd Titan TD4c	10613	8/36	Bolton 36	
974	L26/26R	WH7813	Leyd Titan TD4c	10613	7/36	Bolton 37	
975	L26/26R	WH7814	Leyd Titan TD4c	10614	8/36	Bolton 38	
976	L26/26R	WH7815	Leyd Titan TD4c	10615	7/36	Bolton 39	
977	L26/26R	WH7816	Leyd Titan TD4c	10616	10/36	Bolton 40	
978	L26/26R	WH7817	Leyd Titan TD4c	10617	10/36	Bolton 42	
979	L26/26R	WH7818	Leyd Titan TD4c	10618	7/36	Bolton 43	
980	L26/26R	WH7819	Leyd Titan TD4c	10619	7/36	Bolton 44	
981	L27/26R	WH7820	Leyd Titan TD4c	10620	8/36	Bolton 44	
982	L27/26R	BRM594	Leyd TB4	11397	10/36	Cumberland 11	
983	L27/26R	BRM595	Leyd TB4	11398	10/36	Cumberland 129	
984	L24/26R	BRM596	Leyd TB4	11399	10/36	Cumberland 132	
985*	L24/26R	DJ7428	Leyd TB4	11679	3/37	St Helens 101	
986*	L24/26R	DJ7429	Leyd TB4	11681	3/37	St Helens 102	
987*	L24/26R	DJ7430	Leyd TB4	11680	3/37	St Helens 103	
988*	L24/26R	DJ7431	Leyd TB4	11682	3/37	St Helens 104	
989	L24/26R	DJ7236	Ransomes, S & J D4	2482	12/36	St Helens 142	
990	L24/26R	DJ7237	Ransomes, S & J D4	2483	12/36	St Helens 143	
991	L24/26R	DJ7238	Ransomes, S & J D4	2484	1/37	St Helens 144	
992	H28/24R	BTD121	Leyd Titan TD4	12320	11/36	Widnes 40	
993	H28/24R	BTD122	Leyd Titan TD4	12321	11/36	Widnes 41	
994	H28/24R	BTD123	Leyd Titan TD4	12322	11/36	Widnes 42	
995	H28/24R	BTD124	Leyd Titan TD4	12323	11/36	Widnes 43	
996	H28/24R	BTD125	Leyd Titan TD4	12324	11/36	Widnes 44	
997		-------	Rlwy	N/A	-/37	Walker Brothers, Wigan	
998			Railcar Cab for Sao Paulo	N/A	-/37	Walker Brothers, Wigan	
999	L24/24R	BTD846	Leyd Titan TD4c	12879	1/37	Leigh 58	
1000	L24/24R	BTD847	Leyd Titan TD4c	12880	3/37	Leigh 59	
1001	B32D	BTD848	Leyd Tiger TS7c	12877	3/37	Leigh 60	
1002	B32D	BTD849	Leyd Tiger TS7c	12878	3/37	Leigh 61	
1003	B30R	RJ7004	Leyd Tiger TS7	12873	-/37	Salford 6	
1004	B30R	RJ7005	Leyd Tiger TS7	12874	-/37	Salford 7	
1005	B30R	RJ7006	Leyd Tiger TS7	12875	-/37	Salford 8	
1006*	L24/24R	JP2025	Leyd Titan TD4	12830	3/37	Wigan 87	
1007*	L24/24R	JP2026	Leyd Titan TD4	12831	3/37	Wigan 88	
1008*	L24/24R	JP2027	Leyd Titan TD4	12832	3/37	Wigan 89	
1009*	L24/24R	JP2030	Leyd Titan TD4	12835	3/37	Wigan 92	
1010*	L24/24R	JP2031	Leyd Titan TD4	12836	3/37	Wigan 93	
1011	H24/24R	PV4061	Ransomes, S & J D	2501	8/37	Ipswich 68	
1012	H24/24R	PV4062	Ransomes, S & J D	2502	7/37	Ipswich 69	
1013	H24/24R	PV4063	Ransomes, S & J D	2503	7/37	Ipswich 70	
1014	H24/24R	PV4063	Ransomes, S & J D	2505	7/37	Ipswich 71	

No	Config	Regn	Chassis Make	Chassis No	New	Location	Note
1016	H24/24R	PV4066	Ransomes, S & J D	2506	7/37	Ipswich 73	
1017	H30/24R	BG5501	Leyd Titan TD4c	14258	6/37	Birkenhead 219	
1018	H30/24R	BG5502	Leyd Titan TD5c	13573	6/37	Birkenhead 220	
1019	H30/24R	BG5503	Leyd Titan TD5c	13574	7/37	Birkenhead 221	
1020	H30/24R	BG5504	Leyd Titan TD5c	13575	7/37	Birkenhead 222	
1021	H30/24R	BG5505	Leyd Titan TD5c	13576	6/37	Birkenhead 223	
1022	H30/24R	BG5506	Leyd Titan TD5c	13577	7/37	Birkenhead 224	
1023	H30/24R	BG5507	Leyd Titan TD5c	13578	7/37	Birkenhead 225	
1024	H30/24R	BG5508	Leyd Titan TD5c	13579	7/37	Birkenhead 226	
1025	H30/24R	BG5509	Leyd Titan TD5c	13580	7/37	Birkenhead 227	
1026	H30/24R	BG5510	Leyd Titan TD5c	13581	7/37	Birkenhead 228	
1027	H30/24R	BG5511	Leyd Titan TD5c	13582	7/37	Birkenhead 229	
1028	H30/24R	BG5512	Leyd Titan TD5c	13583	7/37	Birkenhead 230	
1029	H30/24R	BG5513	Leyd Titan TD5c	13584	7/37	Birkenhead 231	
1030	H30/24R	BG5514	Leyd Titan TD5c	13585	7/37	Birkenhead 232	
1031	H30/24R	BG5515	Leyd Titan TD5c	13586	7/37	Birkenhead 233	
1032	H30/24R	BG5516	Leyd Titan TD5c	13587	7/37	Birkenhead 234	
1033	H30/24R	BG5517	Leyd Titan TD5c	13588	8/37	Birkenhead 235	
1034	H30/24R	BG5518	Leyd Titan TD5c	13589	7/37	Birkenhead 236	
1035	H30/24R	BG5519	Leyd Titan TD5c	13590	7/37	Birkenhead 237	
1036	H30/24R	BG5520	Leyd Titan TD5c	13592	7/37	Birkenhead 238	
1037	L24/24R	JP2196	Leyd Titan TD4	13759	4/37	Wigan 95	
1038	H30/24R	BG5521	Leyd Titan TD5c	13591	10/37	Birkenhead 239	
1039	H30/24R	BG5522	Leyd Titan TD5c	14239	10/37	Birkenhead 240	
1040	H30/24R	BG5523	Leyd Titan TD5c	14240	10/37	Birkenhead 241	
1041	H30/24R	BG5524	Leyd Titan TD5c	14241	10/37	Birkenhead 242	
1042	H30/24R	BG5525	Leyd Titan TD5c	14242	10/37	Birkenhead 243	
1043	H30/24R	BG5526	Leyd Titan TD5c	14243	10/37	Birkenhead 244	
1044	H30/24R	BG5527	Leyd Titan TD5c	14244	10/37	Birkenhead 245	
1045	H30/24R	BG5528	Leyd Titan TD5c	14245	10/37	Birkenhead 246	
1046	H30/24R	BG5529	Leyd Titan TD5c	14246	10/37	Birkenhead 247	
1047	H30/24R	BG5530	Leyd Titan TD5c	14247	10/37	Birkenhead 248	
1048	H30/24R	BG5531	Leyd Titan TD5c	14248	10/37	Birkenhead 249	
1049	H30/24R	BG5532	Leyd Titan TD5c	14249	10/37	Birkenhead 250	
1050	H30/24R	BG5533	Leyd Titan TD5c	14250	10/37	Birkenhead 251	
1051	H30/24R	BG5534	Leyd Titan TD5c	14251	12/37	Birkenhead 252	
1052	H30/24R	BG5535	Leyd Titan TD5c	14252	12/37	Birkenhead 253	
1053	H30/24R	BG5536	Leyd Titan TD5c	14253	12/37	Birkenhead 254	
1054	H30/24R	BG5537	Leyd Titan TD5c	14254	10/37	Birkenhead 255	
1055	H30/24R	BG5538	Leyd Titan TD5c	14255	12/37	Birkenhead 256	
1056	H30/24R	BG5539	Leyd Titan TD5c	14256	12/37	Birkenhead 257	
1057	H30/24R	BG5540	Leyd Titan TD5c	14257	12/37	Birkenhead 258	
1058	------	------	Railcar body for Trujillo Peru	N/A	-/37	Walker Brothers, Wigan	
1059*	H29/26R	CWM567	Leyd Titan TD5c	13962	8/37	Southport 51	22
1060*	H29/26R	CWM568	Leyd Titan TD5c	13963	7/37	Southport 52	22
1061*	H29/26R	CWM569	Leyd Titan TD5c	13964	8/37	Southport 53	22
1062*	H29/26R	CWM570	Leyd Titan TD5c	13965	8/37	Southport 54	22
1063*	H29/26R	CWM571	Leyd Titan TD5c	13966	8/37	Southport 55	
1064*	H28/26R	WH9216	Leyd Titan TD5c	14440	9/37	Bolton 118	
1065*	H28/26R	WH9217	Leyd Titan TD5c	14441	9/37	Bolton 119	
1066*	H28/26R	WH9218	Leyd Titan TD5c	14442	9/37	Bolton 120	
1067*	H28/26R	WH9219	Leyd Titan TD5c	14443	9/37	Bolton 121	
1068*	H28/26R	WH9220	Leyd Titan TD5c	14444	9/37	Bolton 122	
1069*	H28/26R	WH9221	Leyd Titan TD5c	14445	9/37	Bolton 123	
1070*	H28/26R	WH9222	Leyd Titan TD5c	14446	9/37	Bolton 124	
1071*	H28/26R	WH9223	Leyd Titan TD5c	14447	9/37	Bolton 125	
1072*	H28/26R	WH9224	Leyd Titan TD5c	14448	9/37	Bolton 126	
1073*	H28/26R	WH9225	Leyd Titan TD5c	14449	9/37	Bolton 127	
1074	H24/24R	PV4540	Ransomes, S & J D	2507	11/37	Ipswich 74	
1075	H24/24R	PV4541	Ransomes, S & J D	2511	12/37	Ipswich 75	
1076	H24/24R	PV4542	Ransomes, S & J D	2512	12/37	Ipswich 76	
1077	H24/24R	PV4543	Ransomes, S & J D	2509	12/37	Ipswich 77	
1078	H24/24R	PV4544	Ransomes, S & J D	2508	1/38	Ipswich 78	
1079	H24/24R	PV4545	Ransomes, S & J D	2591	3/38	Ipswich 79	
1080	H24/24R	PV4788	Ransomes, S & J D	2590	3/38	Ipswich 80	
1081	H24/24R	PV4789	Ransomes, S & J D	2594	3/38	Ipswich 81	
1082	H24/24R	PV4790	Ransomes, S & J D	2593	3/38	Ipswich 82	
1083	H24/24R	PV4791	Ransomes, S & J D	2595	3/38	Ipswich 83	
1084	H24/24R	PV4792	Ransomes, S & J D	2592	5/38	Ipswich 84	
1085	H24/24R	PV4793	Ransomes, S & J D	2592	5/38	Ipswich 85	
1086*	L24/24R	CTD541	Leyd Titan TD5c	14662	12/37	Leigh 62	
1087*	L24/24R	CTD542	Leyd Titan TD5c	14663	12/37	Leigh 63	
1088*	L24/24R	CTD543	Leyd Titan TD5c	14664	12/37	Leigh 64	
1089*	B32F	CTD544	Leyd Tiger TS8c	14659	2/38	Leigh 65	
1090*	B32F	CTD545	Leyd Tiger TS8c	14660	2/38	Leigh 66	23
1091*	B32F	CTD546	Leyd Tiger TS8c	14661	2/38	Leigh 67	
1092	H28/26R	WH9501	Leyd Titan TD5c	15322	12/37	Bolton 128	
1093	H28/26R	WH9502	Leyd Titan TD5c	15323	12/37	Bolton 129	
1094	H28/26R	WH9503	Leyd Titan TD5c	15324	12/37	Bolton 130	
1095	H28/26R	WH9504	Leyd Titan TD5c	15325	12/37	Bolton 131	
1096	H28/26R	WH9505	Leyd Titan TD5c	15326	12/37	Bolton 132	
1097	------	------	Railcar body for Trujillo Peru	N/A	-/38	Walker Brothers, Wigan	
1098	------	------	Railcar body for Trujillo Peru	N/A	-/38	Walker Brothers, Wigan	
1099*	L24/24R	JP2969	Leyd Titan TD5	16287	2/38	Wigan 100	
1100*	L24/24R	JP2970	Leyd Titan TD5	16288	2/38	Wigan 101	
1101*	L24/24R	JP2971	Leyd Titan TD5	16289	2/38	Wigan 102	
1102*	L24/24R	JP2972	Leyd Titan TD5	16290	2/38	Wigan 103	
1103*	H29/23R	HG6012	Leyd Titan TD5c	15984	12/37	Burnley, Colne & Nelson 151	
1104*	H29/23R	HG6013	Leyd Titan TD5c	15985	12/37	Burnley, Colne & Nelson 152	
1105*	H28/24R	CTF741	Leyd Titan TD5	17338	3/38	Widnes 45	
1106*	H28/24R	CTF742	Leyd Titan TD5	17339	3/38	Widnes 46	
1107*	H28/24R	CTF743	Leyd Titan TD5	17340	3/38	Widnes 47	
1108*	H28/24R	CTF744	Leyd Titan TD5	17341	3/38	Widnes 48	
None	H28/24R	XJ282	Daimler CP6	9098	3/38	Lancaster 3	
1109	B32R	DA064	Leyd Tiger TS8	17803	6/38	Cumberland 138	
1110	B32R	DA065	Leyd Tiger TS8	17804	6/38	Cumberland 139	
1111	B32R	DA066	Leyd Tiger TS8	17805	6/38	Cumberland 140	
1112	B32R	DA067	Leyd Titan TD5	17806	6/38	Cumberland 141	
1113	B32R	DA068	Leyd Titan TD5	17807	6/38	Cumberland 142	
1114	L27/26R	DA048	Leyd Titan TD5	17798	6/38	Cumberland 133	
1115	L27/26R	DA049	Leyd Titan TD5	17799	6/38	Cumberland 134	
1116	L27/26R	DA050	Leyd Titan TD5	17800	6/38	Cumberland 135	
1117	L27/26R	DA051	Leyd Titan TD5	17801	6/38	Cumberland 136	
1118	L27/26R	DA052	Leyd Titan TD5	17802	6/38	Cumberland 137	
1119*	H30/24R	BG6801	Leyd Titan TD5c	17594	7/38	Birkenhead 259	
1120*	H30/24R	BG6802	Leyd Titan TD5c	17595	7/38	Birkenhead 260	
1121*	H30/24R	BG6803	Leyd Titan TD5c	17596	7/38	Birkenhead 261	
1122*	H30/24R	BG6804	Leyd Titan TD5c	17597	7/38	Birkenhead 262	
1123*	H30/24R	BG6805	Leyd Titan TD5c	17598	7/38	Birkenhead 263	
1124*	H30/24R	BG6806	Leyd Titan TD5c	17602	7/38	Birkenhead 264	
1125*	H30/24R	BG6807	Leyd Titan TD5c	17603	7/38	Birkenhead 265	
1126*	H30/24R	BG6808	Leyd Titan TD5c	17604	7/38	Birkenhead 266	
1127*	H30/24R	BG6809	Leyd Titan TD5c	17607	7/38	Birkenhead 267	
1128*	H30/24R	BG6810	Leyd Titan TD5c	17608	7/38	Birkenhead 268	
1129	L24/26R	DJ8120	Ransomes, S & J D4	2608	7/38	St Helens 145	
1130	L24/26R	DJ8121	Ransomes, S & J D4	2609	7/38	St Helens 146	
1131	L24/26R	DJ8122	Ransomes, S & J D4	2614	7/38	St Helens 147	
1132	L24/26R	DJ8123	Ransomes, S & J D4	2613	9/38	St Helens 148	
1133	L24/26R	DJ8124	Ransomes, S & J D4	2612	10/38	St Helens 149	
1134	L24/26R	DJ8125	Ransomes, S & J D4	2615	12/38	St Helens 150	
1135	L24/26R	DJ8126	Ransomes, S & J D4	2607	7/38	St Helens 151	
1136	L24/26R	DJ8127	Ransomes, S & J D4	2611	9/38	St Helens 152	
1137	L24/26R	DJ8128	Ransomes, S & J D4	2610	9/38	St Helens 153	
1138	L24/26R	DJ8129	Ransomes, S & J D4	2616	9/38	St Helens 154	
1139	L24/26R	DJ8130	Ransomes, S & J D4	2618	10/38	St Helens 155	
1140	L24/26R	DJ8131	Ransomes, S & J D4	2617	10/38	St Helens 156	
1141*	B32R	ABN403	Leyd Tiger TS8c	300992	9/38	Bolton 3	
1142*	B32R	ABN404	Leyd Tiger TS8c	300993	9/38	Bolton 4	
1143*	L24/24R	DTD169	Leyd Titan TD5	300662	10/38	Leigh 70	
1144*	L24/24R	DTD170	Leyd Titan TD5	300663	10/38	Leigh 71	
1145*	H28/26R	ABN601	Leyd Titan TD5c	301719	7/38	Bolton 153	
1146*	H28/26R	ABN602	Leyd Titan TD5c	301720	9/38	Bolton 154	
1147*	H28/26R	ABN603	Leyd Titan TD5c	301721	9/38	Bolton 155	
1148*	H28/26R	ABN604	Leyd Titan TD5c	301722	9/38	Bolton 156	
1149*	H28/26R	ABN605	Leyd Titan TD5c	301723	9/38	Bolton 157	
1150*	H28/26R	ABN606	Leyd Titan TD5c	301724	10/38	Bolton 158	
1151*	H28/26R	ABN607	Leyd Titan TD5c	301725	1/39	Bolton 159	
1152*	H28/26R	ABN608	Leyd Titan TD5c	301726	1/39	Bolton 160	
1153*	H28/26R	ABN609	Leyd Titan TD5c	301727	1/39	Bolton 161	
1154*	H28/26R	ABN610	Leyd Titan TD5c	301728	1/39	Bolton 162	
1155*	H28/26R	ABN611	Leyd Titan TD5c	301729	1/39	Bolton 163	
1156*	H28/26R	ABN612	Leyd Titan TD5c	301730	1/39	Bolton 164	
1157*	H28/26R	ABN613	Leyd Titan TD5c	301731	1/39	Bolton 165	
1158*	H28/26R	ABN614	Leyd Titan TD5c	301732	1/39	Bolton 166	
1159*	H28/26R	ABN615	Leyd Titan TD5c	301733	1/39	Bolton 167	
1160*	H28/26R	ABN616	Leyd Titan TD5c	301734	1/39	Bolton 168	
1161*	H28/26R	ABN617	Leyd Titan TD5c	301735	1/39	Bolton 169	

Left table

BNUM	CONFIG	REGN	CHASSIS MAKE	NUMBER	YEAR	OPERATOR	NOTE
1162*	H28/26R	ABN618	Leyd Titan TD5c	301736	1/39	Bolton 170	
1163*	H28/26R	ABN619	Leyd Titan TD5c	301737	1/39	Bolton 171	
1164*	H28/26R	ABN620	Leyd Titan TD5c	301738	1/39	Bolton 172	
1165*	H28/26R	ABN621	Leyd Titan TD5c	301739	1/39	Bolton 173	
1166*	H28/26R	ABN622	Leyd Titan TD5c	301740	1/39	Bolton 174	
1167*	H28/26R	ABN623	Leyd Titan TD5c	301741	1/39	Bolton 175	
1168*	H28/26R	ABN624	Leyd Titan TD5c	301742	1/39	Bolton 176	
1169*	H28/26R	ABN625	Leyd Titan TD5c	301743	1/39	Bolton 177	
1170*	H28/26R	ABN626	Leyd Titan TD5c	301744	8/39	Bolton 178	
1171*	H28/26R	ABN627	Leyd Titan TD5c	301745	8/39	Bolton 179	
1172*	H28/26R	ABN628	Leyd Titan TD5c	301746	8/39	Bolton 180	
1173*	H28/26R	ABN629	Leyd Titan TD5c	301747	8/39	Bolton 181	
1174*	H28/26R	ABN630	Leyd Titan TD5c	301748	8/39	Bolton 182	
1175*	H28/26R	ABN631	Leyd Titan TD5c	301749	8/39	Bolton 183	
1176*	H28/26R	ABN632	Leyd Titan TD5c	301750	8/39	Bolton 184	
1177*	H28/26R	ABN633	Leyd Titan TD5c	301751	8/39	Bolton 185	
1178*	H28/26R	ABN634	Leyd Titan TD5c	301752	8/39	Bolton 186	
1179*	H28/26R	ABN635	Leyd Titan TD5c	301753	8/39	Bolton 187	
1180*	H28/26R	ABN636	Leyd Titan TD5c	301754	8/39	Bolton 188	
1181*	H28/26R	ABN637	Leyd Titan TD5c	301755	8/39	Bolton 189	
1182*	H28/26R	ABN638	Leyd Titan TD5c	301756	8/39	Bolton 190	
1183*	H28/26R	ABN639	Leyd Titan TD5c	301757	8/39	Bolton 191	
1184*	H28/26R	ABN640	Leyd Titan TD5c	301758	8/39	Bolton 192	
1185*	H26/26R	GVW946	AEC Regent	O6616369	3/39	Colchester 30	
1186*	H26/26R	GVW947	AEC Regent	O6616370	3/39	Colchester 31	
1187*	H26/26R	GVW948	AEC Regent	O6616371	3/39	Colchester 32	
1188*	H26/26R	GVW949	AEC Regent	O6616372	3/39	Colchester 33	
1189*	H26/26R	GVW950	AEC Regent	O6616373	3/39	Colchester 34	
1190	H30/26R	DKV223	Daimler COA6	10689	5/39	Coventry 223	
1191	H24/24R	EX5010	Leyd Titan TD5	302315	5/39	Great Yarmouth 10	
1192	H24/24R	EX5011	Leyd Titan TD5	302316	5/39	Great Yarmouth 11	
1193	H24/24R	EX5012	Leyd Titan TD5	302317	5/39	Great Yarmouth 12	
1194	H24/24R	EX5013	Leyd Titan TD5	302318	5/39	Great Yarmouth 13	
1195	L27/26R	DRM7	Leyd Titan TD5	302450	4/39	Cumberland 143	
1196	L27/26R	DRM8	Leyd Titan TD5	302451	4/39	Cumberland 144	
1197	H30/24R	BG7701	Leyd Titan TD5c	302617	7/39	Birkenhead 279	
1198	H30/24R	BG7702	Leyd Titan TD5c	302618	7/39	Birkenhead 280	
1199	H30/24R	BG7703	Leyd Titan TD5c	302619	7/39	Birkenhead 281	
1200	H30/24R	BG7704	Leyd Titan TD5c	302620	7/39	Birkenhead 282	
1201	H30/24R	BG7705	Leyd Titan TD5c	302621	7/39	Birkenhead 283	
1202	H30/24R	BG7706	Leyd Titan TD5c	302622	7/39	Birkenhead 284	
1203	H30/24R	BG7707	Leyd Titan TD5c	302623	7/39	Birkenhead 285	
1204	H30/24R	BG7708	Leyd Titan TD5c	302624	7/39	Birkenhead 286	
1205	H30/24R	BG7709	Leyd Titan TD5c	302625	8/39	Birkenhead 287	
1206	H30/24R	BG7710	Leyd Titan TD5c	302626	8/39	Birkenhead 288	
1207	H30/24R	BG7711	Leyd Titan TD5c	302627	7/39	Birkenhead 289	
1208	H30/24R	BG7712	Leyd Titan TD5c	302628	7/39	Birkenhead 290	
1209	H30/24R	BG7713	Leyd Titan TD5c	302629	7/39	Birkenhead 291	
1210	H30/24R	BG7714	Leyd Titan TD5c	302630	7/39	Birkenhead 292	
1211	H30/24R	BG7715	Leyd Titan TD5c	302631	7/39	Birkenhead 293	
1212	H30/24R	BG7716	Leyd Titan TD5c	302632	7/39	Birkenhead 294	
1213	H30/24R	BG7717	Leyd Titan TD5c	302633	8/39	Birkenhead 295	
1214	H30/24R	BG7718	Leyd Titan TD5c	302634	8/39	Birkenhead 296	
1215	H30/24R	BG7719	Leyd Titan TD5c	302635	8/39	Birkenhead 297	
1216	H30/24R	BG7720	Leyd Titan TD5c	302636	8/39	Birkenhead 298	
1217	H30/24R	BG7721	Leyd Titan TD5c	302637	7/39	Birkenhead 299	
1218	H30/24R	BG7722	Leyd Titan TD5c	302638	8/39	Birkenhead 300	
1219	H30/24R	BG7723	Leyd Titan TD5c	302639	9/39	Birkenhead 301	
1220	H30/24R	BG7724	Leyd Titan TD5c	302640	9/39	Birkenhead 302	
1221	H30/24R	BG7725	Leyd Titan TD5c	302641	9/39	Birkenhead 303	
1222	H30/24R	BG7726	Leyd Titan TD5c	302642	11/39	Birkenhead 304	
1223	H30/24R	BG7727	Leyd Titan TD5c	302643	11/39	Birkenhead 305	
1224	H30/24R	BG7728	Leyd Titan TD5c	302644	11/39	Birkenhead 306	
1225	H30/24R	BG7729	Leyd Titan TD5c	302645	11/39	Birkenhead 307	
1226	H30/24R	BG7730	Leyd Titan TD5c	302646	11/39	Birkenhead 308	
1227	H30/24R	BG7731	Leyd Titan TD5c	302647	1/40	Birkenhead 309	
1228	H30/24R	BG7732	Leyd Titan TD5c	302648	1/40	Birkenhead 310	
1229	H30/24R	BG7733	Leyd Titan TD5c	302649	1/40	Birkenhead 311	
1230	H30/24R	BG7734	Leyd Titan TD5c	302650	1/40	Birkenhead 312	
1231	H30/24R	BG7735	Leyd Titan TD5c	302651	1/40	Birkenhead 313	
1232	H30/24R	BG7736	Leyd Titan TD5c	302652	1/40	Birkenhead 314	
1233	H30/24R	BG7737	Leyd Titan TD5c	302653	1/40	Birkenhead 315	
1234	H30/24R	BG7738	Leyd Titan TD5c	302654	1/40	Birkenhead 316	
1235	H30/24R	BG7739	Leyd Titan TD5c	302655	1/40	Birkenhead 317	

Right table

BNUM	CONFIG	REGN	CHASSIS MAKE	NUMBER	YEAR	OPERATOR	NOTE
1237	DP32R	RM5629	Leyd Tiger TS2	60375	4/39	Cumberland 94	1
1238	DP32R	RM6017	Leyd Tiger TS2	60575	5/39	Cumberland 30	1
1239	C26F	RM6018	Leyd Tiger TS2	60576	5/39	Cumberland 31	1
1240	H28/26R	DFM946	AEC Regent	O6616520	5/39	Chester 31	
1241	H28/26R	DFM947	AEC Regent	O6616521	5/39	Chester 32	
1242	H28/26R	DFM948	AEC Regent	O6616522	5/39	Chester 33	
1243	H28/26R	DFM949	AEC Regent	O6616523	5/39	Chester 34	
1244	H30/26R	FRH570	AEC Regent	O661G6544	10/39	Hull 170	
1245	H30/26R	FRH571	AEC Regent	O661G6545	10/39	Hull 171	
1246	H30/26R	FRH572	AEC Regent	O661G6546	10/39	Hull 172	
1247	H30/26R	FRH573	AEC Regent	O661G6547	10/39	Hull 173	
1248	H30/26R	FRH574	AEC Regent	O661G6548	10/39	Hull 174	
1249	H30/26R	FRH575	AEC Regent	O661G6549	10/39	Hull 175	
1250	H30/26R	FRH576	AEC Regent	O661G6550	11/39	Hull 176	
1251	H30/26R	FRH577	AEC Regent	O661G6551	12/39	Hull 177	
1252	H30/26R	FRH578	AEC Regent	O661G6552	11/39	Hull 178	
1253	H30/26R	FRH579	AEC Regent	O661G6553	1/40	Hull 179	
1254	H30/26R	FRH580	AEC Regent	O661G6554	11/39	Hull 180	
1255	H30/26R	FRH581	AEC Regent	O661G6555	1/40	Hull 181	
1256	H30/26R	FRH582	AEC Regent	O661G6556	1/40	Hull 182	
1257	H30/26R	FRH583	AEC Regent	O661G6557	1/40	Hull 183	
1258	H30/26R	FRH584	AEC Regent	O661G6558	1/40	Hull 184	
1259	H30/26R	FRH585	AEC Regent	O661G6559	1/40	Hull 185	
1260	H30/26R	FRH586	AEC Regent	O661G6560	1/40	Hull 186	
1261	H30/26R	FRH587	AEC Regent	O661G6561	1/40	Hull 187	
1262	H30/26R	FRH588	AEC Regent	O661G6562	1/40	Hull 188	
1263	H30/26R	FRH589	AEC Regent	O661G6563	1/40	Hull 189	
1264	H30/26R	AWH931	Leyd Titan TD5c	303205	10/40	Bolton 193	
1265	H30/26R	AWH932	Leyd Titan TD5c	303206	10/40	Bolton 194	
1266	H30/26R	AWH933	Leyd Titan TD5c	303207	10/40	Bolton 195	
1267	H30/26R	AWH934	Leyd Titan TD5c	303208	10/40	Bolton 196	
1268	H30/26R	AWH935	Leyd Titan TD5c	303209	10/40	Bolton 197	
1269	H30/26R	AWH936	Leyd Titan TD5c	303210	10/40	Bolton 198	
1270	H30/26R	AWH937	Leyd Titan TD5c	303211	10/40	Bolton 199	
1271	H30/26R	AWH938	Leyd Titan TD5c	303212	1/41	Bolton 200	
1272	H30/26R	AWH939	Leyd Titan TD5c	303213	2/41	Bolton 201	
1273	H30/26R	AWH940	Leyd Titan TD5c	303214	2/41	Bolton 202	
1274	H30/26R	AWH941	Leyd Titan TD5c	303215	2/41	Bolton 203	
1275	H30/26R	AWH942	Leyd Titan TD5c	303216	4/41	Bolton 204	
1276	H30/26R	AWH943	Leyd Titan TD5c	303217	4/41	Bolton 205	
1277	H30/26R	AWH944	Leyd Titan TD5c	303218	3/41	Bolton 206	
1278	H30/26R	AWH945	Leyd Titan TD5c	303219	3/41	Bolton 207	
1279	H30/26R	AWH946	Leyd Titan TD5c	303220	4/41	Bolton 208	
1280	H30/26R	AWH947	Leyd Titan TD5c	303221	10/40	Bolton 209	
1281	H30/26R	AWH948	Leyd Titan TD5c	303222	10/40	Bolton 210	
1282	H30/26R	AWH949	Leyd Titan TD7c	303223	1/42	Bolton 211	
1283	H30/26R	AWH950	Leyd Titan TD7c	303224	10/40	Bolton 212	
1284	H30/26R	AWH951	Leyd Titan TD7c	303225	3/41	Bolton 213	
1285	H30/26R	AWH952	Leyd Titan TD7c	303226	1/42	Bolton 214	
1286	H30/26R	AWH953	Leyd Titan TD7c	303227	10/40	Bolton 215	
1287	H30/26R	AWH954	Leyd Titan TD7c	303228	10/40	Bolton 216	
1288	H30/26R	AWH955	Leyd Titan TD7c	303229	10/40	Bolton 217	
1289	H30/26R	BBN176	Leyd Titan TD7c	303230	3/41	Bolton 218	
1290	H30/26R	BBN177	Leyd Titan TD7c	303231	3/41	Bolton 219	
1291	H30/26R	BBN178	Leyd Titan TD7c	303232	3/41	Bolton 220	
1292	H30/26R	BBN179	Leyd Titan TD7c	303233	3/41	Bolton 221	
1293	H30/26R	BBN180	Leyd Titan TD7c	303234	3/41	Bolton 222	
1294	H30/26R	BBN181	Leyd Titan TD7c	303235	5/41	Bolton 223	
1295	H30/26R	BBN182	Leyd Titan TD7c	303236	8/40	Bolton 224	
1296	H30/26R	BBN183	Leyd Titan TD7c	303237	5/41	Bolton 225	
1297	H30/26R	BBN184	Leyd Titan TD7c	303238	8/40	Bolton 226	
1298	H30/26R	BBN185	Leyd Titan TD7c	303239	11/39	Bolton 227	
1299	H30/26R	BBN186	Leyd Titan TD7c	303240	5/41	Bolton 228	
1300	H30/26R	BBN187	Leyd Titan TD7c	303241	5/41	Bolton 229	
1301	H30/26R	BBN188	Leyd Titan TD7c	303242	10/41	Bolton 230	
1302	H30/26R	BBN189	Leyd Titan TD7c	303243	10/41	Bolton 231	
1303	H30/26R	BBN190	Leyd Titan TD7c	303244	10/41	Bolton 232	
1304	H30/26R	BBN191	Leyd Titan TD7c	303245	10/41	Bolton 233	
1305	H30/26R	BBN192	Leyd Titan TD7c	303246	10/41	Bolton 234	
1306	H30/26R	BBN193	Leyd Titan TD7c	303247	10/41	Bolton 235	
1307	H30/26R	BBN194	Leyd Titan TD7c	303248	8/40	Bolton 236	
1308	H30/26R	BBN195	Leyd Titan TD7c	303249	11/41	Bolton 237	
1309	H30/26R	BBN196	Leyd Titan TD7c	303250	11/41	Bolton 238	
1310	H30/26R	BBN197	Leyd Titan TD7c	303251	8/40	Bolton 239	

Left section:

No	Body	Chassis	Reg	Serial	Date	Operator	Notes
1312	H30/26R	Leyd Titan TD7c	BBN199	303253	8/40	Bolton 241	
1313	H30/26R	Leyd Titan TD7c	BBN200	303254	11/41	Bolton 242	
1314	Lorry	Horse	JP4821	?	-/41	Wigan Corporation	
1315	H24/24R	Ransomes, S & J Light	PV6426	2704	6/40	Ipswich 86	
1316	H28/26R	AEC Regent	EFM909	O6616900	6/40	Chester 37	
1317	H28/26R	AEC Regent	EFM910	O6616930	6/40	Chester 38	
1318	H28/26R	AEC Regent	EFM911	O6616979	6/40	Chester 39	
1319	H28/26R	Leyd Titan TD7c	FFM113	306833	4/41	Chester 40	
1320	L27/26R	Leyd Titan TD7c	FFM114	306834	5/41	Chester 41	
1321	H28/26R	Leyd Titan TD7c	FFM115	306835	6/41	Chester 42	
1322	L27/26R	Leyd Titan TD7	EAO699	306818	2/41	Cumberland 159	
1323	L27/26R	Leyd Titan TD7	EAO700	306819	2/41	Cumberland 160	
1324	L27/26R	Leyd Titan TD7	EAO701	306820	3/41	Cumberland 161	
1325	L27/26R	Leyd Titan TD7	EAO702	306821	3/41	Cumberland 162	
1326	L27/26R	Leyd Titan TD7	EAO703	306822	5/41	Cumberland 163	
1327*	L24/26R	Sunbeam MF2	DJ9005	13105	6/42	St Helens 157	
1328*	L24/26R	Sunbeam MF2	DJ9006	13103	6/42	St Helens 158	
1329*	L24/26R	Sunbeam MF2	DJ9007	13099	6/42	St Helens 159	
1330*	L24/26R	Sunbeam MF2	DJ9008	13100	6/42	St Helens 160	24
1331*	L24/26R	Sunbeam MF2	DJ9009	13101	6/42	St Helens 161	
1332	Lorry	Dodge 30-cwt (Flatbed lorry)	???	?	-/41	Ashton Brothers, Wigan	
1333*	L27/26R	Leyd Titan TD7	DWY391	307603	11/41	Todmorden 21	
1334*	L27/26R	Leyd Titan TD7	DWY392	307604	11/41	Todmorden 28	
1335*	L27/26R	Leyd Titan TD7	DWY393	307605	11/41	Todmorden 29	
1336*	L27/28R	Leyd Titan TD7	DWY394	307606	11/41	Todmorden 32	
1337	L27/28R	Leyd Titan TD7	VS4213	307631	2/42	Greenock Motor Services	
1338	L27/28R	Leyd Titan TD7	VS4214	307760	2/42	Greenock Motor Services	
1339	L27/28R	Leyd Titan TD5c	ERM127	311699	1/42	Cumberland 176	
1340*	L24/26R	Sunbeam MF2	DJ9010	13102	7/42	St Helens 162	
1341*	L24/26R	Sunbeam MF2	DJ9011	13098	8/42	St Helens 163	
1342*	L24/26R	Sunbeam MF2	DJ9012	13104	8/42	St Helens 164	24
1343*	L24/26R	Sunbeam MF2	DJ9013	13097	10/42	St Helens 165	
1344*	L24/26R	Sunbeam MF2	DJ9014	13106	10/42	St Helens 166	
1345	Lorry					Not built	
1346	H30/26R	AEC Regent	HWA145	O6616984	3/42	Sheffield A465	
1347	H30/26R	AEC Regent	HWA146	O6616985	3/42	Sheffield A466	
1348	H30/26R	AEC Regent	HWA147	O6616986	3/42	Sheffield A467	
1349	H30/26R	AEC Regent	HWA148	O6616987	3/42	Sheffield A468	
1350	H30/26R	Daimler COG6	HWA141	11156	4/42	Sheffield A461	
1351	H30/24R	Leyd Titan TD4c	BG3432	7368	-/42	Birkenhead 207	
1352*	H30/24R	Leyd Titan TD4c	BG4382	10134	-/42	Birkenhead 209	
1353*	H30/24R	Leyd Titan TD5c	BG7729	302645	-/42	Birkenhead 307	
1354	H30/26R	Guy Arab I	FFM232	FD25512	9/42	Chester 43	
1355	H30/26R	Guy Arab I	FFM233	FD25516	9/42	Chester 44	
1356	H30/26R	Guy Arab I	CU4510	FD25521	8/42	South Shields 125	
1357	H30/26R	Guy Arab I	EF7407	FD25523	9/42	West Hartlepool 37	25
1358	H30/26R	Guy Arab I	JTN505	FD25573	10/42	Newcastle 245	25
1359	H30/26R	Guy Arab I	JTN506	FD25568	10/42	Newcastle 246	25
1360	H30/26R	Guy Arab I	CN9696	FD25596	10/42	Northern General 996	
1361	H30/26R	Guy Arab I	CDT175	FD25603	-/42	Doncaster 80	
1362	H30/26R	Guy Arab I	RC8311	FD25629	11/42	Derby 1	
1363	H30/26R	Guy Arab I	RC8312	FD25610	11/42	Derby 2	
1364	H30/26R	Guy Arab I	CDT186	FD25660	11/42	Doncaster 81	
1365	H30/26R	Guy Arab I	HDH941	FD25664	11/42	Walsall 192	
1366	H30/26R	Guy Arab I	HDH942	FD25607	11/42	Walsall 195	
1367	H30/26R	Guy Arab I	CDT197	FD25689	11/42	Doncaster 82	
1368	H30/26R	Guy Arab I	EKV300	FD25694	11/42	Coventry 300	
1369	H30/26R	Guy Arab I	EKV301	FD25776	11/42	Coventry 301	
1370	H30/26R	Guy Arab I	CDT198	FD25734	1/43	Doncaster 83	
1371	H30/26R	Guy Arab I	KRE849	FD25755	-/42	Harper, Heath Hayes 24	
1372	H30/26R	Guy Arab I	EO7906	FD25734	-/43	Barrow 88	
1373	H30/26R	Guy Arab I	EO7907	FD25756	1/43	Barrow 89	
1374	H30/26R	Guy Arab I	EO7908	FD25771	1/43	Barrow 90	
1375	H30/26R	Guy Arab I	GKH702	FD25777	2/43	Hull 207	
1376	H30/26R	Guy Arab I	GKH703	FD25732	2/43	Hull 208	
1377	H30/26R	Guy Arab I	CN9716	FD25689	2/43	Northern General 1046	
1378	H30/26R	Guy Arab I	FTC715	FD25791	3/43	Ashton 13	
1379	H30/26R	Guy Arab I	GAL245	FD25823	3/43	Baker, Warsop 33	
1380	H30/26R	Guy Arab I	GTV408	FD25856	2/43	Nottingham 88	
1381	H30/26R	Guy Arab I	ASD94	FD25763	4/43	Western SMT	
1382	H30/26R	Guy Arab I	ASD95	FD25861	4/43	Western SMT	
1383	H30/26R	Guy Arab I	HE9774	FD25981	3/43	Yorkshire Traction 705	
1384	H30/26R	Guy Arab I	HD7348	FD25894	5/43	Yorkshire Woollen 483	

Right section:

No	Body	Chassis	Reg	Serial	Date	Operator
1385	H30/26R	Guy Arab I	XS5526	FD25889	5/43	Young, Paisley 132
1386	H30/26R	Guy Arab I	XS5527	FD25895	5/43	Young, Paisley 133
1387	H30/26R	Daimler CWG5	DKY468	11310	1/43	Western SMT
1388	H30/26R	Daimler CWG5	DKY468	11311	2/43	Bradford 468
1389	H30/26R	Daimler CWG5	EO7904	11320	2/43	Barrow 91
1390	H30/26R	Daimler CWG5	EO7905	11321	2/43	Barrow 92
1391	H30/26R	Daimler CWG5	ASD121	11322	1/43	Western SMT
1392	H30/26R	Daimler CWG5	DKY469	11323	2/43	Bradford 469
1393	H30/26R	Daimler CWG5	DKY470	11332	3/43	Bradford 470
1394	H30/26R	Daimler CWG5	DWS82	11333	3/43	Edinburgh G62
1395	H30/26R	Daimler CWG5	GR7707	11334	3/43	Sunderland 60
1396	H30/26R	Daimler CWG5	EKV822	11335	3/43	Coventry 322
1397	H30/26R	Daimler CWG5	DWS83	11344	3/43	Edinburgh G63
1398	H30/26R	Daimler CWG5	DGB448	11345	3/43	Glasgow 101
1399	H30/26R	Daimler CWG5	DGB449	11346	3/43	Glasgow 102
1400	H30/26R	Daimler CWG5	GR7708	11347	4/43	Sunderland 61
1401	H30/26R	Daimler CWG5	HWA675	11356	5/43	Sheffield A485
1402	H30/26R	Daimler CWG5	FTD70	11357	6/43	Lancaster 44
1403	H30/26R	Daimler CWG5	BRG838	11358	6/43	Aberdeen 136
1404	H30/26R	Daimler CWG5	DKY471	11359	6/43	Bradford 471
1405	H30/26R	Daimler CWG5	CU4548	11368	5/43	South Shields 128
1406	H30/26R	Daimler CWG5	HMA12	11369	5/43	SHMD 190
1407	H30/26R	Daimler CWG5	EDK771	11370	6/43	Rochdale 187
1408	H30/26R	Daimler CWG5	FFM270	11371	6/43	Chester 45
1409	H30/26R	Daimler CWG5	BRG839	11380	6/43	Aberdeen 137
1410	H30/26R	Daimler CWG5	ASD122	11381	6/43	Western SMT
1411	H30/26R	Daimler CWG5	DKY472	11382	7/43	Bradford 472
1412	H30/26R	Daimler CWG5	DKY473	11378	7/43	Bradford 473
1413	H30/26R	Daimler CWG5	JP5049	11398	6/43	Everingham, Pocklington 49
1414	H30/26R	Daimler CWG5	EWO473	11399	7/43	Red & White 473
1415	H30/26R	Daimler CWG5	EKV821	11400	7/43	Coventry 321
1416	H30/26R	Daimler CWG5	ASD123	11401	7/43	Western SMT
1417	H30/26R	Guy Arab II	EWT664	FD25964	7/43	Severn & Sons, Stainforth
1418	H30/26R	Guy Arab II	GTV414	FD25984	7/43	Nottingham 94
1419	H30/26R	Guy Arab II	GTV415	FD25985	7/43	West Monmouthshire 21
1420	H30/26R	Guy Arab II	EWO579	FD26003	6/43	Nottingham 95
1421	H30/26R	Guy Arab II	FTD287	FD26019	8/43	Ashton 14
1422	H30/26R	Guy Arab II	ASD252	FD26036	7/43	Western SMT
1423	H30/26R	Guy Arab II	ASD253	FD26069	7/43	Western SMT
1424	H30/26R	Guy Arab II	GR7722	FD26065	7/43	Sunderland 62
1425	H30/26R	Guy Arab II	DWS312	FD26097	8/43	Edinburgh G3
1426	H30/26R	Guy Arab II	GR7723	FD26124	7/43	Sunderland 63
1427	H30/26R	Guy Arab II	JA7609	FD26125	9/43	Stockport 209
1428	H30/26R	Guy Arab II	JA7610	FD26158	9/43	Stockport 210
1429	H30/26R	Guy Arab II	GTV416	FD26129	8/43	Nottingham 96
1430	H30/26R	Guy Arab II	FFM278	FD26142	9/43	Chester 46
1431	H30/26R	Guy Arab II	DWS313	FD26165	8/43	Edinburgh G2
1432	H30/26R	Guy Arab II	HG8070	FD26189	10/43	Rawtenstall 37
1433	H30/26R	Guy Arab II	HG8070	FD26204	10/43	Burnley, Colne & Nelson 66
1434	H30/26R	Guy Arab II	GKH932	FD26224	10/43	Hull 209
1435	H30/26R	Guy Arab II	GKH933	FD26201	10/43	Hull 210
1436	H30/26R	Guy Arab II	GR7739	FD26216	10/43	Sunderland 64
1437	H30/26R	Guy Arab II	GR7740	FD26268	10/43	Sunderland 65
1438	H30/26R	Guy Arab II	HE9805	FD26295	11/43	Yorkshire Traction 708
1439	H30/26R	Guy Arab II	FTD645	FD26299	12/43	Ashton 15
1440	H30/26R	Guy Arab II	HE9806	FD26293	12/43	Yorkshire Traction 709
1441	H30/26R	Guy Arab II	GRH31	FD26294	12/43	Hull 211
1442	H30/26R	Guy Arab II	BG8554	FD26353	1/44	Birkenhead 321
1443	H30/26R	Guy Arab II	FTD751	FD26307	1/44	Ashton 16
1444	H30/26R	Guy Arab II	GR7741	FD26382	12/43	Sunderland 66
1445	H30/26R	Guy Arab II	GR7744	FD26390	12/43	Sunderland 69
1446	H30/26R	Guy Arab II	GR7745	FD26393	1/44	Sunderland 70
1447	H30/26R	Guy Arab II	BG8555	FD26387	1/44	Birkenhead 322
1448	H30/26R	Guy Arab II	BG8556	FD26388	1/44	Birkenhead 323
1449	H30/26R	Guy Arab II	BG8557	FD26418	1/44	Birkenhead 324
1450	H30/26R	Guy Arab II	BG8558	FD26425	1/44	Birkenhead 325
1451	H30/26R	Guy Arab II	EO7932	FD26426	1/44	Barrow 93
1452	H30/26R	Guy Arab II	JV8642	FD25989	1/44	Grimsby 71
1453	L27/28R	Guy Arab II	ASD254	FD26040	10/43	Western SMT
1454	L27/28R	Guy Arab II	BVD177	FD26079	10/43	Lanarkshire H7
1455	L27/28R	Guy Arab II	ASD255	FD26079	10/43	Western SMT
1456	L27/28R	Guy Arab II	BVD180	FD26079	10/43	Lanarkshire H8
1457	L27/28R	Guy Arab II	ASD256	FD26110	10/43	Western SMT
1458	L27/28R	Guy Arab II	BVD181	FD26133	10/43	Lanarkshire H9
1459	L27/28R	Guy Arab II	BVD189	FD26249	2/44	Central SMT H10

Left table (BNUM 1460–1532):

BNUM	CONFIG	REGN	CHASSIS MAKE	NUMBER	YEAR	OPERATOR	NOTE
1460	L27/28R	BVD190	Guy Arab II	FD26402	2/44	Central SMT H11	
1461	L27/28R	DWS355	Guy Arab II	FD26435	2/44	Scottish Motor Traction E8	
1462	L27/28R	DWS354	Guy Arab II	FD26534	2/44	Scottish Motor Traction E7	
1463	L27/28R	BVD194	Guy Arab II	FD26535	3/44	Central SMT H15	
1464	L27/28R	BVD195	Guy Arab II	FD26059	2/44	Central SMT H16	
1465	L27/28R	FAO59	Guy Arab II	FD26411	2/44	Cumberland 216	
1466	L27/28R	FAO60	Guy Arab II	FD26416	2/44	Cumberland 217	
1467	H30/26R	HMA155	Daimler CWA6	11408	9/43	SHMD 191	
1468	H30/26R	HMA156	Daimler CWA6	11409	9/43	SHMD 192	
1469	H30/26R	EN8407	Daimler CWA6	11415	9/43	Bury 11	
1470	H30/26R	EN8408	Daimler CWA6	11420	9/43	Bury 28	
1471	H30/26R	HMA157	Daimler CWA6	11421	-/43	SHMD 193	
1472	H30/26R	YJ7953	Daimler CWA6	11434	11/43	Dundee 28	
1473	H30/26R	YJ7954	Daimler CWA6	11435	12/43	Dundee 29	
1474	H30/26R	YJ7955	Daimler CWA6	11436	12/43	Dundee 30	
1475	H30/26R	EN8414	Daimler CWA6	11446	12/43	Bury 33	
1476	H30/26R	HG8073	Daimler CWA6	11447	10/43	Burnley, Colne & Nelson 67	
1477	H30/26R	HG8076	Daimler CWA6	11448	10/43	Burnley, Colne & Nelson 68	
1478	H30/26R	HG8085	Daimler CWA6	11461	12/43	Burnley, Colne & Nelson 69	
1479	H30/26R	HG8086	Daimler CWA6	11462	12/43	Burnley, Colne & Nelson 70	
1480	H30/26R	FTD681	Daimler CWA6	11463	12/43	Widnes 49	
1481	H30/26R	DWS420	Daimler CWA6	11476	12/43	Edinburgh G64	
1482	H30/26R	DWS421	Daimler CWA6	11477	12/43	Edinburgh G65	
1483	H30/26R	FTD682	Daimler CWA6	11478	12/43	Widnes 50	
1484	H30/26R	FTD683	Daimler CWA6	11495	12/43	Widnes 51	
1485	H30/26R	YJ7956	Daimler CWA6	11496	1/44	Dundee 31	
1486	H30/26R	DWS422	Daimler CWA6	11497	12/43	Edinburgh G66	
1487	H30/26R	FTD684	Daimler CWA6	11516	12/43	Widnes 52	
1488	H30/26R	FTD685	Daimler CWA6	11517	12/43	Widnes 53	
1489	H30/26R	DGB450	Daimler CWA6	11518	12/43	Glasgow 106	
1490	H30/26R	XS5564	Guy Arab II	FD26569	3/44	Young, Paisley 138	
1491	H30/26R	XS5563	Guy Arab II	FD26553	3/44	Young, Paisley 137	
1492	H30/26R	GAL832	Guy Arab II	FD26460	3/44	Baker, Warsop 34	
1493	H30/26R	GR7770	Guy Arab II	FD26537	3/44	Young, Paisley 139	
1494	H30/26R	XS5565	Guy Arab II	FD26570	5/44	Hull 212	
1495	H30/26R	GRH32	Guy Arab II	FD26621	3/44	Hull 213	
1496	H30/26R	GRH33	Guy Arab II	FD26622	3/44	Sunderland 75	
1497	H30/26R	GR7771	Guy Arab II	FD26549	3/44	Chester 51	
1498	H30/26R	FFM295	Guy Arab II	FD26548	3/44	Chester 52	
1499	H30/26R	FFM296	Guy Arab II	FD26603	3/44	Chester 53	
1500	H30/26R	FFM297	Guy Arab II	FD26619	4/44	Chester 54	
1501	H30/26R	FFM298	Guy Arab II	FD26630	4/44	Chester 55	
1502	H30/26R	FFM299	Guy Arab II	FD26647	3/44	Accrington 96	
1503	H30/26R	FTE51	Guy Arab II	FD26705	4/44	Accrington 97	
1504	H30/26R	FTE52	Guy Arab II	FD26656	3/44	Birkenhead 326	
1505	H30/26R	BG8628	Guy Arab II	FD26661	3/44	Birkenhead 327	
1506	H30/26R	BG8629	Guy Arab II	FD26662	3/44	Birkenhead 328	
1507	H30/26R	BG8630	Guy Arab II	FD26677	3/44	Birkenhead 329	
1508	H30/26R	BG8631	Guy Arab II	FD26679	3/44	Birkenhead 330	
1509	H30/26R	BG8632	Guy Arab II	FD26685	4/44	Lancaster 47	
1510	H30/26R	FTE66	Guy Arab II	FD26658	4/44	Lancaster 48	
1511	H30/26R	FTE67	Guy Arab II	FD26700	4/44	Sunderland 76	
1512	H30/26R	GR7772	Guy Arab II	FD26701	4/44	Sunderland 77	
1513	H30/26R	GR7773	Guy Arab II	FD26734	4/44	Sunderland 78	
1514	H30/26R	GR7774	Guy Arab II	FD26739	4/44	Sunderland 79	
1515	H30/26R	GR7775	Guy Arab II	FD26781	4/44	Hull 216	
1516	H30/26R	GRH131	Guy Arab II	FD26782	5/44	Hull 217	
1517	H30/26R	GRH132	Guy Arab II	FD26738	4/44	Birkenhead 332	
1518	H30/26R	BG8642	Guy Arab II	FD26720	4/44	Birkenhead 331	
1519	H30/26R	BG8641	Guy Arab II	FD26743	4/44	Birkenhead 333	
1520	H30/26R	BG8643	Guy Arab II	FD26744	4/44	Birkenhead 334	
1521	H30/26R	BG8644	Guy Arab II	FD26751	4/44	West Hartlepool 41	
1522	H30/26R	EF7453	Guy Arab II	FD26753	4/44	Lancaster 49	
1523	H30/26R	FTE181	Guy Arab II	FD26755	5/44	Lancaster 50	
1524	H30/26R	FTE182	Guy Arab II	FD26725	5/44	Lancashire United 308	
1525	H30/26R	FTE329	Guy Arab II	FD26775	7/44	Brown, Garelochhead	
1526	H30/26R	SN9682	Guy Arab II	FD26805	6/44	McGregor, Stevenston (Clyde Coast, Ardrossan)	
1527	H30/26R	ASD568	Guy Arab II	FD26806	6/44	Blackburn 58	
1528	H30/26R	ABV950	Guy Arab II	FD26813	6/44	Blackburn 59	
1529	H30/26R	ABV951	Guy Arab II	FD26855	6/44	Blackburn 60	
1530	H30/26R	ABV952	Guy Arab II	FD26860	6/44	Burnley, Colne & Nelson 25	
1531	H30/26R	HG8108	Guy Arab II	FD26858	6/44	Burnley, Colne & Nelson 24	
1532	H30/26R	HG8107	Guy Arab II		6/44		

Right table (BNUM 1534–1607):

BNUM	CONFIG	REGN	CHASSIS MAKE	NUMBER	YEAR	OPERATOR	NOTE
1534	H30/26R	HG8109	Guy Arab II	FD26861	6/44	Burnley, Colne & Nelson 26	
1535	H30/26R	HG8111	Guy Arab II	FD26866	6/44	Burnley, Colne & Nelson 28	
1536	H30/26R	HG8112	Guy Arab II	FD26875	7/44	Burnley, Colne & Nelson 29	
1537	H30/26R	FTE330	Guy Arab II	FD26909	8/44	Lancashire United 309	
1538	H30/26R	FTE531	Guy Arab II	FD26911	8/44	Lancashire United 310	
1539	H30/26R	FTE332	Guy Arab II	FD26912	8/44	Lancashire United 311	
1540	H30/26R	FTE333	Guy Arab II	FD26916	8/44	Lancashire United 312	
1541	H30/26R	FTE183	Guy Arab II	FD26764	5/44	Ashton 41	
1542	H30/26R	FTE185	Guy Arab II	FD26766	5/44	Ashton 43	
1543	H30/26R	FTE184	Guy Arab II	FD26765	5/44	Ashton 42	
1544	H30/26R	FTE186	Guy Arab II	FD26817	6/44	Ashton 44	
1545	H30/26R	BG8645	Guy Arab II	FD26840	6/44	Birkenhead 335	
1546	H30/26R	BG8646	Guy Arab II	FD26842	6/44	Birkenhead 336	
1547	H30/26R	BG8647	Guy Arab II	FD26884	6/44	Birkenhead 337	
1548	H30/26R	BG8648	Guy Arab II	FD26887	7/44	Birkenhead 338	
1549	H30/26R	FTE334	Guy Arab II	FD26910	8/44	Lancashire United 313	
1550	H30/26R	FTE461	Guy Arab II	FD26963	8/44	Accrington 98	
1551	H30/26R	FTE462	Guy Arab II	FD26965	8/44	Accrington 99	
1552	H30/26R	GR7806	Guy Arab II	FD26972	8/44	Sunderland 80	
1553	H30/26R	GR7807	Guy Arab II	FD26977	8/44	Sunderland 81	
1554	H30/26R	ABV983	Guy Arab II	FD26970	9/44	Blackburn 61	
1555	H30/26R	ABV985	Guy Arab II	FD27022	9/44	Blackburn 62	
1556	H30/26R	ABV986	Guy Arab II	FD27030	9/44	Blackburn 63	
1557	H30/26R	JDH199	Guy Arab II	FD26945	9/44	Walsall 50	
1558	H30/26R	JDH200	Guy Arab II	FD26952	9/44	Walsall 52	
1559	H30/26R	JDH201	Guy Arab II	FD26953	9/44	Walsall 51	
1560	H30/26R	JDH202	Guy Arab II	FD26999	9/44	Walsall 56	
1561	H30/26R	JDH203	Guy Arab II	FD27000	9/44	Walsall 33	
1562	H30/26R	JA7611	Guy Arab II	FD27012	10/44	Stockport 211	
1563	H30/26R	JA7612	Guy Arab II	FD27015	10/44	Stockport 212	
1564	H30/26R	JA7613	Guy Arab II	FD27019	11/44	Stockport 213	
1565	H30/26R	EWW188	Guy Arab II	FD27064	9/44	Severn & Sons, Stainforth	
1566	H30/26R	ABV988	Guy Arab II	FD27035	10/44	Blackburn 64	
1567	H30/26R	JDH204	Guy Arab II	FD27064	11/44	Walsall 63	
1568	H30/26R	JDH205	Guy Arab II	FD27068	11/44	Walsall 67	
1569	H30/26R	JDH206	Guy Arab II	FD27080	11/44	Walsall 69	
1570	H30/26R	JDH207	Guy Arab II	FD27081	11/44	Walsall 71	
1571	H30/26R	JA7614	Guy Arab II	FD27085	11/44	Stockport 214	
1572	H30/26R	JA7615	Guy Arab II	FD27081	11/44	Stockport 215	
1573	H30/26R	JA7616	Guy Arab II	FD27102	12/44	Stockport 216	
1574	H30/26R	FPT854	Guy Arab II	FD27105	11/44	Northern General 1054	
1575	H30/26R	FPT855	Guy Arab II	FD27139	11/44	Northern General 1055	
1576	H30/26R	FPT856	Guy Arab II	FD27140	11/44	Northern General 1056	
1577	H30/26R	JV8732	Guy Arab II	FD27155	11/44	Grimsby 78	
1578	H30/26R	JV8733	Guy Arab II	FD27159	10/44	Grimsby 79	
1579	H30/26R	GNN328	Guy Arab II	FD27164	1/45	Baker, Warsop 35	
1580	H30/26R	JA7617	Guy Arab II	FD27166	12/44	Stockport 217	
1581	H30/26R	JA7618	Guy Arab II	FD27192	1/45	Stockport 218	
1582	H30/26R	JDH251	Guy Arab II	FD27194	11/44	Walsall 64	
1583	H30/26R	JDH252	Guy Arab II	FD27195	11/44	Walsall 68	
1584	H30/26R	JDH253	Guy Arab II	FD27207	11/44	Walsall 72	
1585	H30/26R	JDH254	Guy Arab II	FD27221	11/44	Walsall 59	
1586	H30/26R	JDH255	Guy Arab II	FD27227	11/44	Walsall 58	
1587	H30/26R	CN9768	Guy Arab II	FD27230	12/44	Northern General 1058	
1588	H30/26R	CN9767	Guy Arab II	FD27234	1/45	Northern General 1057	
1589	H30/26R	CN9769	Guy Arab II	FD27242	12/44	Northern General 1059	
1590	H30/26R	JDH256	Guy Arab II	FD27255	11/44	Walsall 101	
1591	H30/26R	JDH257	Guy Arab II	FD27263	11/44	Walsall 32	
1592	H30/26R	CN9771	Guy Arab II	FD27266	1/45	Northern General 1061	
1593	H30/26R	BVD570	Guy Arab II	FD27281	12/44	Northern General 1060	
1594	H30/26R	JDH266	Guy Arab II	FD27278	1/45	Laurie, Hamilton 12	
1595	H30/26R	JDH267	Guy Arab II	FD27283	1/45	Walsall 1	
1596	H30/26R	JDH268	Guy Arab II	FD27273	1/45	Walsall 104	
1597	H30/26R	JDH269	Guy Arab II	FD27285	1/45	Walsall 3	
1598	H30/26R	JDH270	Guy Arab II	FD27292	1/45	Walsall 34	
1599	H30/26R	JDH271	Guy Arab II	FD27298	1/45	Walsall 31	
1600	H30/26R	XS5624	Guy Arab II	FD27302	1/45	Graham, Paisley 21	
1601	H30/26R	XS5625	Guy Arab II	FD27311	1/45	Graham, Paisley 22	
1602	H30/26R	XS5626	Guy Arab II	FD27301	1/45	Graham, Paisley 23	
1603	H30/26R	XS5627	Guy Arab II	FD27352	1/45	Graham, Paisley 24	
1604	H30/26R	JNU242	Guy Arab II	FD27342	1/45	Truman, Shirebrook 20	
1605	H30/26R	JNU243	Guy Arab II	FD27344	1/45	Truman, Shirebrook 21	
1606	H30/26R	FTE885	Guy Arab II	FD27342	2/45	Ashton 67	
1607	H30/26R	FTE886	Guy Arab II	FD27344	3/45	Ashton 68	

No.	Chassis no.	Chassis	Reg.	Body	Owner	Date
1609	FTE887	Guy Arab II	—	H30/26R	Ashton 69	3/45
1610	FTE890	Guy Arab II	—	H30/26R	Ashton 72	3/45
1611	FTE888	Guy Arab II	—	H30/26R	Ashton 71	3/45
1612	FTE891	Guy Arab II	—	H30/26R	Ashton 74	3/45
1613	FTE889	Guy Arab II	—	H30/26R	Ashton 70	3/45
1614	JA7619	Guy Arab II	—	H30/26R	Stockport 219	7/45
1615	JA7620	Guy Arab II	—	H30/26R	Stockport 220	7/45
1616	JA7621	Guy Arab II	—	H30/26R	Stockport 221	7/45
1617	JA7622	Guy Arab II	—	H30/26R	Stockport 222	7/45
1618	JA7623	Guy Arab II	—	H30/26R	Stockport 223	11/45
1619	JA7624	Guy Arab II	—	H30/26R	Stockport 224	12/45
1620	ACB47	Guy Arab II	—	H30/26R	Blackburn 65	11/45
1621	ACB48	Guy Arab II	—	H30/26R	Blackburn 66	11/45
1622	HG8157	Guy Arab II	—	H30/26R	Burnley, Colne & Nelson 21	3/45
1623	HG8158	Guy Arab II	—	H30/26R	Burnley, Colne & Nelson 22	3/45
1624	HG8159	Guy Arab II	—	H30/26R	Burnley, Colne & Nelson 23	3/45
1625	EWW639	Guy Arab II	—	H30/26R	Severn & Sons, Stainforth	3/45
1626	FBJ369	Guy Arab II	—	H30/26R	Lowestoft 1	5/45
1627	FBJ370	Guy Arab II	—	H30/26R	Lowestoft 2	5/45
1628	FBJ371	Guy Arab II	—	H30/26R	Lowestoft 3	5/45
1629	FBJ372	Guy Arab II	—	H30/26R	Lowestoft 4	5/45
1630	FBJ373	Guy Arab II	—	H30/26R	Lowestoft 5	5/45
1631	FBJ374	Guy Arab II	—	H30/26R	Lowestoft 6	5/45
1632	GYL313	Guy Arab II	—	H30/26R	London Transport G174	5/45
1633	GYL314	Guy Arab II	—	H30/26R	London Transport G175	5/45
1634	GYL315	Guy Arab II	—	H30/26R	London Transport G176	5/45
1635	GYL316	Guy Arab II	—	H30/26R	London Transport G177	5/45
1636	GYL317	Guy Arab II	—	H30/26R	London Transport G178	5/45
1637	GYL318	Guy Arab II	—	H30/26R	London Transport G179	5/45
1638	GYL319	Guy Arab II	—	H30/26R	London Transport G180	5/45
1639	GYL320	Guy Arab II	—	H30/26R	London Transport G181	6/45
1640	GYL321	Guy Arab II	—	H30/26R	London Transport G182	6/45
1641	GYL323	Guy Arab II	—	H30/26R	London Transport G183	6/45
1642	GYL324	Guy Arab II	—	H30/26R	London Transport G184	6/45
1643	GYL325	Guy Arab II	—	H30/26R	London Transport G185	6/45
1644	GYL322	Guy Arab II	—	H30/26R	London Transport G186	6/45
1645	GYL326	Guy Arab II	—	H30/26R	London Transport G187	6/45
1646	GYL327	Guy Arab II	—	H30/26R	London Transport G188	6/45
1647	GYL329	Guy Arab II	—	H30/26R	London Transport G189	6/45
1648	GYL328	Guy Arab II	—	H30/26R	London Transport G190	6/45
1649	GYL330	Guy Arab II	—	H30/26R	London Transport G191	7/45
1650	GYL331	Guy Arab II	—	H30/26R	London Transport G192	7/45
1651	GYL332	Guy Arab II	—	H30/26R	London Transport G193	7/45
1652	GYL397	Guy Arab II	—	H30/26R	London Transport G258	7/45
1653	GYL398	Guy Arab II	—	H30/26R	London Transport G259	8/45
1654	GYL399	Guy Arab II	—	H30/26R	London Transport G260	8/45
1655	GYL400	Guy Arab II	—	H30/26R	London Transport G261	8/45
1656	GYL401	Guy Arab II	—	H30/26R	London Transport G262	8/45
1657	GYL402	Guy Arab II	—	H30/26R	London Transport G263	8/45
1658	GYL403	Guy Arab II	—	H30/26R	London Transport G264	8/45
1659	GYL404	Guy Arab II	—	H30/26R	London Transport G265	8/45
1660	GYL405	Guy Arab II	—	H30/26R	London Transport G266	8/45
1661	GYL406	Guy Arab II	—	H30/26R	London Transport G267	8/45
1662	GYL407	Guy Arab II	—	H30/26R	London Transport G268	8/45
1663	GRH375	Guy Arab II	—	H30/26R	Hull 230	6/45
1664	GRH376	Guy Arab II	—	H30/26R	Hull 231	6/45
1665	GRH377	Guy Arab II	—	H30/26R	Hull 232	6/45
1666	GRH378	Guy Arab II	—	H30/26R	Hull 234	7/45
1667	GRH379	Guy Arab II	—	H30/26R	Hull 235	7/45
1668	GRH380	Guy Arab II	—	H30/26R	Hull 236	8/45
1669	GRH381	Guy Arab II	—	H30/26R	Hull 237	8/45
1670	GRH382	Guy Arab II	—	H30/26R	Hull 238	8/45
1671	GRH383	Guy Arab II	—	H30/26R	Hull 239	8/45
1672	GRH384	Guy Arab II	—	H30/26R	London Transport G312	7/45
1673	GYL452	Guy Arab II	—	H30/26R	London Transport G313	8/45
1674	GYL453	Guy Arab II	—	H30/26R	London Transport G314	8/45
1675	GYL454	Guy Arab II	—	H30/26R	London Transport G315	8/45
1676	GYL455	Guy Arab II	—	H30/26R	London Transport G316	8/45
1677	GYL456	Guy Arab II	—	H30/26R	London Transport G317	8/45
1678	GYL457	Guy Arab II	—	H30/26R	London Transport G318	8/45
1679	GYL458	Guy Arab II	—	H30/26R	London Transport G319	8/45
1680	CRX595	Guy Arab II	—	H30/26R	Newbury & District 105	10/45
1681	CRX596	Guy Arab II	—	H30/26R	Newbury & District 106	10/45
1682	HGC137	Guy Arab II	—	H30/26R	London Transport G358	8/45
1683	HGC141	Guy Arab II	—	H30/26R	London Transport G362	9/45

No.	Chassis no.	Chassis	Reg.	Body	Owner	Date
1684	FD27864	Guy Arab II	HGC142	H30/26R	London Transport G363	9/45
1685	FD27865	Guy Arab II	HGC143	H30/26R	London Transport G364	9/45
1686	FD27866	Guy Arab II	HGC144	H30/26R	London Transport G365	9/45
1687	FD27867	Guy Arab II	HGC145	H30/26R	London Transport G366	9/45
1688	FD27811	Guy Arab II	HGC138	H30/26R	London Transport G359	8/45
1689	FD27849	Guy Arab II	HGC139	H30/26R	London Transport G360	9/45
1690	FD27855	Guy Arab II	HGC140	H30/26R	London Transport G361	9/45
1691	FD27856	Guy Arab II	HGC146	H30/26R	London Transport G367	9/45
1692	FD27857	Guy Arab II	HGC147	H30/26R	London Transport G368	9/45
1693	12338	Daimler CWD6	EDK921	H30/26R	Rochdale 21	11/45
1694	12366	Daimler CWD6	EDK922	H30/26R	Rochdale 22	11/45
1695	12367	Daimler CWD6	EDK923	H30/26R	Rochdale 23	11/45
1696	12381	Daimler CWA6D	EDK925	H30/26R	Rochdale 25	11/45
1697	12382	Daimler CWA6D	EDK926	H30/26R	Rochdale 26	11/45
1698	12396	Daimler CWA6D	EDK927	H30/26R	Rochdale 27	11/45
1699	12380	Daimler CWD6	EDK924	H30/26R	Rochdale 24	11/45
1700	12397	Daimler CWA6D	EDK928	H30/26R	Rochdale 28	11/45
1701	12398	Daimler CWA6D	EDK929	H30/26R	Rochdale 29	11/45
1702	12411	Daimler CWA6D	EDK930	H30/26R	Rochdale 30	11/45
1703	12412	Daimler CWA6D	JVK613	H30/26R	Newcastle 13	12/45
1704	12413	Daimler CWA6D	JVK614	H30/26R	Newcastle 14	12/45
1705	12427	Daimler CWA6D	JVK615	H30/26R	Newcastle 15	12/45
1706	12428	Daimler CWA6D	JVK616	H30/26R	Newcastle 16	12/45
1707	12429	Daimler CWA6D	JVK617	H30/26R	Newcastle 17	12/45
1708	12442	Daimler CWA6	JVK618	H30/26R	Newcastle 18	4/46
1709	12443	Daimler CWA6	JVK619	H30/26R	Newcastle 19	1/46
1710	12455	Daimler CWA6	JVK620	H30/26R	Newcastle 20	2/46
1711	12456	Daimler CWA6	JVK621	H30/26R	Newcastle 21	2/46
1712	12474	Daimler CWA6	JVK622	H30/26R	Newcastle 22	2/46
1713	12496	Daimler CWA6D	JVK625	H30/26R	Newcastle 25	4/46
1714	12490	Daimler CWA6D	JVK623	H30/26R	Newcastle 23	2/46
1715	12491	Daimler CWA6D	JVK624	H30/26R	Newcastle 24	2/46
1716	12511	Daimler CWA6D	JVK626	H30/26R	Newcastle 26	2/46
1717	12512	Daimler CWD6	EF7529	H30/26R	West Hartlepool 45	2/46
1718	12530	Daimler CWD6	EF7530	H30/26R	West Hartlepool 46	2/46
1719	12531	Daimler CWD6	EF7531	H30/26R	West Hartlepool 47	2/46
1720	13247	Daimler CWD6	GR8097	H30/26R	Sunderland 15	3/46
1721	13248	Daimler CWD6	GR8098	H30/26R	Sunderland 16	3/46
1722	13249	Daimler CWD6	GR8099	H30/26R	Sunderland 17	5/46
1723	13250	Daimler CWD6	GR8100	H30/26R	Sunderland 18	3/46
1724	12549	Daimler CWA6	CSA342	L27/28R	Sutherland, Peterhead 100	3/46
1725	12550	Daimler CWD6	JNU830	L27/28R	Chesterfield 115	3/46
1726	12570	Daimler CWD6	JNU831	L27/28R	Chesterfield 116	3/46
1727	12571	Daimler CWD6	JNU832	L27/28R	Chesterfield 117	3/46
1728	12597	Daimler CWD6	JNU833	L27/28R	Chesterfield 118	3/46
1729	12617	Daimler CWA6	JNU834	L27/28R	Chesterfield 119	3/46
1730	12638	Daimler CWD6	JNU835	L27/28R	Chesterfield 120	3/46
1731	12658	Daimler CWA6	CSA343	L27/26RD	Sutherland, Peterhead 99	3/46
1732	10137	Leyland Titan TD4c	BG4385	H30/24R	Birkenhead 212	2/46
1733	3200	Daimler CWD6	GRR919	H30/26R	Baker, Warsop 37	4/46
1734	FD29096	Guy Arab III	JVK651	B34F	Newcastle 51	6/46
1735	FD29097	Guy Arab III	JVK652	B34F	Newcastle 52	6/46
1736	FD29098	Guy Arab III	JVK653	B34F	Newcastle 53	6/46
1737	FD29115	Guy Arab III	JVK654	B34F	Newcastle 54	6/46
1738	FD29116	Guy Arab III	JVK655	B34F	Newcastle 55	6/46
1739	FD29117	Guy Arab III	JVK656	B34F	Newcastle 56	6/46
1740	FD29118	Guy Arab III	JVK657	B34F	Newcastle 57	6/46
1741	FD29182	Guy Arab III	JVK658	B34F	Newcastle 58	6/46
1742	FD29111	Guy Arab III	AMS561	DP35F	Alexander G31	7/46
1743	FD29112	Guy Arab III	AMS562	DP35F	Alexander G32	7/46
1744	FD29133	Guy Arab III	AMS563	DP35F	Alexander G33	7/46
1745	FD29134	Guy Arab III	AMS564	DP35F	Alexander G34	7/46
1746	FD29135	Guy Arab III	AMS565	DP35F	Alexander G35	7/46
1747	FD29169	Guy Arab III	AMS566	DP33F	Alexander G36	7/46
1748	FD29196	Guy Arab III	AMS567	DP33F	Alexander G37	7/46
1749	FD29205	Guy Arab III	AMS568	DP33F	Alexander G38	8/46
1750	FD29207	Guy Arab III	AMS569	DP33F	Alexander G39	8/46
1751	FD29208	Guy Arab III	AMS570	DP33F	Alexander G40	8/46
1752	O6624690	AEC Regal I	FFM660	B32F	Chester 64	6/46
1753	O6624838	AEC Regal I	FFM661	B32R	Chester 65	6/46
1754	O6624735	AEC Regal I	KEH123	DP37F	Stoke-on-Trent Motors 19	7/46
1755	O6624734	AEC Regal I	KEH124	DP37F	Stoke-on-Trent Motors 40	7/46
1756	O6624471	AEC Regal I	GYO865	DP37F	Bevan & Barker, Mansfield	8/46
1757	O6624662	AEC Regal I	GYO866	DP35F	Baker, Warsop 38	8/46
1758	O6617741	AEC Regent II	BJN94	L27/28R	Southend 236	10/46

Upper table

BNUM	CONFIG	REGN	CHASSIS MAKE	NUMBER	YEAR	OPERATOR	NOTE
	B35F	LEH693	AEC Regal I	O6625438	9/47	Stoke-on-Trent Motors	
	B35F	LEH694	AEC Regal I	O6625646	9/47	Stoke-on-Trent Motors	
	B32F	HFM176	AEC Regal I	O6625630	10/47	Chester 68	
	B32F	HFM177	AEC Regal I	O6625631	10/47	Chester 69	
	DP35F	JAL516	Daimler CVD6	13627	11/47	Baker, Warsop 39	
	H30/26R	EX5931	Leyd Titan PD1A	470420	5/48	Great Yarmouth 51	
	H30/26R	EX5932	Leyd Titan PD1A	470433	5/48	Great Yarmouth 52	
	H30/26R	EX5933	Leyd Titan PD1A	470434	5/48	Great Yarmouth 53	
	H30/26R	EX5934	Leyd Titan PD1A	470441	1/48	Great Yarmouth 54	
	H30/26R	EX5935	Leyd Titan PD1A	470442	1/48	Great Yarmouth 55	
	H30/26R	EX5936	Leyd Titan PD1A	470443	1/48	Great Yarmouth 56	
	H30/26R	EX5937	Leyd Titan PD1A	470470	1/48	Great Yarmouth 57	
	H30/26R	EX5938	Leyd Titan PD1A	470512	1/48	Great Yarmouth 58	
	H30/26R	EX5939	Leyd Titan PD1A	470526	5/48	Great Yarmouth 59	
	H30/26R	EX5940	Leyd Titan PD1A	470525	1/48	Great Yarmouth 60	
	DP35F	LVT193	Albion CX13	58029F	12/47	Rowley, Bignall End	
	DP35F	FD29204	Guy Arab III	FD29230	12/47	Alexander G62	
	DP35F	BMS585	Guy Arab III	FD29243	1/48	Alexander G63	
	DP35F	BMS586	Guy Arab III	FD29273	1/48	Alexander G64	
	DP35F	BMS587	Guy Arab III	FD29486	1/48	Alexander G65	
	DP35F	BMS588	Guy Arab III	FD29488	1/48	Alexander G66	
	DP35F	BMS589	Guy Arab III	FD29489	1/48	Alexander G67	
	DP35F	BMS590	Guy Arab III	FD29501	1/48	Alexander G68	
	DP35F	BMS591	Guy Arab III	FD29511	1/48	Alexander G69	
	DP35F	BMS592	Guy Arab III	FD29512	2/48	Alexander G70	
	DP35F	BMS593	Guy Arab III	13581	1/48	Alexander G71	
	H30/24R	BG5510	Leyd Titan TD5c	14343	2/48	Birkenhead 228	
	H30/26R	HFM976	Daimler CWD6	12678	2/48	Chester 70	
	H30/26R	HFM977	Daimler CVA6	13613	3/48	Chester 71	
	L27/26R	CHJ439	Daimler CVA6	13614	3/48	Southend 239	
	L27/26R	CHJ440	Daimler CVA6	13615	3/48	Southend 240	
	L27/26R	CHJ441	Daimler CVA6	462502	3/48	Southend 241	
	L27/26R	GAO756	Leyd Titan PD1A	462503	3/48	Cumberland 218	
	L27/26R	GAO757	Leyd Titan PD1A	462507	3/48	Cumberland 219	
	L27/26R	GAO758	Leyd Titan PD1A	462508	3/48	Cumberland 220	
	L27/26R	GAO759	Leyd Titan PD1A	462964	3/48	Cumberland 221	
	L27/26R	GAO760	Leyd Titan PD1A	470988	3/48	Cumberland 222	
	L27/26R	GAO781	Leyd Titan PD1A	471057	3/48	Cumberland 243	
	L27/26R	GAO782	Leyd Titan PD1A	471161	3/48	Cumberland 244	
	L27/26R	GAO783	Leyd Titan PD1A	471162	3/48	Cumberland 245	
	L27/26R	GAO784	Leyd Titan PD1A	471276	3/48	Cumberland 246	
	L27/26R	GAO785	Leyd Titan PD1A	471276	3/48	Cumberland 247	
	B33R	GWO422	AEC Regent III	O961884	4/48	West Monmouthshire 17	
	B33R	ACM107	Leyd Tiger PS1	470701	6/48	Birkenhead 98	
	B33R	ACM108	Leyd Tiger PS1	470702	6/48	Birkenhead 99	
	B33R	ACM109	Leyd Tiger PS1	470699	6/48	Birkenhead 100	
	B35F	ACM194	Leyd Tiger PS1	470700	6/48	Birkenhead 97	
	H30/26R	MEH384	Leyd Titan PS1	472050	7/48	Stoke-on-Trent Motors 25	
	H30/26R	GR9920	Daimler CVG6	14536	7/48	Sunderland 88	
	H30/26R	GR9921	Daimler CVG6	14537	7/48	Sunderland 89	
	H30/26R	GR9922	Daimler CVG6	14538	9/48	Sunderland 90	
	H30/26R	GR9923	Daimler CVG6	14539	7/48	Sunderland 91	
	H30/26R	GR9924	Daimler CVG6	14540	7/48	Sunderland 92	
	H30/26R	GR9925	Daimler CVG6	14541	7/48	Sunderland 93	
	H30/26R	GR9926	Daimler CVG6	14542	9/48	Sunderland 94	
	H30/26R	GR9927	Daimler CVG6	14543	8/48	Sunderland 95	
	H30/26R	GR9928	Daimler CVG6	14544	8/48	Sunderland 96	
	H30/26R	GR9929	Daimler CVG6	14545	9/48	Sunderland 97	
	H30/26R	GR9930	Daimler CVG6	14546	8/48	Sunderland 98	
	H30/26R	GR9931	Daimler CVG6	14547	8/48	Sunderland 99	
	B33R	JVO473	AEC Regent III	O9612093	9/48	Bevan & Barker, Mansfield	
	H30/26R	ACM301	Leyd Titan PD1A	481530	8/48	Birkenhead 126	
	H30/26R	ACM302	Leyd Titan PD1A	481706	9/48	Birkenhead 127	
	H30/26R	ACM303	Leyd Titan PD1A	481707	9/48	Birkenhead 128	
	H30/26R	ACM304	Leyd Titan PD1A	481715	10/48	Birkenhead 129	
	H30/26R	ACM305	Leyd Titan PD1A	481716	12/48	Birkenhead 130	
	H30/26R	ACM306	Leyd Titan PD1A	481876	10/48	Birkenhead 131	
	H30/26R	ACM307	Leyd Titan PD1A	481877	9/48	Birkenhead 132	
	H30/26R	ACM308	Leyd Titan PD1A	481952	12/48	Birkenhead 133	
	H30/26R	ACM309	Leyd Titan PD1A	481953	12/48	Birkenhead 134	
	H30/26R	ACM310	Leyd Titan PD1A	481954	12/48	Birkenhead 135	
	H30/26R	ACM311	Leyd Titan PD1A	481955	10/48	Birkenhead 136	
	H30/26R	ACM312	Leyd Titan PD1A	481956	11/48	Birkenhead 137	
	H30/26R	ACM313	Leyd Titan PD1A	481957	11/48	Birkenhead 138	

Lower table

BNUM	CONFIG	REGN	CHASSIS MAKE	NUMBER	YEAR	OPERATOR	NOTE
	L27/28R	BJN95	AEC Regent II	O6617742	10/46	Southend 237	
	L27/28R	BJN96	AEC Regent II	O6617743	10/46	Southend 238	
	L27/28R	BVD991	Guy Arab II	FD28273	10/46	Greenshields, Salsburgh 6	
	H30/26R	BG9221	Leyd Titan PD1	460526	11/46	Birkenhead 101	
	H30/26R	BG9222	Leyd Titan PD1	460527	10/46	Birkenhead 102	
	H30/26R	BG9223	Leyd Titan PD1	460542	10/46	Birkenhead 103	
	H30/26R	BG9224	Leyd Titan PD1	460598	11/46	Birkenhead 104	
	H30/26R	BG9225	Leyd Titan PD1	460599	11/46	Birkenhead 105	
	H30/26R	BG9226	Leyd Titan PD1	460647	11/46	Birkenhead 106	
	H30/26R	BG9227	Leyd Titan PD1	460688	11/46	Birkenhead 107	
	H30/26R	BG9228	Leyd Titan PD1	460811	12/46	Birkenhead 108	
	H30/26R	BG9229	Leyd Titan PD1	460840	12/46	Birkenhead 109	
	H30/26R	BG9230	Leyd Titan PD1	460856	12/46	Birkenhead 110	
	H30/26R	BG9231	Leyd Titan PD1	460879	12/46	Birkenhead 111	
	H30/26R	BG9232	Leyd Titan PD1	460944	10/46	Birkenhead 112	
	L27/24R	CTH471	Leyd Titan TD4	460534	-/46	Williams, Llandilo	
	L27/28R	VH0081	Leyd Titan TD5c	75593	12/46	Hansons Buses, Huddersfield 76	1
	H32/25F	DDK113	Daimler CWD6	17811	12/46	Rochdale 143	1
	H30/26R	GPT920	Daimler CWD6	13338	1/47	Stockton 40	
	H30/26R	GPT921	Daimler CWD6	13339	2/47	Stockton 41	
	H30/26R	GPT922	Daimler CWD6	13340	2/47	Stockton 42	
	H30/26R	GPT923	Daimler CWD6	13341	1/47	Stockton 43	
	H30/26R	GPT924	Daimler CWD6	13342	1/47	Stockton 44	
	H30/26R	GPT925	Daimler CWD6	13343	1/47	Stockton 45	
	H30/26R	GUP556	Guy Arab II	FD28291	2/47	Stockton 104	
	H30/26R	GUP557	Guy Arab III	FD28299	2/47	Stockton 105	
	H30/26R	GUP558	Guy Arab III	FD28330	2/47	Stockton 106	
	H30/26R	GUP559	Guy Arab III	FD28331	2/47	Stockton 107	
	H30/26R	GUP560	Guy Arab III	FD28332	2/47	Stockton 108	
	H30/26R	GUP561	Guy Arab III	FD28335	2/47	Stockton 109	
	H30/26R	GUP562	Guy Arab III	FD28336	2/47	Stockton 110	
	H30/26R	GUP563	Guy Arab III	FD28337	2/47	Stockton 111	
	B32F	JC8427	Guy Arab III	FD28352	c4/47	Roberts (Purple Motors), Bethesda 8	
	B32F	GAO501	Leyd Tiger PS1	461126	3/47	Cumberland 1	
	B32F	GAO502	Leyd Tiger PS1	462070	3/47	Cumberland 9	
	B32F	GAO503	Leyd Tiger PS1	462105	3/47	Cumberland 58	
	B32F	GAO504	Leyd Tiger PS1	462738	3/47	Cumberland 70	
	B32F	GAO505	Leyd Tiger PS1	462739	3/47	Cumberland 73	
	H30/26R	KPU515	AEC Regent II	O6617813	4/47	Colchester 51	
	H30/26R	KPU516	AEC Regent II	O6617814	4/47	Colchester 52	
	H30/26R	KPU517	AEC Regent II	O6617815	4/47	Colchester 53	
	H30/26R	KPU518	AEC Regent II	O6617816	3/47	Colchester 54	
	H30/26R	DPY568	Leyd Titan PD1A	462504	4/47	Tees-Side 32	
	H30/26R	DPY569	Leyd Titan PD1A	461587	4/47	Tees-Side 33	
	H30/26R	HFM170	Daimler CVA6	14340	5/47	Chester 60	
	H30/26R	HFM171	Daimler CVA6	14341	5/47	Chester 61	
	H30/26R	HFM172	Daimler CWD6	12676	7/47	Chester 62	
	H30/26R	HFM173	Daimler CWD6	12677	8/47	Chester 63	
	H30/26R	HFM174	Daimler CVA6	12679	8/47	Chester 66	
	H30/26R	HFM175	Daimler CVA6	14342	8/47	Chester 67	
	H30/26R	BG9531	Leyd Titan PD1A	470100	5/47	Birkenhead 122	
	H30/26R	BG9532	Leyd Titan PD1A	461680	5/47	Birkenhead 114	
	H30/26R	BG9533	Leyd Titan PD1A	461681	5/47	Birkenhead 115	
	H30/26R	BG9534	Leyd Titan PD1A	470101	5/47	Birkenhead 123	
	H30/26R	BG9535	Leyd Titan PD1A	463057	5/47	Birkenhead 121	
	H30/26R	BG9536	Leyd Titan PD1A	462490	8/47	Birkenhead 120	
	H30/26R	BG9672	Leyd Titan PD1A	461632	8/47	Birkenhead 113	
	H30/26R	BG9673	Leyd Titan PD1A	461633	8/47	Birkenhead 116	
	H30/26R	BG9674	Leyd Titan PD1A	462487	8/47	Birkenhead 117	
	H30/26R	BG9675	Leyd Titan PD1A	462489	8/47	Birkenhead 119	
	H30/26R	BG9676	Leyd Titan PD1A	462488	9/47	Birkenhead 118	
	H30/26R	BG9677	Leyd Titan PD1A	470163	9/47	Birkenhead 125	
	H30/26R	BG9678	Leyd Titan PD1A	470162	9/47	Birkenhead 124	
	H30/26R	HPT430	Bristol K6G	W3183	7/47	Stockton 9	
	H30/26R	HPT431	Bristol K6G	W3184	7/47	Stockton 10	
	H30/26R	HPT432	Bristol K6G	W3185	7/47	Stockton 11	
	H30/26R	HPT433	Bristol K6G	W3186	7/47	Stockton 12	
	H30/26R	HB6263	Bristol K6G	62063	7/47	Merthyr Tydfil 7	
	H30/26R	HB6264	Bristol K6G	62064	7/47	Merthyr Tydfil 8	
	H30/26R	HB6265	Bristol K6G	62070	7/47	Merthyr Tydfil 9	
	B35F	NRF950	Leyd Tiger PS1	462687	9/47	Milton Bus Service, Stoke-on-Trent 10	
	B35F	NRF951	Leyd Tiger PS1	462689	9/47	Milton Bus Service, Stoke-on-Trent 11	
	DP35F	NRF954	Leyd Tiger PS1	462113	9/47	Mainwaring, Bignall End 20	
	DP35F	NRF955	Leyd Tiger PS1	462401	9/47	Mainwaring, Bignall End 21	

Type	Reg	Chassis	Chassis No.	Date	Operator
H30/26R	ACM315	Leyd Titan PD1A	481977	11/48	Birkenhead 140
H30/26R	ACM316	Leyd Titan PD1A	481978	12/48	Birkenhead 141
H30/26R	ACM317	Leyd Titan PD1A	481979	11/48	Birkenhead 142
H30/26R	ACM318	Leyd Titan PD1A	481980	10/48	Birkenhead 143
H30/26R	ACM319	Leyd Titan PD1A	481981	11/48	Birkenhead 144
H30/26R	ACM320	Leyd Titan PD1A	481982	11/48	Birkenhead 145
H30/26R	JFM745	Foden PVD6	27292	11/48	Chester 72
B35R	KPU519	Crossley DD42/3T	93840	11/48	Colchester 55
B35R	HG9660	Leyd Tiger PS1	463044	6/48	Burnley, Colne & Nelson 15
B35R	HG9661	Leyd Tiger PS1	463045	6/48	Burnley, Colne & Nelson 16
B35R	HG9662	Leyd Tiger PS1	473458	5/48	Burnley, Colne & Nelson 17
B35R	HG9663	Leyd Tiger PS1	473459	6/48	Burnley, Colne & Nelson 18
B35R	HG9664	Leyd Tiger PS1	480583	5/48	Burnley, Colne & Nelson 19
B35R	HG9665	Leyd Tiger PS1	480584	6/48	Burnley, Colne & Nelson 20
L27/26R	ETH104	Guy Arab III	FD28449	12/48	Rees & Williams, Tycroes
H30/26R	LVK87	AEC Regent III	9612E1769	11/48	Newcastle 87
H30/26R	LVK88	AEC Regent III	9612E1770	11/48	Newcastle 88
H30/26R	LVK89	AEC Regent III	9612E1771	11/48	Newcastle 89
H30/26R	LVK90	AEC Regent III	9612E1772	11/48	Newcastle 90
H30/26R	LVK91	AEC Regent III	9612E1773	11/48	Newcastle 91
H30/26R	LVK92	AEC Regent III	9612E1774	11/48	Newcastle 92
H30/26R	LVK93	AEC Regent III	9612E1775	11/48	Newcastle 93
H30/26R	LVK94	AEC Regent III	9612E1776	11/48	Newcastle 94
H30/26R	LVK95	AEC Regent III	9612E1763	1/49	Newcastle 95
H30/26R	LVK96	AEC Regent III	9612E1767	1/49	Newcastle 96
H30/26R	LVK97	AEC Regent III	9612E1765	1/49	Newcastle 97
H30/26R	LVK98	AEC Regent III	9612E1768	1/49	Newcastle 98
H30/26R	LVK99	AEC Regent III	9612E1764	1/49	Newcastle 99
H30/26R	LVK100	AEC Regent III	9612E1766	2/49	Newcastle 100
H30/26R	LVK101	AEC Regent III	9612E1778	2/49	Newcastle 101
H30/26R	LVK102	AEC Regent III	9612E1780	2/49	Newcastle 102
H30/26R	LVK103	AEC Regent III	9612E1777	2/49	Newcastle 103
H30/26R	LVK104	AEC Regent III	9612E1779	2/49	Newcastle 104
H30/26R	LVK105	AEC Regent III	9612E1781	2/49	Newcastle 105
H30/26R	LVK106	AEC Regent III	9612E1787	2/49	Newcastle 106
H30/26R	LVK107	AEC Regent III	9612E1786	3/49	Newcastle 107
H30/26R	LVK108	AEC Regent III	9612E1782	3/49	Newcastle 108
H30/26R	LVK109	AEC Regent III	9612E1783	3/49	Newcastle 109
H30/26R	LVK110	AEC Regent III	9612E1785	3/49	Newcastle 110
H30/26R	LVK111	AEC Regent III	9612E1788	3/49	Newcastle 111
H30/26R	LVK112	AEC Regent III	9612E1790	3/49	Newcastle 112
H30/26R	LVK113	AEC Regent III	9612E1789	3/49	Newcastle 113
H30/26R	LVK114	AEC Regent III	9612E1784	3/49	Newcastle 114
H30/26R	JFM746	Foden PVD6	27714	3/49	Chester 73
H30/26R	JFM747	Foden PVD6	27716	3/49	Chester 74
H30/26R	JFM748	Foden PVD6	27758	3/49	Chester 75
H30/26R	JFM749	Foden PVD6	28750	3/49	Chester 76
H30/26R	ACM604	Guy Arab III	FD36034	5/49	Birkenhead 146
H30/26R	ACM605	Guy Arab III	FD36035	5/49	Birkenhead 147
H30/26R	ACM606	Guy Arab III	FD36045	5/49	Birkenhead 148
H30/26R	ACM607	Guy Arab III	FD36046	5/49	Birkenhead 149
H30/26R	ACM608	Guy Arab III	FD36051	5/49	Birkenhead 150
H30/26R	ACM609	Guy Arab III	FD36058	5/49	Birkenhead 151
H30/26R	ACM610	Guy Arab III	FD36059	5/49	Birkenhead 152
H30/26R	ACM611	Guy Arab III	FD36060	5/49	Birkenhead 153
H30/26R	ACM612	Guy Arab III	FD36069	5/49	Birkenhead 154
H30/26R	ACM613	Guy Arab III	FD36241	5/49	Birkenhead 155
H30/26R	ACM614	Guy Arab III	FD36242	6/49	Birkenhead 156
H30/26R	ACM615	Guy Arab III	FD36243	6/49	Birkenhead 157
H30/26R	ACM616	Guy Arab III	FD36244	6/49	Birkenhead 158
H30/26R	ACM617	Guy Arab III	FD36245	6/49	Birkenhead 159
H30/26R	ACM618	Guy Arab III	FD36246	7/49	Birkenhead 160
H30/26R	KPT751	Leyd Titan PD2/3	491955	10/49	Stockton 46
H30/26R	KPT752	Leyd Titan PD2/3	492166	10/49	Stockton 47
H30/26R	KPT753	Leyd Titan PD2/3	492165	10/49	Stockton 48
H30/26R	KPT754	Leyd Titan PD2/3	492408	10/49	Stockton 49
H30/26R	KPT755	Leyd Titan PD2/3	492409	10/49	Stockton 50
H30/26R	KPT756	Leyd Titan PD2/3	492410	10/49	Stockton 51
H30/26R	KPT757	Leyd Titan PD2/3	492407	10/49	Stockton 52
H30/26R	KPT758	Leyd Titan PD2/3	493021	10/49	Stockton 53
H30/26R	KPT759	Leyd Titan PD2/3	493019	10/49	Stockton 54
H30/26R	KPT760	Leyd Titan PD2/3	493020	10/49	Stockton 55
H30/26R	KPT761	Leyd Titan PD2/3	493018	10/49	Stockton 56
H30/26R	KPT762	Leyd Titan PD2/3	493148	10/49	Stockton 57
H30/26R	KPT763	Leyd Titan PD2/3	493148	10/49	Stockton 58
H30/26R	KPT764	Leyd Titan PD2/3	493149	11/49	Stockton 59
H30/26R	KPT765	Leyd Titan PD2/3	493152	10/49	Stockton 60
H30/26R	KPT766	Leyd Titan PD2/3	493151	10/49	Stockton 61
H30/26R	KPT767	Leyd Titan PD2/3	493150	11/49	Stockton 62
H30/26R	KPT768	Leyd Titan PD2/3	494098	12/49	Stockton 63
H30/26R	KPT769	Leyd Titan PD2/3	494099	12/49	Stockton 64
H30/26R	KPT770	Leyd Titan PD2/3	494151	12/49	Stockton 65
H30/26R	KPT771	Leyd Titan PD2/3	494356	12/49	Stockton 66
H30/26R	KPT772	Leyd Titan PD2/3	494357	12/49	Stockton 67
H30/26R	KPT773	Leyd Titan PD2/3	493022	12/49	Stockton 68
H30/26R	KPT774	Leyd Titan PD2/3	494358	12/49	Stockton 69
H30/26R	KPT775	Leyd Titan PD2/3	494152	12/49	Stockton 70
L27/26R	DHJ427	Daimler CVD6	15248	6/49	Southend 251
L27/26R	DHJ431	Daimler CVD6	15252	6/49	Southend 256
L27/26R	DHJ430	Daimler CVD6	15251	6/49	Southend 255
L27/26R	DHJ429	Daimler CVD6	15250	6/49	Southend 254
L27/26R	DHJ428	Daimler CVD6	15249	6/49	Southend 253
H30/26R	ACM630	Daimler CVG6	15222	8/49	Birkenhead 172
H30/26R	ACM625	Daimler CVG6	15217	8/49	Birkenhead 167
H30/26R	ACM624	Daimler CVG6	15214	8/49	Birkenhead 164
H30/26R	ACM622	Daimler CVG6	15216	8/49	Birkenhead 166
H30/26R	ACM619	Daimler CVG6	15211	8/49	Birkenhead 161
H30/26R	ACM620	Daimler CVG6	15212	9/49	Birkenhead 162
H30/26R	ACM621	Daimler CVG6	15213	9/49	Birkenhead 163
H30/26R	ACM631	Daimler CVG6	15225	9/49	Birkenhead 175
H30/26R	ACM633	Daimler CVG6	15223	9/49	Birkenhead 173
H30/26R	ACM632	Daimler CVG6	15221	9/49	Birkenhead 171
H30/26R	ACM629	Daimler CVG6	15220	9/49	Birkenhead 170
H30/26R	ACM628	Daimler CVG6	15219	9/49	Birkenhead 169
H30/26R	ACM627	Daimler CVG6	15218	9/49	Birkenhead 168
H30/26R	ACM626	Daimler CVG6	15215	9/49	Birkenhead 165
H30/26R	FDM568	Foden PVD6	27764	4/49	Lloyd, Bagillt
H30/26R	FDM724	Foden PVD6	28790	7/49	Phillips, Holywell
H30/26R	RRF773	AEC Regent III	FD36139M	5/49	Stevenson, Spath 3
L27/26RD	FAV827	AEC Regent III	9612E4331	9/49	Sutherland, Peterhead 124
L27/26RD	FAV826	AEC Regent III	9612E4330	9/49	Sutherland, Peterhead 123
H30/26R	OFM33	Foden PVD6	32252	12/51	Chester 81
H30/26R	ABG181	Daimler CVG6	16964	1/50	Birkenhead 181
H30/26R	ABG179	Daimler CVG6	16962	1/50	Birkenhead 179
H30/26R	ABG187	Daimler CVG6	16970	1/50	Birkenhead 187
H30/26R	ABG190	Daimler CVG6	16973	1/50	Birkenhead 190
H30/26R	ABG185	Daimler CVG6	16968	1/50	Birkenhead 185
H30/26R	ABG186	Daimler CVG6	16969	1/50	Birkenhead 186
H30/26R	ABG183	Daimler CVG6	16966	1/50	Birkenhead 183
H30/26R	ABG177	Daimler CVG6	16960	2/50	Birkenhead 177
H30/26R	ABG178	Daimler CVG6	16961	2/50	Birkenhead 178
H30/26R	ABG176	Daimler CVG6	16959	2/50	Birkenhead 176
H30/26R	ABG188	Daimler CVG6	16971	2/50	Birkenhead 188
H30/26R	ABG182	Daimler CVG6	16965	2/50	Birkenhead 182
H30/26R	ABG180	Daimler CVG6	16963	2/50	Birkenhead 180
H30/26R	ABG184	Daimler CVG6	16967	2/50	Birkenhead 184
H30/26R	ABG189	Daimler CVG6	16972	2/50	Birkenhead 189
H30/26R	ABG293	Guy Arab III	FD70191	3/50	Birkenhead 193
H30/26R	ABG294	Guy Arab III	FD70193	3/50	Birkenhead 194
H30/26R	ABG291	Guy Arab III	FD70166	3/50	Birkenhead 191
H30/26R	ABG303	Guy Arab III	FD70248	3/50	Birkenhead 203
H30/26R	ABG304	Guy Arab III	FD70249	3/50	Birkenhead 204
H30/26R	ABG296	Guy Arab III	FD70196	5/50	Birkenhead 196
H30/26R	ABG302	Guy Arab III	FD70245	5/50	Birkenhead 202
H30/26R	ABG292	Guy Arab III	FD70178	5/50	Birkenhead 192
H30/26R	ABG297	Guy Arab III	FD70212	5/50	Birkenhead 197
H30/26R	ABG298	Guy Arab III	FD70214	5/50	Birkenhead 198
H30/26R	ABG299	Guy Arab III	FD70217	5/50	Birkenhead 199
H30/26R	ABG305	Guy Arab III	FD70268	5/50	Birkenhead 205
H30/26R	ABG295	Guy Arab III	FD70194	5/50	Birkenhead 195
H30/26R	ABG300	Guy Arab III	FD70220	5/50	Birkenhead 200
H30/26R	ABG301	Guy Arab III	FD70239	10/50	Birkenhead 201
H30/26R	HER784	Daimler CVD6	17178	1/50	Mansfield (Burwell & District), Burwell
B35R	AHG55	Leyd Tiger PS1	495561	4/50	Burnley, Colne & Nelson 34
B35R	AHG56	Leyd Tiger PS1	495562	4/50	Burnley, Colne & Nelson 35
B35R	AHG53	Leyd Tiger PS1	495204	3/50	Burnley, Colne & Nelson 32
B35R	AHG51	Leyd Tiger PS1	495559	4/50	Burnley, Colne & Nelson 30
B35R	AHG52	Leyd Tiger PS1	495558	5/50	Burnley, Colne & Nelson 31

Top table (BNUM 2128–2200)

BNUM	CONFIG	REGN	CHASSIS MAKE	NUMBER	YEAR	OPERATOR	NOTE
2128	L27/28R	HGF952	Daimler CWA6	12903	4/54	Southend 265	1
2129	L27/28R	HGF923	Daimler CWA6	12874	4/54	Southend 262	1
2130	L27/28R	HGC286	Daimler CWA6	12525	6/54	Southend 268	1
2131	L27/28R	GLX913	Daimler CWA6	11845	6/54	Southend 263	1
2132	L27/28R	HGC276	Daimler CWA6	12486	6/54	Southend 264	1
2133	L27/28R	HGF905	Daimler CWA6	12856	7/54	Southend 275	1
2134	L27/28R	GYE60	Daimler CWA6	12086	7/54	Southend 270	1
2135	L27/28R	HGC263	Daimler CWA6	12465	7/54	Southend 271	1
2136	L27/28R	GYE100	Daimler CWA6	12145	7/54	Southend 274	1
2137	L27/28R	GXV783	Daimler CWA6	11989	7/54	Southend 272	1
2138	L27/28R	HGF879	Daimler CWA6	12830	7/54	Southend 269	1
2139	L27/28R	GXV784	Daimler CWA6	11990	7/54	Southend 273	1
2140	L27/28R	HJN838	Leyd Titan PD2/20	540653	10/54	Southend 278	
2141	L27/28R	HJN836	Leyd Titan PD2/20	540651	10/54	Southend 276	
2142	L27/28R	HJN837	Leyd Titan PD2/20	540652	10/54	Southend 277	
2143	L27/28R	HJN839	Leyd Titan PD2/20	540654	10/54	Southend 279	
2144	Van	HJN840	Austin goods	540655	10/54	Southend 280	
2145	B31F	CEK444	Foden PVSC6	33868 ?	--/54	Moorfield, Pemberton for HP Birmingham	
2146	N/A	N/A	Vanmaster Trailer	N/A	--/55	Wankie Colliery, Southern Rhodesia	
2147	H33/28RD	RAL795	Daimler CVG6	18688	8/54	Southend Corporation	28
2148	B44F	OTG517	Leyd Royal Tiger PSU1/13	541305	12/54	Gash, Newark DD10	
2149	B44F	OTG518	Leyd Royal Tiger PSU1/13	541306	12/54	Caerphilly 7	
2150	H30/26R	UFM860	Guy Arab IV	FD72315	11/54	Caerphilly 8	
2151	H30/26R	UFM862	Guy Arab IV	FD72318	1/55	Chester 9	
2152	H30/26R	UFM863	Guy Arab IV	FD72319	1/55	Chester 11	
2153	H30/26R	UFM858	Guy Arab IV	FD72303	1/55	Chester 12	
2154	H30/26R	UFM861	Guy Arab IV	FD72316	10/54	Chester 7	
2155	H30/26R	UFM859	Guy Arab IV	FD72304	11/54	Chester 8	
2156	L27/28R	KVA657	Leyd Titan PD2/10	541283	9/54	Baxter, Airdrie 56	
2157	L27/28R	KVA658	Leyd Titan PD2/10	541284	9/54	Baxter, Airdrie 57	
2158	H30/28R	KVD286	Leyd Titan PD2/10	541549	5/55	Baxter, Airdrie 58	
2159	H30/28R	EX9073	Leyd Titan PD2/22	550462	5/55	Great Yarmouth 73	
2160	H30/28R	EX9075	Leyd Titan PD2/22	550465	7/55	Great Yarmouth 75	
2161	H30/28R	EX9072	Leyd Titan PD2/22	550464	6/55	Great Yarmouth 72	
2162	H30/28R	EX9074	Leyd Titan PD2/22	550461	7/55	Great Yarmouth 74	
2163	H30/28R	EX9071	Leyd Titan PD2/22	550463	6/55	Great Yarmouth 71	
2164	H31/28R	DCM976	Guy Arab III	FD72483	6/55	Birkenhead 356	1
2165	H31/28R	DCM975	Guy Arab III	FD72482	5/55	Birkenhead 357	1
2166	H31/28R	DCM977	Guy Arab III	FD72485	5/55	Birkenhead 355	1
2167	H31/28R	DCM979	Guy Arab II	FD72488	5/55	Birkenhead 359	1
2168	H31/28R	DCM980	Guy Arab II	FD72489	5/55	Birkenhead 360	1
2169	H31/28R	DCM978	Guy Arab II	FD72487	5/55	Birkenhead 358	1
2170	H31/28R	DCM...	Guy Arab II	FD72491	5/55	Birkenhead 361	1
2171	H30/28R	CHS271	Guy Arab II	D26978	--/55	McGill, Barrhead	
2172	H30/28R	CHS272	Guy Arab II	D26973	--/55	McGill, Barrhead	
2173	H30/28R	CHS254	Guy Arab II	D26716	--/55	McGill, Barrhead	
2174	H30/28R	CHS355	Guy Arab II	D27919	--/55	McGill, Barrhead	
2175	H33/28R	DVD878	Guy Arab III	D28406	--/55	Laurie, Hamilton 37	
2176	DP43F	BEO397	Leyd Royal Tiger PSU1/13	550129	7/55	Barrow 52	
2177	L27/28RD	LBX250	Guy Arab IV	FD72518	4/55	Rees & Williams, Tycroes	
2178	L27/28RD	CBX796	Guy Arab IV	FD28107	--/55	Rees & Williams, Tycroes	1
2179	H32/26R	XFM522	Leyd Titan PD2/20	FD72604	9/55	Chester 14	
2180	H32/26R	XFM524	Leyd Titan PD2/20	FD72606	8/55	Chester 16	
2181	H32/26R	XFM526	Leyd Titan PD2/20	FD72613	9/55	Chester 18	
2182	H32/26R	XFM525	Leyd Titan PD2/20	FD72612	9/55	Chester 17	
2183	H32/26R	XFM523	Leyd Titan PD2/20	FD72605	10/55	Chester 15	
2184	H32/26R	XFM521	Leyd Titan PD2/20	FD72584	10/55	Chester 13	
2185	H33/28RD	MDM626	Guy Arab IV	FD72777	9/55	Lloyd, Bagillt	
2186	H33/28R	WKP71	Leyd Titan PD2/20	556426	3/56	Maidstone 1	
2187	H33/28R	WKP73	Leyd Titan PD2/20	560033	3/56	Maidstone 5	
2188	H33/28R	WKP75	Leyd Titan PD2/20	560338	4/56	Maidstone 6	
2189	H33/28R	WKP76	Leyd Titan PD2/20	560339	4/56	Maidstone 4	
2190	H33/28R	WKP74	Leyd Titan PD2/20	560337	4/56	Maidstone 2	
2191	H33/28R	WKP72	Leyd Titan PD2/20	560032	4/56	Maidstone	
2192	H31/28R	EBG59	Guy Arab IV	FD73129	6/56	Birkenhead 372	
2193	H31/28R	EBG62	Guy Arab IV	FD73118	6/56	Birkenhead 375	
2194	H31/28R	EBG60	Guy Arab IV	FD73125	6/56	Birkenhead 373	
2195	H31/28R	EBG64	Guy Arab IV	FD73134	6/56	Birkenhead 377	
2196	H31/28R	EBG63	Guy Arab IV	FD73136	6/56	Birkenhead 376	
2197	H31/28R	EBG61	Guy Arab IV	FD73128	6/56	Birkenhead 374	
2198	H31/28R	EBG750	Guy Arab IV	FD73295	10/56	Birkenhead 378	
2199	H31/28R	EBG751	Guy Arab IV	FD73351	10/56	Birkenhead 379	
2200	H31/28R	EBG751	Guy Arab IV	FD73371	10/56	Birkenhead 380	

Bottom table (BNUM 2059–2126*)

BNUM	CONFIG	REGN	CHASSIS MAKE	NUMBER	YEAR	OPERATOR	NOTE
2059	B35R	AHG54	Leyd Tiger PS1	495560	5/50	Burnley, Colne & Nelson 33	
2060	L27/26R	EHJ446	AEC Regent III	6811A099	7/50	Southend 262	
2061	L27/26R	EHJ444	AEC Regent III	6811A097	7/50	Southend 260	
2062	L27/26R	EHJ445	AEC Regent III	6811A098	7/50	Southend 261	
2063	L27/26R	EHJ443	AEC Regent III	6811A096	8/50	Southend 259	
2064	L27/26R	EHJ442	AEC Regent III	6811A095	8/50	Southend 258	
2065	L27/26R	EHJ441	AEC Regent III	6811A094	8/50	Southend 257	
2066	H30/26R	EN7702	Leyd Titan TD5 rebuilt from TS8c	300744	11/51	Bury 73	1
2067	H30/26R	EN7701	Leyd Titan TD5 rebuilt from TS8c	300743	11/51	Bury 72	1
2068	H30/26R	EN7703	Leyd Titan TD5 rebuilt from TS8c	300745	11/51	Bury 74	1
2069	H30/26R	EN7704	Leyd Titan TD5 rebuilt from TS8c	300746	11/51	Bury 75	1
2070	H30/26R	MFM556	Foden PVD6	30630	11/50	Chester 77	
2071	H30/26R	MFM557	Foden PVD6	30668	12/50	Chester 78	
2072	L27/26R	LBJ743	AEC Regent III	6812A106	1/51	Lowestoft 28	
2073	H30/26R	LBJ744	AEC Regent III	6812A107	1/51	Lowestoft 29	
2074	L29/26R	NMB314	Guy Arab III	FD70807	5/51	Naylor, Stockton Heath	
2075	L27/26RD	JVE447	Daimler CVD6	14199	6/51	Mansfield (Burwell & District), Burwell	
2076	DP39F	KTX631	Leyd Tiger PS2/3	501267	4/51	Thomas (Llynfi), Maesteg 59	
2077	FC37F	XRE979	Foden PVSC6	30626	8/52	Whieldon (Green Bus), Rugeley 25	
2078	FDP43F	MRR601	Barton BTS/1	BTL30/51/1101	10/51	Barton Transport 651	1
2079	H32/26RD	FBW886	Daimler CVD6	17181	1/52	Smith, Upper Heyford 8	
2080	H32/26RD	FBW887	Daimler CVD6	17183	3/52	Smith, Upper Heyford 9	
2081	H30/26R	FFM299	Guy Arab II	FD26630	5/52	Chester 55	
2082	H30/26R	JYS466	Foden PVD6	33816	5/52	SCWS, Glasgow (Smith, Barrhead)	
2083	B35F	LTX311	Leyd Tiger PS2/5	520623	6/52	Caerphilly 1	
2084	H30/26R	XRE590	Foden PVD6	32258	8/52	Rowbotham, Harriseahead 7	
2085	H30/26R	FOP355	Guy Arab II	FD26429	11/52	Rowbotham, Harriseahead 5	
2086	L29/28R	BHJ807	Daimler CWA6	11873	12/52	Southend 233	
2087	H30/26R	BHJ805	Daimler CWA6	11871	12/52	Southend 231	
2088	L29/28R	BHJ804	Daimler CWA6	11865	12/52	Southend 230	
2089	L29/28R	BHJ806	Daimler CWA6	11872	12/52	Southend 232	
2090	H30/26R	BHJ808	Daimler CWA6	11891	12/52	Southend 234	
2091	L29/28R	BHJ809	Daimler CWA6	11892	12/52	Southend 235	
2092	H30/26R	FFM278	Guy Arab II	FD26129	3/53	Chester 46	
2093	H31/28R	BG8557	Guy Arab II	FD26388	5/53	Birkenhead 242	
2094	H31/28R	BG8556	Guy Arab II	FD26381	5/53	Birkenhead 241	
2095	H31/28R	BG8628	Guy Arab II	FD26656	5/53	Birkenhead 244	
2096	H31/28R	BG8558	Guy Arab II	FD26418	5/53	Birkenhead 243	1
2097	H31/28R	BG8629	Guy Arab II	FD26661	5/53	Birkenhead 245	1
2098	H31/28R	BG8630	Guy Arab II	FD26662	5/53	Birkenhead 246	1
2099	H31/28R	BG8631	Guy Arab II	FD26677	5/53	Birkenhead 247	1
2100	H31/28R	BG8632	Guy Arab II	FD26679	5/53	Birkenhead 248	1
2101	H31/28R	BG8641	Guy Arab II	FD26738	5/53	Birkenhead 249	1
2102	H32/26RD	BG8645	Guy Arab II	FD26840	5/53	Birkenhead 253	
2103	H31/28R	BG8646	Guy Arab II	FD26842	5/53	Birkenhead 254	
2104	H31/28R	BG8647	Guy Arab II	FD26884	5/53	Birkenhead 255	
2105	H31/28R	BG8642	Guy Arab II	FD26720	5/53	Birkenhead 250	
2106	H31/28R	BG8643	Guy Arab II	FD26743	5/53	Birkenhead 251	
2107	H31/28R	BG8644	Guy Arab II	FD26743	5/53	Birkenhead 252	
2108	H30/26RD	GBW336	Daimler CVD6	18484	3/53	Smith, Upper Heyford 12	
2109	H32/26RD	GBW337	Daimler CVD6	18485	9/53	Smith, Upper Heyford 13	
2110	Cancelled		Cancelled			Cancelled	
2111	Cancelled		Cancelled			Cancelled	
2112	B31F	RFM641	Foden PVSC6	33848 ?	--/53	Wankie Colliery, Southern Rhodesia	
2113	H30/26R	RFM642	Guy Arab IV	FD71864	6/53	Chester 1	
2114	H30/26R	RFM643	Guy Arab IV	FD71863	6/53	Chester 2	
2115	H30/26R	WPU732	Guy Arab IV	FD71865	7/53	Chester 3	
2116	H30/26R	WPU733	AEC Regent III	6812A108	9/53	Colchester 10	
2117	H30/26R	WPU734	AEC Regent III	6812A109	9/53	Colchester 11	
2118	H30/26RD		AEC Regent III	6812A110	12/53	Colchester 12	
2119*	B53D		Foden FG6/12	35256	--/54	Mozambique Railway	
2120*	B53D		Foden FG6/12	35258	--/54	Mozambique Railway	
2121*	B53D	MZQ0102	Foden FG6/12	35260	--/54	Mozambique Railway	
2122*	B53D		Foden FG6/12	35262	--/54	Mozambique Railway	
2123*	B53D		Foden FG6/12	35264	--/54	Mozambique Railway	
2124*	B53D		Foden FG6/12	35266	--/54	Mozambique Railway	
2125*	B53D	MZQ0113	Foden FG6/12	35268	--/54	Mozambique Railway	
2126*	B53D		Foden FG6/12	35270	--/54	Mozambique Railway	

BNUM	CONFIG	REGN	CHASSIS MAKE	NUMBER	YEAR	OPERATOR	NOTE
2203	L27/28R	LHJ396	Leyd Titan PD2/12	551556	2/56	Southend 294	
2204	L27/28R	LHJ400	Leyd Titan PD2/12	551560	12/55	Southend 298	
2205	L27/28R	LHJ394	Leyd Titan PD2/12	551499	12/55	Southend 292	
2206	L27/28R	LHJ399	Leyd Titan PD2/12	551559	12/55	Southend 297	
2207	L27/28R	LHJ398	Leyd Titan PD2/12	551558	2/56	Southend 296	
2208	L27/28R	LHJ395	Leyd Titan PD2/12	551555	2/56	Southend 293	
2209	L27/28R	LHJ390	Leyd Titan PD2/12	551492	2/56	Southend 288	
2210	L27/28R	LHJ391	Leyd Titan PD2/12	551496	2/56	Southend 289	
2211	L27/28R	LHJ389	Leyd Titan PD2/12	551456	2/56	Southend 287	
2212	L27/28R	LHJ393	Leyd Titan PD2/12	551498	5/56	Southend 291	
2213	L27/28R	LHJ397	Leyd Titan PD2/12	551557	5/56	Southend 295	
2214	L27/28R	LHJ392	Leyd Titan PD2/12	551497	5/56	Southend 290	
2215	H30/28R	EX9826	AEC Regent V	MD3RV299	6/56	Great Yarmouth 26	
2216	H30/28R	EX9828	AEC Regent V	MD3RV301	6/56	Great Yarmouth 28	
2217	H30/28R	EX9830	AEC Regent V	MD3RV303	7/56	Great Yarmouth 30	
2218	H30/28R	EX9829	AEC Regent V	MD3RV302	7/56	Great Yarmouth 29	
2219	H30/28R	EX9827	AEC Regent V	MD3RV300	7/56	Great Yarmouth 27	
2220	H33/28R	681HEV	AEC Regent V	D3RV142	8/56	Colchester 15	
2221	H33/28R	682HEV	AEC Regent V	D3RV143	9/56	Colchester 16	
2222	H33/28R	679HEV	AEC Regent V	D3RV140	9/56	Colchester 13	
2223	H33/28R	680HEV	AEC Regent V	D3RV141	8/56	Colchester 14	
2224	B35F	EVJ807	AEC Regal I	O6625437	--/56	Baxter, Airdrie 34	1
2225	Van	CJP34	Austin 5-ton	?	--/56	Moorfield, Pemberton for HP Birmingham	
2226	H30/26R	NVD608	Guy Arab IV	FD73177	--/56	Duncan,Law	
2227	H30/26R	791ATD	AEC Regent V	MD3RV379	12/56	Morecambe & Heysham 82	
2228	H30/26RD	793ATD	AEC Regent V	MD3RV381	1/57	Morecambe & Heysham 84	
2229	H30/26R	794ATD	AEC Regent V	MD3RV382	1/57	Morecambe & Heysham 85	
2230	H30/26R	795ATD	AEC Regent V	MD3RV383	1/57	Morecambe & Heysham 86	
2231	H30/26R	792ATD	AEC Regent V	MD3RV380	12/56	Morecambe & Heysham 83	
2232	B39F	DBX28	Leyd Tiger PS1	462684	6/56	Rees & Williams, Tycroes	1
2233	L27/28R	NVD861	Leyd Titan PD2/10	560734	11/56	Baxter, Airdrie 61	
2234	L27/28R	NVD863	Leyd Titan PD2/10	560733	11/56	Baxter, Airdrie 63	
2235	L27/28R	NVD862	Leyd Titan PD2/10	560735	11/56	Baxter, Airdrie 62	
2236	Van	DEK139	Austin 5-ton	?	--/56	Moorfield, Pemberton for HP Birmingham	
2237	B44F	UTX9	Leyd Royal Tiger PSU1/13	511325	11/56	Caerphilly 9	
2238	L27/28R	VTX24	Leyd Titan PD2/40	571087	7/57	Caerphilly 24	
2239	L27/28R	VTX25	Leyd Titan PD2/40	571088	7/57	Caerphilly 25	
2240	H30/28R	AEX333	Leyd Titan PD2/22	562666	5/57	Great Yarmouth 33	
2241	H30/28R	AEX332	Leyd Titan PD2/22	562665	5/57	Great Yarmouth 32	
2242	H30/28R	AEX334	Leyd Titan PD2/22	562667	5/57	Great Yarmouth 34	
2243	H30/28R	AEX331	Leyd Titan PD2/22	562664	5/57	Great Yarmouth 31	
2244	H30/28R	AEX335	Leyd Titan PD2/22	562668	5/57	Great Yarmouth 35	
2245	H32/28R	714CFM	Guy Arab IV	FD73591	4/57	Chester 20	
2246	H32/28R	716CFM	Guy Arab IV	FD73595	5/57	Chester 22	
2247	H32/28R	713CFM	Guy Arab IV	FD73590	3/57	Chester 19	
2248	H32/28R	717CFM	Guy Arab IV	FD73597	3/57	Chester 23	
2249	H32/28R	715CFM	Guy Arab IV	FD73594	3/57	Chester 21	
2250	H30/26R	TFJ808	Guy Arab IV	FD73287	11/56	Exeter 50	
2251	H30/26R	UFJ291	Guy Arab IV	FD73679	6/57	Exeter 51	
2252	H30/26R	UFJ292	Guy Arab IV	FD73680	6/57	Exeter 52	
2253	H30/26R	UFJ294	Guy Arab IV	FD73687	6/57	Exeter 54	
2254	H30/26R	UFJ293	Guy Arab IV	FD73686	7/57	Exeter 53	
2255	H31/28R	FCM992	Leyd Titan PD2/40	571267	7/57	Birkenhead 2	
2256	H31/28R	FCM997	Leyd Titan PD2/40	571320	7/57	Birkenhead 7	
2257	H31/28R	FBG915	Leyd Titan PD2/40	571372	11/57	Birkenhead 15	
2258	H31/28R	FCM993	Leyd Titan PD2/40	571268	12/57	Birkenhead 3	
2259	H31/28R	FCM996	Leyd Titan PD2/40	571319	11/57	Birkenhead 6	
2260	H31/28R	FCM991	Leyd Titan PD2/40	571266	12/57	Birkenhead 1	
2261	H31/28R	FCM998	Leyd Titan PD2/40	571321	12/57	Birkenhead 8	
2262	H31/28R	FCM994	Leyd Titan PD2/40	571269	12/57	Birkenhead 4	
2263	H31/28R	FBG909	Leyd Titan PD2/40	571322	1/58	Birkenhead 9	
2264	H31/28R	FBG914	Leyd Titan PD2/40	571371	1/58	Birkenhead 14	
2265	H31/28R	FBG911	Leyd Titan PD2/40	571368	2/58	Birkenhead 11	
2266	H31/28R	FBG913	Leyd Titan PD2/40	571370	1/58	Birkenhead 13	
2267	H31/28R	FBG912	Leyd Titan PD2/40	571369	2/58	Birkenhead 12	
2268	H31/28R	FBG910	Leyd Titan PD2/40	571367	3/58	Birkenhead 10	
2269	H31/28R	FCM995	Leyd Titan PD2/40	571318	3/58	Birkenhead 5	
2270	L27/28R	OVA864	Leyd Titan PD2/12	571616	3/57	Baxter, Airdrie 64	
2271	L27/28R	OVA866	Leyd Titan PD2/12	571618	6/57	Baxter, Airdrie 66	
2272	L27/28R	OVA865	Leyd Titan PD2/12	571617	3/57	Baxter, Airdrie 65	
2273	H33/28R	1296 F	AEC Regent V	D3RV410	5/57	Colchester 18	
2274	H33/28R	1298 F	AEC Regent V	D3RV412	5/57	Colchester 20	
2275	H33/28R	1297 F	AEC Regent V	D3RV411	5/57	Colchester 19	
2276	H33/28R	1295 F	AEC Regent V	D3RV409	6/57	Colchester 17	
2277	L29/28R	RAX583	AEC Regent V	MD3RV461	4/57	Bedwas & Machen 10	

BNUM	CONFIG	REGN	CHASSIS MAKE	NUMBER	YEAR	OPERATOR	NOTE
2278	H32/26RD	DEK107	Leyd Titan PD2/20	571235	9/57	Wigan 6	
2279	H32/26RD	DEK105	Leyd Titan PD2/20	571196	10/57	Wigan 2	
2280	H32/26RD	DEK106	Leyd Titan PD2/20	571197	10/57	Wigan 4	
2281	L27/28R	OHJ77	Leyd Titan PD2/40	571383	9/57	Southend 307	
2282	L27/28R	OHJ76	Leyd Titan PD2/40	571382	8/57	Southend 306	
2283	L27/28R	OHJ79	Leyd Titan PD2/40	571385	9/57	Southend 309	
2284	L27/28R	OHJ78	Leyd Titan PD2/40	571384	8/57	Southend 308	
2285	L27/28R	OHJ80	Leyd Titan PD2/40	571386	8/57	Southend 310	
2286	L27/28R	OHJ75	Leyd Titan PD2/40	571381	8/57	Southend 305	
2287	H33/28R	998AKT	Leyd Titan PD2/30	571437	10/57	Maidstone 8	
2288	H33/28R	997AKT	Leyd Titan PD2/30	571436	10/57	Maidstone 7	
2289	H33/28R	999AKT	Leyd Titan PD2/30	571438	10/57	Maidstone 9	
2290	H33/28R	410DKM	Leyd Titan PD2/30	571369	9/58	Maidstone 10	
2291	H33/28R	411DKM	Leyd Titan PD2/30	571370	9/58	Maidstone 11	
2292	H33/28R	412DKM	Leyd Titan PD2/30	571387	9/58	Maidstone 12	
2293	H33/28R	245TRF	Leyd Titan PD2/30	572928	12/57	Turner, Brown Edge 11	
2294	L27/28R	PVD568	AEC Regent V	MD3RV482	12/57	Baxter, Airdrie 68	
2295	L27/28R	PVD567	AEC Regent V	MD3RV481	12/57	Baxter, Airdrie 67	
2296	H30/28R	BEX239	AEC Regent V	MD3RV527	5/58	Great Yarmouth 39	
2297	H30/28R	BEX238	AEC Regent V	MD3RV525	5/58	Great Yarmouth 38	
2298	H30/28R	BEX237	AEC Regent V	MD3RV524	5/58	Great Yarmouth 37	
2299	H30/28R	BEX236	AEC Regent V	MD3RV526	5/58	Great Yarmouth 36	
2300	H33/28R	DCS616	Daimler CVD6SD	16519	3/58	A1, Ardrossan (Hunter, Dreghorn) 16A	1
2301	L27/28R	RVD469	Leyd Titan PD2/40	572917	5/58	Baxter, Airdrie 69	
2302	H40/33RD	RDM200	Guy Arab IV	FD73863	5/58	Lloyd, Bagillt	
2303	L35/33R	PHJ951	Leyd Titan PD3/6	580829	6/58	Southend 312	
2304	L35/33R	PHJ955	Leyd Titan PD3/6	580864	6/58	Southend 316	
2305	L35/33R	PHJ952	Leyd Titan PD3/6	580830	7/58	Southend 313	
2306	L35/33R	PHJ950	Leyd Titan PD3/6	580828	7/58	Southend 311	
2307	L35/33R	PHJ953	Leyd Titan PD3/6	580831	6/58	Southend 314	
2308	L35/33R	PHJ954	Leyd Titan PD3/6	580863	7/58	Southend 315	
2309	H41/31F	YTG304	Leyd Titan PD3/4	571786	7/58	Thomas (Llynfi), Maesteg 72	
2310	L29/28R	YNY922	Leyd Titan PD2/40	581705	11/58	Caerphilly 22	
2311	L29/28R	YNY923	Leyd Titan PD2/40	581706	11/58	Caerphilly 23	
2312	H33/28RD	DJP753	Leyd Titan PD2/30	581263	8/58	Wigan 10	
2313	H33/28RD	DJP751	Leyd Titan PD2/30	581308	9/58	Wigan 7	
2314	H33/28RD	DJP752	Leyd Titan PD2/30	581309	8/58	Wigan 9	
2315	L34/33RD	RBX700	Guy Arab IV	FD73869	6/58	West Wales, Tycroes 39	
2316	L34/33R	8935NO	Guy Arab IV	FD74120	10/58	Moore, Kelvedon	
2317	L34/33R	8936NO	Guy Arab IV	FD74124	10/58	Moore, Kelvedon	
2318	L27/28RD	ETH104	Guy Arab III	FD28449	--/58	Rees & Williams, Tycroes	1
2319	H33/28R	HFA574	Guy Arab IV	FD74155	1/59	Burton 74	
2320	H33/28R	HFA575	Guy Arab IV	FD74157	1/59	Burton 75	
2321	H33/28R	HFA573	Guy Arab IV	FD74154	1/59	Burton 73	
2322	L27/28R	TVA70	Leyd Titan PD2/41	583417	1/59	Baxter, Airdrie 70	
2323	L27/28R	TVA71	Leyd Titan PD2/41	583418	1/59	Baxter, Airdrie 71	
2324	H33/28RD	KAL579	Daimler CVD6	15227	10/58	Gash, Newark DD2	1
2325	H33/28RD	KAL580	Daimler CVD6	16745	11/58	Gash, Newark DD3	1
2326	H33/28RD	KNN622	Daimler CVD6	16746	12/58	Gash, Newark DD4	1
2327	L31/28R	SVD676	AEC Regent V	MD3RV532	11/58	Greenshields, Salsburgh	
2328	H33/28R	195MNO	AEC Regent V	D3RV665	2/59	Colchester 23	
2329	H33/28R	194MNO	AEC Regent V	D3RV664	2/59	Colchester 22	
2330	H33/28R	193MNO	AEC Regent V	D3RV663	2/59	Colchester 21	
2331	H33/28R	CEX46	AEC Regent V	MD3RV531	3/59	Great Yarmouth 46	
2332	H33/28R	CEX43	AEC Regent V	MD3RV528	3/59	Great Yarmouth 43	
2333	H33/28R	CEX45	AEC Regent V	MD3RV530	3/59	Great Yarmouth 45	
2334	H33/28R	CEX44	AEC Regent V	MD3RV529	3/59	Great Yarmouth 44	
2335	L27/28R	TVD72	Leyd Titan PD2/41	581966	4/59	Baxter, Airdrie 72	
2336	L27/28R	TVD73	Leyd Titan PD2/41	581967	5/59	Baxter, Airdrie 73	
2337	H33/28R	NHS764	Leyd Titan PD2/30	572980	3/59	McGill, Barrhead	
2338	H40/33RD	SDM663	Leyd Titan PD3/1	583831	3/59	Lloyd, Bagillt	
2339	B39F	JXT496	Leyd Tiger PS1/1	483013	2/59	Davies,Tonmawr	1
2340	L31/28R	UWO498	AEC Regent V	MD3RV498	6/59	Bedwas & Machen 11	
2341	H41/31F	1212RE	Leyd Titan PD3/1	583970	6/59	Turner, Brown Edge 12	
2342	H33/28R	HCM516	Leyd Titan PD2/40	583796	4/59	Birkenhead 16	
2343	H33/28R	HCM517	Leyd Titan PD2/40	583816	4/59	Birkenhead 17	
2344	H33/28R	HCM520	Leyd Titan PD2/40	583827	5/59	Birkenhead 20	
2345	H33/28R	HCM519	Leyd Titan PD2/40	583826	5/59	Birkenhead 19	
2346	H33/28R	HCM518	Leyd Titan PD2/40	583825	5/59	Birkenhead 18	
2347	H33/28R	HCM525	Leyd Titan PD2/40	583903	9/59	Birkenhead 25	
2348	H33/28R	HCM522	Leyd Titan PD2/40	583900	9/59	Birkenhead 22	
2349	H33/28R	HCM523	Leyd Titan PD2/40	583901	10/59	Birkenhead 23	
2350	H33/28R	HCM521	Leyd Titan PD2/40	583899	9/59	Birkenhead 21	
2351	H33/28R	HCM524	Leyd Titan PD2/40	583902	10/59	Birkenhead 24	
2352	H33/28R	HCM527	Leyd Titan PD2/40	583910	11/59	Birkenhead 27	

BNUM	CONFIG	REGN	CHASSIS MAKE	NUMBER	YEAR	OPERATOR	NOTE
2353	H33/28R	HCM530	Leyd Titan PD2/40	583965	11/59	Birkenhead 30	
2354	H33/28R	HCM529	Leyd Titan PD2/40	583935	1/60	Birkenhead 29	
2355	H33/28R	HCM528	Leyd Titan PD2/40	583934	1/60	Birkenhead 28	
2356	H33/28R	HCM526	Leyd Titan PD2/40	583909	12/59	Birkenhead 26	
2357	DP39F	EEO468	Leyd Tiger Cub PSUC1/1	594056	8/59	Barrow 53	
2358	H33/28R	OHS980	Daimler CVG6	19595	1/60	McGill, Barrhead	
2359	H33/28R	OHS979	Daimler CVG6	19594	1/60	McGill, Barrhead	
2360	H41/31F	UVA638	Leyd Titan PD3/2	572844	--/59	Laurie, Hamilton 69	
2361	L34/33R	20PVX	Guy Arab IV	FD74288	7/59	Moore, Kelvedon	
2362	L34/33R	19PVX	Guy Arab IV	FD74286	7/59	Moore, Kelvedon	
2363	H41/31F	EJP504	Leyd Titan PD3/2	590595	7/59	Wigan 62	
2364	H41/31F	EJP501	Leyd Titan PD3/2	590577	9/59	Wigan 5	
2365	H41/31F	EJP503	Leyd Titan PD3/2	590594	8/59	Wigan 61	
2366	H41/31F	EJP502	Leyd Titan PD3/2	590578	9/59	Wigan 60	
2367	H33/28R	413GKT	Leyd Titan PD2/30	590744	9/59	Maidstone 13	
2368	H33/28R	414GKT	Leyd Titan PD2/30	590745	10/59	Maidstone 14	
2369	H33/28R	415GKT	Leyd Titan PD2/30	590746	9/59	Maidstone 15	
2370	H33/28R	CXS104	Guy Arab IV	FD74410	12/59	Graham, Paisley 45	
2371	L31/28RD	UTH78	Guy Arab IV	FD74470	1/60	Rees & Williams, Tycroes	
2372	L29/27F	VVD74	Leyd Titan PD2/37	591771	2/60	Baxter, Airdrie 74	
2373	H33/28R	FA9716	Guy Arab III	FD36252	1/60	Burton 16	1
2374	H33/28R	FA9715	Guy Arab III	FD36253	2/60	Burton 15	1
2375	H33/28R	FA9718	Guy Arab III	FD70039	3/60	Burton 18	1
2376	H37/27F	33MTD	Leyd Titan PD2/37	592831	3/60	Morecambe & Heysham 87	
2377	H37/27F	35MTD	Leyd Titan PD2/37	592856	3/60	Morecambe & Heysham 89	
2378	H37/27F	34MTD	Leyd Titan PD2/37	592855	3/60	Morecambe & Heysham 88	
2379	H31/26R	972AFJ	Guy Arab IV	FD74588	6/60	Exeter 72	
2380	H31/26R	971AFJ	Guy Arab IV	FD74587	6/60	Exeter 71	
2381	H31/26R	970AFJ	Guy Arab IV	FD74585	6/60	Exeter 70	
2382	H31/26R	973AFJ	Guy Arab IV	FD74589	7/60	Exeter 73	
2383	H31/26R	974AFJ	Guy Arab IV	FD74590	7/60	Exeter 74	
2384	H35/28R	JBG531	Leyd Titan PD2/40	600615	4/60	Birkenhead 31	
2385	H35/28R	JBG535	Leyd Titan PD2/40	600628	5/60	Birkenhead 35	
2386	H35/28R	JBG533	Leyd Titan PD2/40	600617	5/60	Birkenhead 33	
2387	H35/28R	JBG536	Leyd Titan PD2/40	600672	5/60	Birkenhead 36	
2388	H35/28R	JBG532	Leyd Titan PD2/40	600616	5/60	Birkenhead 32	
2389	H35/28R	JBG539	Leyd Titan PD2/40	600683	8/60	Birkenhead 39	
2390	H35/28R	JBG534	Leyd Titan PD2/40	600627	7/60	Birkenhead 34	
2391	H35/28R	JBG537	Leyd Titan PD2/40	600673	8/60	Birkenhead 37	
2392	H35/28R	JBG542	Leyd Titan PD2/40	600860	9/60	Birkenhead 42	
2393	H35/28R	JBG538	Leyd Titan PD2/40	600682	8/60	Birkenhead 38	
2394	H35/28R	JBG540	Leyd Titan PD2/40	600684	1/61	Birkenhead 40	
2395	H35/28R	JBG543	Leyd Titan PD2/40	600861	1/61	Birkenhead 43	
2396	H35/28R	JBG544	Leyd Titan PD2/40	600862	1/61	Birkenhead 44	
2397	H35/28R	JBG541	Leyd Titan PD2/40	600859	2/61	Birkenhead 41	
2398	H35/28R	JBG545	Leyd Titan PD2/40	600895	2/61	Birkenhead 45	
2399	L29/28R	LPU611	Guy Arab III	FD28324	4/60	Moore, Kelvedon	1
2400	L29/28R	JTW447	Guy Arab I	FD25917	10/60	Moore, Kelvedon	1
2401	L29/28R	JVW999	Guy Arab II	FD26955	5/60	Moore, Kelvedon	1
2402	L29/27F	WVA75	Leyd Titan PD2/37	592672	5/60	Baxter, Airdrie 75	
2403	H33/28R	9668VX	Leyd Titan PD2/31	601946	11/60	Colchester 25	
2404	H33/28R	9669VX	Leyd Titan PD2/31	601983	12/60	Colchester 26	
2405	H33/28R	9671VX	Leyd Titan PD2/31	602084	2/61	Colchester 28	
2406	H33/28R	9670VX	Leyd Titan PD2/31	601984	12/60	Colchester 27	
2407	H33/28R	9667VX	Leyd Titan PD2/31	601945	12/60	Colchester 24	
2408	L35/33R	827HNY	Leyd Titan PD3/4	601332	9/60	Caerphilly 27	
2409	L35/33R	828HNY	Leyd Titan PD3/4	601333	9/60	Caerphilly 28	
2410	H41/29F	GJP8	Leyd Titan PD3/2	601890	10/60	Wigan 1	
2411	H41/29F	GJP19	Leyd Titan PD3/2	602096	10/60	Wigan 144	
2412	H41/29F	GJP9	Leyd Titan PD3/2	601891	10/60	Wigan 137	
2413	H41/29F	GJP10	Leyd Titan PD3/2	601892	10/60	Wigan 138	29
2414	H41/29F	GJP17	Leyd Titan PD3/2	602094	11/60	Wigan 141	
2415	H41/29F	GJP18	Leyd Titan PD3/2	602095	10/60	Wigan 143	
2416	L29/27F	XVA276	Leyd Titan PD2/37	600573	7/60	Baxter, Airdrie 76	
2417	L29/27F	YVD77	Leyd Titan PD2/37	600574	5/61	Baxter, Airdrie 77	
2418	H31/26R	475CFJ	Leyd Titan PD2A/30	610082	4/61	Exeter 75	
2419	H31/26R	477CFJ	Leyd Titan PD2A/30	610084	4/61	Exeter 77	
2420	H31/26R	478CFJ	Leyd Titan PD2A/30	610090	4/61	Exeter 78	
2421	H31/26R	476CFJ	Leyd Titan PD2A/30	610083	4/61	Exeter 76	
2422	H31/26R	479CFJ	Leyd Titan PD2A/30	610091	4/61	Exeter 79	
2423	H33/28R	NFA878	Guy Arab IV	FD74963	6/61	Burton 78	
2424	H33/28R	NFA877	Guy Arab IV	FD74962	6/61	Burton 77	
2425	H33/28R	NFA876	Guy Arab IV	FD74961	6/61	Burton 76	
2426	B40F	J 26611	Leyd Tiger Cub PSUC1/5	614353	4/61	Jersey MT 611	

BNUM	CONFIG	REGN	CHASSIS MAKE	NUMBER	YEAR	OPERATOR	NOTE
2428	B40F	J 26613	Leyd Tiger Cub PSUC1/5	614355	5/61	Jersey MT 613	30
2429	B40F	J 26614	Leyd Tiger Cub PSUC1/5	614366	5/61	Jersey MT 614	
2430	B40F	J 26615	Leyd Tiger Cub PSUC1/5	614367	4/61	Jersey MT 615	
2431	L34/33R	373WPU	Guy Arab IV	FD74911	6/61	Moore, Kelvedon	
2432	L34/33R	372WPU	Guy Arab IV	FD74910	6/61	Moore, Kelvedon	
2433	H41/32F	326VFM	Guy Arab IV	FD74918	7/61	Chester 26	
2434	H41/32F	325VFM	Guy Arab IV	FD74917	6/61	Chester 25	
2435	H41/32F	324VFM	Guy Arab IV	FD74916	7/61	Chester 24	
2436	L27/28RD	260BAX	Leyd Titan PD2/40	603177	6/61	West Monmouthshire 21	
2437	H37/27F	HEO278	Leyd Titan PD2A/27	611309	10/61	Barrow 8	
2438	H37/27F	HEO275	Leyd Titan PD2A/27	611302	9/61	Barrow 5	
2439	H37/27F	HEO274	Leyd Titan PD2A/27	611301	9/61	Barrow 4	
2440	H37/27F	HEO272	Leyd Titan PD2A/27	611299	9/61	Barrow 2	
2441	H37/27F	HEO280	Leyd Titan PD2A/27	611311	9/61	Barrow 10	
2442	H37/27F	HEO276	Leyd Titan PD2A/27	611307	10/61	Barrow 6	
2443	H37/27F	HEO277	Leyd Titan PD2A/27	611308	11/61	Barrow 7	
2444	H37/27F	HEO273	Leyd Titan PD2A/27	611300	11/61	Barrow 3	
2445	H37/27F	HEO279	Leyd Titan PD2A/27	611310	10/61	Barrow 9	
2446	H37/27F	HEO271	Leyd Titan PD2A/27	611298	10/61	Barrow 1	
2447	H41/29F	HEK705	Leyd Titan PD3A/2	610873	7/61	Wigan 57	
2448	H41/29F	HEK706	Leyd Titan PD3A/2	610874	7/61	Wigan 58	
2449	H41/29F	HEK707	Leyd Titan PD3A/2	611431	8/61	Wigan 59	
2450	H41/29F	HJP3	Leyd Titan PD3A/2	611433	1/62	Wigan 42	
2451	H41/29F	HJP4	Leyd Titan PD3A/2	611434	1/62	Wigan 49	
2452	H41/29F	HJP2	Leyd Titan PD3A/2	611432	1/62	Wigan 40	
2453	H41/29F	HJP1	Leyd Titan PD3A/2	611430	1/62	Wigan 39	
2454	H33/28R	518RKR	Leyd Titan PD2A/30	611704	12/61	Maidstone 18	
2455	H33/28R	517RKR	Leyd Titan PD2A/30	611703	12/61	Maidstone 17	
2456	H33/28R	516RKR	Leyd Titan PD2A/30	611702	12/61	Maidstone 16	
2457	L35/33R	557MNY	Leyd Titan PD3/4	611535	11/61	Caerphilly 29	
2458	L35/33R	558MNY	Leyd Titan PD3/4	611536	11/61	Caerphilly 30	
2459	L31/28RD	YTH815	Guy Arab IV	FD74812	1/62	Rees & Williams, Tycroes	
2460	L31/28R	422CAX	AEC Regent V	MD3RV565	12/61	Bedwas & Machen 5	
2461	H33/28R	PFA81	Daimler CSG5	19889	2/62	Burton 81	
2462	H33/28R	PFA80	Daimler CSG5	19888	2/62	Burton 80	
2463	H33/28R	PFA79	Daimler CSG5	19887	2/62	Burton 79	
2464	H37/27F	436XTF	Leyd Titan PD2A/27	613769	4/62	Morecambe & Heysham 91	
2465	H37/27F	435XTF	Leyd Titan PD2A/27	613623	4/62	Morecambe & Heysham 90	
2466	H31/26R	482EFJ	Leyd Titan PD2A/30	620423	4/62	Exeter 82	
2467	H31/26R	484EFJ	Leyd Titan PD2A/30	620425	4/62	Exeter 84	
2468	H31/26R	480EFJ	Leyd Titan PD2A/30	620405	4/62	Exeter 80	
2469	H31/26R	481EFJ	Leyd Titan PD2A/30	620406	4/62	Exeter 81	
2470	H31/26R	483EFJ	Leyd Titan PD2A/30	620424	4/62	Exeter 83	
2471	L27/28RD	204CWO	Leyd Titan PD2/40	613250	3/62	West Monmouthshire 27	
2472	L27/28RD	203CWO	Leyd Titan PD2/40	613249	3/62	West Monmouthshire 14	
2473	B40F	J 28623	Leyd Tiger Cub PSUC1/11	624867	5/62	Jersey MT 623	30
2474	B40F	J 28622	Leyd Tiger Cub PSUC1/11	624855	6/62	Jersey MT 622	30
2475	B40F	J 28624	Leyd Tiger Cub PSUC1/11	624868	6/62	Jersey MT 624	30
2476	B40F	J 28625	Leyd Tiger Cub PSUC1/11	624919	6/62	Jersey MT 625	30
2477	B40F	J 28621	Leyd Tiger Cub PSUC1/11	624854	6/62	Jersey MT 621	30
2478	H35/30R	MCM964	Leyd Titan PD2/40	621336	7/62	Birkenhead 64	
2479	H35/30R	MCM972	Leyd Titan PD2/40	621463	8/62	Birkenhead 72	
2480	H35/30R	MCM962	Leyd Titan PD2/40	621306	7/62	Birkenhead 62	
2481	H35/30R	MCM975	Leyd Titan PD2/40	621497	9/62	Birkenhead 75	
2482	H35/30R	MCM973	Leyd Titan PD2/40	621464	7/62	Birkenhead 73	
2483	H35/30R	MCM974	Leyd Titan PD2/40	621496	9/62	Birkenhead 74	
2484	H35/30R	MCM961	Leyd Titan PD2/40	621305	9/62	Birkenhead 61	
2485	H35/30R	MCM969	Leyd Titan PD2/40	621431	9/62	Birkenhead 69	
2486	H35/30R	MCM971	Leyd Titan PD2/40	621433	9/62	Birkenhead 71	
2487	H35/30R	MCM970	Leyd Titan PD2/40	621432	9/62	Birkenhead 70	
2488	H35/30R	MCM966	Leyd Titan PD2/40	621361	12/62	Birkenhead 66	
2489	H35/30R	MCM967	Leyd Titan PD2/40	621398	12/62	Birkenhead 67	
2490	H35/30R	MCM963	Leyd Titan PD2/40	621335	12/62	Birkenhead 63	
2491	H35/30R	MCM968	Leyd Titan PD2/40	621399	11/62	Birkenhead 68	
2492	H35/30R	MCM965	Leyd Titan PD2/40	621360	11/62	Birkenhead 65	
2493	H33/28R	20UKK	Leyd Titan PD2A/30	621275	7/62	Maidstone 20	
2494	H33/28R	22UKK	Leyd Titan PD2A/30	621304	7/62	Maidstone 22	
2495	H33/28R	21UKK	Leyd Titan PD2A/30	621303	8/62	Maidstone 21	
2496	H33/28R	19UKK	Leyd Titan PD2A/30	621274	8/62	Maidstone 19	
2497	H41/32F	328YFM	Guy Arab IV	FD75127	6/62	Chester 28	
2498	H41/32F	327YFM	Guy Arab IV	FD75125	6/62	Chester 27	
2499	H41/32F	329YFM	Guy Arab IV	FD75128	6/62	Chester 29	
2500	H41/32F	330YFM	Guy Arab IV	FD75129	6/62	Chester 30	
2501	H41/31F	961GBF	Leyd Titan PD3/4	621571	9/62	Turner, Brown Edge 6	

BNUM	CONFIG	REGN	CHASSIS MAKE	NUMBER	YEAR	OPERATOR	NOTE
2503	H37/27F	JJP504	Leyd Titan PD2A/27	622128	11/62	Wigan 37	
2504	H37/27F	JJP505	Leyd Titan PD2A/27	622129	10/62	Wigan 145	
2505	H37/27F	JJP502	Leyd Titan PD2A/27	622126	10/62	Wigan 35	
2506	H37/27F	JJP503	Leyd Titan PD2A/27	622127	11/62	Wigan 36	
2507	H33/28R	SFA84	Daimler CCG5	19933	3/63	Burton 84	
2508	H33/28R	SFA83	Daimler CCG5	19932	3/63	Burton 83	
2509	H33/28R	SFA82	Daimler CCG5	19931	3/63	Burton 82	
2510	L34/33R	581AOO	Guy Arab IV	FD75265	3/63	Eastern National 1049	31
2511	L34/33R	582AOO	Guy Arab IV	FD75266	3/63	Eastern National 1050	31
2512	H33/28R	MWC129	Leyd Titan PD2A/31	623611	1/63	Colchester 29	
2513	H33/28R	MWC132	Leyd Titan PD2A/31	623766	3/63	Colchester 32	
2514	H33/28R	MWC134	Leyd Titan PD2A/31	623698	2/63	Colchester 34	
2515	H33/28R	MWC133	Leyd Titan PD2A/31	623767	2/63	Colchester 33	
2516	H33/28R	MWC131	Leyd Titan PD2A/31	623765	3/63	Colchester 31	
2517	H33/28R	MWC135	Leyd Titan PD2A/31	623699	3/63	Colchester 35	
2518	H33/28R	MWC130	Leyd Titan PD2A/31	623612	3/63	Colchester 30	
2519	H33/28R	918NRT	AEC Regent V	MD3RV593	1/63	Lowestoft 8	
2520	H33/28R	917NRT	AEC Regent V	MD3RV592	1/63	Lowestoft 7	
2521	L35/33RD	31SNY	Leyd Titan PD3/4	629094	3/63	Caerphilly 31	
2522	B55F	12SNY	Leyd Leopard PSU3/1R	L00475	5/63	Caerphilly 12	
2523	B55F	13SNY	Leyd Leopard PSU3/1R	L00476	7/63	Caerphilly 13	
2524	H31/26R	88GFJ	Leyd Titan PD2A/30	L00527	5/63	Exeter 88	
2525	H31/26R	85GFJ	Leyd Titan PD2A/30	L00490	5/63	Exeter 85	
2526	H31/26R	89GFJ	Leyd Titan PD2A/30	L00528	5/63	Exeter 89	
2527	H31/26R	86GFJ	Leyd Titan PD2A/30	L00491	5/63	Exeter 86	
2528	H31/26R	87GFJ	Leyd Titan PD2A/30	L00526	5/63	Exeter 87	
2529	H33/28RD	KAL578	Daimler CVD6	15226	12/62	Gash, Newark DD1	1
2530	H35/30R	OCM979	Leyd Titan PD2/40	L00774	6/63	Birkenhead 79	
2531	H35/30R	OCM986	Leyd Titan PD2/40	L01079	12/63	Birkenhead 86	
2532	H35/30R	OCM987	Leyd Titan PD2/40	L01092	12/63	Birkenhead 87	
2533	H35/30R	OCM980	Leyd Titan PD2/40	L00800	6/63	Birkenhead 80	
2534	H35/30R	OCM982	Leyd Titan PD2/40	L00901	9/63	Birkenhead 82	
2535	H35/30R	OCM988	Leyd Titan PD2/40	L01093	11/63	Birkenhead 88	
2536	H35/30R	OCM977	Leyd Titan PD2/40	L00772	6/63	Birkenhead 77	
2537	H35/30R	OCM976	Leyd Titan PD2/40	L00771	6/63	Birkenhead 76	
2538	H35/30R	OCM978	Leyd Titan PD2/40	L00773	6/63	Birkenhead 78	
2539	H35/30R	OCM985	Leyd Titan PD2/40	L01078	9/63	Birkenhead 85	
2540	H35/30R	OCM989	Leyd Titan PD2/40	L01094	11/63	Birkenhead 89	
2541	H35/30R	OCM981	Leyd Titan PD2/40	L00801	9/63	Birkenhead 81	
2542	H35/30R	OCM983	Leyd Titan PD2/40	L00902	8/63	Birkenhead 83	
2543	H35/30R	OCM990	Leyd Titan PD2/40	L01095	11/63	Birkenhead 90	
2544	H35/30R	OCM984	Leyd Titan PD2/40	L00903	7/63	Birkenhead 84	
2545	H37/27F	KEK742	Leyd Titan PD2A/27	L00507	7/63	Wigan 45	
2546	H37/27F	KEK739	Leyd Titan PD2A/27	L00504	7/63	Wigan 41	
2547	H37/27F	KEK744	Leyd Titan PD2A/27	L00550	8/63	Wigan 48	
2548	H37/27F	KEK743	Leyd Titan PD2A/27	L00549	8/63	Wigan 47	
2549	H37/27F	KEK740	Leyd Titan PD2A/27	L00505	9/63	Wigan 43	
2550	H37/27F	KEK741	Leyd Titan PD2A/27	L00506	9/63	Wigan 44	
2551	H41/32F	4832FM	Guy Arab V	FD75383	11/63	Chester 32	
2552	H41/32F	4834FM	Guy Arab V	FD75398	11/63	Chester 34	
2553	H41/32F	4833FM	Guy Arab V	FD75397	11/63	Chester 33	
2554	H41/32F	4831FM	Guy Arab V	FD75382	11/63	Chester 31	
2555	H33/28R	26YKO	Leyd Titan PD2A/30	L01579	10/63	Maidstone 26	
2556	H33/28R	23YKO	Leyd Titan PD2A/30	L01576	10/63	Maidstone 23	
2557	H33/28R	24YKO	Leyd Titan PD2A/30	L01577	11/63	Maidstone 24	
2558	H33/28R	25YKO	Leyd Titan PD2A/30	L01578	10/63	Maidstone 25	
2559	H33/28R	TFA987	Daimler CCG5	20060	1/64	Burton 87	
2560	H33/28R	TFA985	Daimler CCG5	20058	1/64	Burton 85	
2561	H33/28R	TFA986	Daimler CCG5	20059	1/64	Burton 86	
2562	H37/27F	CTF627B	Leyd Titan PD2A/27	L03683	5/64	Lytham 70	
2563	H37/27F	CTF625B	Leyd Titan PD2A/27	L03681	5/64	Lytham 68	
2564	H37/27F	CTF626B	Leyd Titan PD2A/27	L03682	5/64	Lytham 69	
2565	H31/26R	AFJ93B	Leyd Titan PD2A/30	L20548	6/64	Exeter 93	
2566	H31/26R	AFJ92B	Leyd Titan PD2A/30	L20547	6/64	Exeter 92	
2567	H31/26R	AFJ94B	Leyd Titan PD2A/30	L20549	6/64	Exeter 94	
2568	H31/26R	AFJ91B	Leyd Titan PD2A/30	L20494	6/64	Exeter 91	
2569	H31/26R	AFJ90B	Leyd Titan PD2A/30	L20493	6/64	Exeter 90	
2570	B42D	RCM492	Leyd Leopard L1	L04466	5/64	Birkenhead 92	
2571	B42D	RCM491	Leyd Leopard L1	L04465	5/64	Birkenhead 91	
2572	B42D	RCM493	Leyd Leopard L1	L04497	5/64	Birkenhead 93	
2573	B42D	RCM494	Leyd Leopard L1	L04498	5/64	Birkenhead 94	
2574	H37/27F	AEK2B	Leyd Titan PD2A/27	L21126	9/64	Wigan 147	
2575	H37/27F	AEK1B	Leyd Titan PD2A/27	L21125	9/64	Wigan 146	
2576	H37/27F	AEK3B	Leyd Titan PD2A/27	L21127	9/64	Wigan 148	
2577	H37/27F	AEK5B	Leyd Titan PD2A/27	L21190	9/64	Wigan 150	

BNUM	CONFIG	REGN	CHASSIS MAKE	NUMBER	YEAR	OPERATOR	NOTE
2578	H37/27F	AEK4B	Leyd Titan PD2A/27	L21189	8/64	Wigan 149	
2579	H37/27F	KRE266B	Leyd Titan PD2/37	L20798	6/64	Turner, Brown Edge 10	
2580	H33/28R	CWC37B	Leyd Titan PD2A/30Spl	L20810	7/64	Colchester 37	
2581	H33/28R	CWC36B	Leyd Titan PD2A/30Spl	L20809	6/64	Colchester 36	
2582	H33/28R	CWC38B	Leyd Titan PD2A/30Spl	L20811	7/64	Colchester 38	
2583	H43/31F	AAG312B	Daimler Fleetline CRG6LX	60528	6/64	A1, Ardrossan (Brown, Dreghorn)	
2584	H37/28R	ADX63B	AEC Regent V	2D2RA1606	11/64	Ipswich 63	
2585	H37/28R	ADX64B	AEC Regent V	2D2RA1607	11/64	Ipswich 64	
2586	L31/28R	BWO585B	AEC Regent V	2MD3RA609	9/64	Bedwas & Machen 8	
2587	B55F	ATX514B	Leyd Leopard PSU3/1R	L21421	10/64	Caerphilly 14	
2588	B55F	ATX515B	Leyd Leopard PSU3/1R	L21422	10/64	Caerphilly 15	
2589	H37/28RD	ASD887B	AEC Regent V	2D2RA1655	11/64	A1, Ardrossan (JC Stewart,Stevenston) 35	
2590	H37/28RD	ASD888B	AEC Regent V	2D2RA1654	11/64	A1, Ardrossan (Dunn,Stevenston) 33	
2591	H37/28RD	BCS371C	Leyd Titan PD2A/27	L23663	1/65	A1, Ardrossan (McMenemy, Kilwinning)	
2592	H37/27F	AEK8B	Leyd Titan PD2A/27	L21662	12/64	Wigan 24	
2593	H37/27F	AEK9B	Leyd Titan PD2A/27	L21866	12/64	Wigan 29	
2594	H37/27F	AEK10B	Leyd Titan PD2A/27	L21867	12/64	Wigan 31	
2595	H37/27F	AEK7B	Leyd Titan PD2A/27	L21661	12/64	Wigan 11	
2596	H37/27F	AEK6B	Leyd Titan PD2A/27	L21660	12/64	Wigan 3	
2597	H38/32R	CJN435C	Leyd Titan PD3/6	L23728	2/65	Southend 335	
2598	H38/32R	CJN444C	Leyd Titan PD3/6	L23886	2/65	Southend 344	
2599	H38/32R	CJN437C	Leyd Titan PD3/6	L23782	2/65	Southend 337	
2600	H38/32R	CJN439C	Leyd Titan PD3/6	L23815	2/65	Southend 339	
2601	H38/32R	CJN440C	Leyd Titan PD3/6	L23816	1/65	Southend 340	
2602	H38/32R	CJN434C	Leyd Titan PD3/6	L23712	1/65	Southend 334	
2603	H38/32R	CJN438C	Leyd Titan PD3/6	L23783	3/65	Southend 338	
2604	H38/32R	CJN436C	Leyd Titan PD3/6	L23729	3/65	Southend 336	
2605	H38/32R	CJN441C	Leyd Titan PD3/6	L23883	4/65	Southend 341	
2606	H38/32R	CJN433C	Leyd Titan PD3/6	L23711	4/65	Southend 333	
2607	H38/32R	CJN443C	Leyd Titan PD3/6	L23885	4/65	Southend 343	
2608	H38/32R	CJN442C	Leyd Titan PD3/6	L23884	3/65	Southend 342	
2609	H33/28R	BFA588B	Daimler CCG5	20136	1/65	Burton 88	
2610	H33/28R	BFA590B	Daimler CCG5	20138	1/65	Burton 90	
2611	H33/28R	BFA589B	Daimler CCG5	20137	12/64	Burton 89	
2612	H33/28R	BFA591B	Daimler CCG5	20139	12/64	Burton 91	
2613	H36/30R	BBG112C	Leyd Titan PD2/40	L40919	5/65	Birkenhead 112	
2614	H36/30R	BBG118C	Leyd Titan PD2/40	L41559	6/65	Birkenhead 118	
2615	H36/30R	BBG110C	Leyd Titan PD2/40	L40917	5/65	Birkenhead 110	
2616	H36/30R	BBG111C	Leyd Titan PD2/40	L40918	5/65	Birkenhead 111	
2617	H36/30R	BBG114C	Leyd Titan PD2/40	L41122	5/65	Birkenhead 114	
2618	H36/30R	BBG113C	Leyd Titan PD2/40	L40920	5/65	Birkenhead 113	
2619	H36/30R	BBG116C	Leyd Titan PD2/40	L41124	6/65	Birkenhead 116	
2620	H36/30R	BBG115C	Leyd Titan PD2/40	L41123	6/65	Birkenhead 115	
2621	H36/30R	BBG119C	Leyd Titan PD2/40	L41560	6/65	Birkenhead 119	
2622	H36/30R	BBG117C	Leyd Titan PD2/40	L41558	6/65	Birkenhead 117	
2623	H36/30R	BBG120C	Leyd Titan PD2/40	L41583	8/65	Birkenhead 120	
2624	H36/30R	BBG123C	Leyd Titan PD2/40	L41731	9/65	Birkenhead 123	
2625	H36/30R	BBG124C	Leyd Titan PD2/40	L41814	9/65	Birkenhead 124	
2626	H36/30R	BBG121C	Leyd Titan PD2/40	L41584	9/65	Birkenhead 121	
2627	H36/30R	BBG122C	Leyd Titan PD2/40	L41730	9/65	Birkenhead 122	
2628	H37/28R	DFJ897C	Leyd Titan PD2A/30	L41918	9/65	Exeter 97	
2629	H37/28R	DFJ896C	Leyd Titan PD2A/30	L41917	10/65	Exeter 96	
2630	H37/28R	DFJ895C	Leyd Titan PD2A/30	L41916	10/65	Exeter 95	
2631	H37/28R	DFJ898C	Leyd Titan PD2A/30	L42168	10/65	Exeter 98	
2632	H37/28R	DFJ899C	Leyd Titan PD2A/30	L42169	10/65	Exeter 99	
2633	L27/28RD	EWO195C	Leyd Titan PD2/40	L24300	4/65	West Monmouthshire 15	
2634	H43/31F	EKP234C	Leyd Atlantean PDR1/1	L42269	1/66	Maidstone 34	
2635	H43/31F	EKP227C	Leyd Atlantean PDR1/1	L42129	1/66	Maidstone 27	
2636	H43/31F	EKP230C	Leyd Atlantean PDR1/1	L42143	1/66	Maidstone 30	
2637	H43/31F	EKP228C	Leyd Atlantean PDR1/1	L42130	1/66	Maidstone 28	
2638	H43/31F	EKP233C	Leyd Atlantean PDR1/1	L42268	12/65	Maidstone 33	
2639	H43/31F	EKP229C	Leyd Atlantean PDR1/1	L42142	12/65	Maidstone 29	
2640	H43/31F	EKP231C	Leyd Atlantean PDR1/1	L42144	12/65	Maidstone 31	
2641	H43/31F	EKP232C	Leyd Atlantean PDR1/1	L42267	12/65	Maidstone 32	
2642	H41/32F	FFM137C	Guy Arab V	FD76144	8/65	Chester 37	
2643	H41/32F	FFM138C	Guy Arab V	FD76149	8/65	Chester 38	
2644	H41/32F	FFM136C	Guy Arab V	FD76128	7/65	Chester 36	
2645	H41/32F	FFM135C	Guy Arab V	FD76148	7/65	Chester 35	
2646	L35/33RD	GNY433C	Leyd Titan PD3/4	L42818	11/65	Caerphilly 33	
2647	L35/33RD	GNY432C	Leyd Titan PD3/4	L42817	10/65	Caerphilly 32	
2648	L35/33RD	GTX734C	Leyd Titan PD3/4	L42822	12/65	Caerphilly 34	
2649	L27/28RD	GWO351C	Leyd Titan PD2/40	L41695	12/65	West Monmouthshire 17	
2650	H33/28R	OVX144D	Leyd Titan PD2A/30	L43644	2/66	Colchester 44	
2651	H33/28R	OVX142D	Leyd Titan PD2A/30	L43642	2/66	Colchester 42	
2652	H33/28R	OVX143D	Leyd Titan PD2A/30	L43643	2/66	Colchester 43	

Left table:

BNUM	CONFIG	REGN	CHASSIS MAKE	NUMBER	YEAR	OPERATOR	NOTE
2653	H33/28R	OVX139D	Leyd Titan PD2A/30	L43611	3/66	Colchester 39	
2654	H33/28R	OVX140D	Leyd Titan PD2A/30	L43612	2/66	Colchester 40	
2655	H33/28R	OVX141D	Leyd Titan PD2A/30	L43613	3/66	Colchester 41	
2656	H33/28R	EFA293D	Daimler CCG5	20162	3/66	Burton 93	
2657	H33/28R	EFA294D	Daimler CCG5	20163	3/66	Burton 94	
2658	H33/28R	EFA295D	Daimler CCG5	20164	3/66	Burton 95	
2659	H33/28R	EFA292D	Daimler CCG5	20161	3/66	Burton 92	
2660	H36/30R	DBG125D	Leyd Titan PD2/40	L60361	4/66	Birkenhead 125	
2661	H36/30R	DBG126D	Leyd Titan PD2/40	L60362	4/66	Birkenhead 126	
2662	H36/30R	DBG127D	Leyd Titan PD2/40	L60318	5/66	Birkenhead 127	
2663	H36/30R	DBG128D	Leyd Titan PD2/40	L60794	5/66	Birkenhead 128	
2664	H36/30R	DBG129D	Leyd Titan PD2/40	L60795	5/66	Birkenhead 129	
2665	H36/30R	DBG133D	Leyd Titan PD2/40	L61390	6/66	Birkenhead 133	
2666	H36/30R	DBG132D	Leyd Titan PD2/40	L61282	6/66	Birkenhead 132	
2667	H36/30R	DBG134D	Leyd Titan PD2/40	L61521	6/66	Birkenhead 134	
2668	H36/30R	DBG130D	Leyd Titan PD2/40	L61063	5/66	Birkenhead 130	
2669	H36/30R	DBG131D	Leyd Titan PD2/40	L61085	6/66	Birkenhead 131	
2670	H36/30R	DBG137D	Leyd Titan PD2/40	L61809	7/66	Birkenhead 137	
2671	H36/30R	DBG138D	Leyd Titan PD2/40	L61985	7/66	Birkenhead 138	
2672	H36/30R	DBG139D	Leyd Titan PD2/40	L62066	8/66	Birkenhead 139	
2673	H36/30R	DBG135D	Leyd Titan PD2/40	L61567	6/66	Birkenhead 135	
2674	H36/30R	DBG136D	Leyd Titan PD2/40	L61739	6/66	Birkenhead 136	
2675	B41D	GFJ601D	Leyd Leopard PSU4/2R	L62213	10/66	Exeter 1	
2676	B41D	GFJ602D	Leyd Leopard PSU4/2R	L62532	10/66	Exeter 5	
2677	B41D	GFJ605D	Leyd Leopard PSU4/2R	L62644	10/66	Exeter 3	
2679	B41D	GFJ603D	Leyd Leopard PSU4/2R	L62533	10/66	Exeter 3	
2680	L27/28RD	UWO688	Guy Arab V	583400	6/66	West Monmouthshire 13	1
2681	L31/29RD	LNY535D	Leyd Tiger Cub PSUC1/12	L62783	10/66	Caerphilly 35	
2682	L31/29RD	LNY536D	Leyd Tiger Cub PSUC1/12	L62869	10/66	Caerphilly 36	
2683	B40D	LFM152D	Leyd Panther Cub	L62941	8/66	Chester 52	
2684	H37/27F	DEK2D	Leyd Titan PD2/37	L62942	12/66	Wigan 139	
2685	H37/27F	DEK3D	Leyd Titan PD2/37	L62631	12/66	Wigan 140	
2686	H41/32F	LFM141D	Guy Arab V	FD76655	12/66	Chester 41	
2687	H41/32F	LFM139D	Guy Arab V	FD76656	9/66	Chester 39	
2688	H41/32F	LFM140D	Guy Arab V	FD76657	9/66	Chester 40	
2689	B45F	YTE951D	Leyd Tiger Cub PSUC1/12	L70319	12/66	Fishwick 2	
2690	B45F	YTE952D	Leyd Tiger Cub PSUC1/12	L70320	12/66	Fishwick 3	
2691	L27/28RD	KWO134D	Guy Arab V	L61971	12/66	West Monmouthshire 28	
2692	B43D	DJP468E	Leyd Panther Cub	L72703	7/67	Wigan 20	
2693	B43D	EEK1F	Leyd Panther Cub	L72750	8/67	Wigan 22	
2694	H33/28R	GFA97D	Daimler CCG5	20183	12/66	Burton 97	
2695	H33/28R	GFA96D	Daimler CCG5	20185	12/66	Burton 96	
2696	H33/28R	GFA99D	Daimler CCG5	20184	1/67	Burton 99	
2697	H33/28R	GFA98D	Daimler CCG5	20184	1/67	Burton 98	
2698	H43/31F	JKE336G	Leyd Atlantean PDR1/1	L63927	2/67	Maidstone 36	
2699	H43/31F	JKE341E	Leyd Atlantean PDR1/1	L64234	2/67	Maidstone 41	
2700	H43/31F	JKE339E	Leyd Atlantean PDR1/1	L64192	3/67	Maidstone 39	
2701	H43/31F	JKE342E	Leyd Atlantean PDR1/1	L64235	3/67	Maidstone 42	
2702	H43/31F	JKE337E	Leyd Atlantean PDR1/1	L64009	4/67	Maidstone 37	
2703	H43/31F	JKE340E	Leyd Atlantean PDR1/1	L64193	4/67	Maidstone 40	
2704	H43/31F	JKE338E	Leyd Atlantean PDR1/1	L64010	4/67	Maidstone 38	
2705	H43/31F	JKE335E	Leyd Atlantean PDR1/1	L63783	4/67	Maidstone 35	
2706	H36/30R	GCM140E	Leyd Titan PD2/37	700383	4/67	Birkenhead 140	
2707	H36/30R	GCM141E	Leyd Titan PD2/37	700579	4/67	Birkenhead 141	
2708	H36/30R	GCM142E	Leyd Titan PD2/37	700696	4/67	Birkenhead 142	
2709	H36/30R	GCM143E	Leyd Titan PD2/37	700903	5/67	Birkenhead 143	
2710	H36/30R	GCM145E	Leyd Titan PD2/37	701008	5/67	Birkenhead 145	
2711	H36/30R	GCM144E	Leyd Titan PD2/37	701007	5/67	Birkenhead 144	
2712	H36/30R	GCM146E	Leyd Titan PD2/37	701234	6/67	Birkenhead 146	
2713	H36/30R	GCM147E	Leyd Titan PD2/37	701235	6/67	Birkenhead 147	
2714	H36/30R	GCM151E	Leyd Titan PD2/37	701398	7/67	Birkenhead 151	
2715	H36/30R	GCM149E	Leyd Titan PD2/37	701247	7/67	Birkenhead 149	
2716	H36/30R	GCM150E	Leyd Titan PD2/37	701249	7/67	Birkenhead 150	

Right table:

BNUM	CONFIG	REGN	CHASSIS MAKE	NUMBER	YEAR	OPERATOR	NOTE
2717	H36/30R	GCM153E	Leyd Titan PD2/37	701578	9/67	Birkenhead 153	
2718	H36/30R	GCM152E	Leyd Titan PD2/37	701399	9/67	Birkenhead 152	
2719	H36/30R	GCM154E	Leyd Titan PD2/37	701579	9/67	Birkenhead 154	
2720	H36/30R	GCM148E	Leyd Titan PD2/47	701248	11/67	Birkenhead 148	
2721	H34/28R	PBJ2F	Leyd Titan PD2/47	701793	9/67	Lowestoft 12	
2722	H34/28R	PBJ1F	Leyd Titan PD2/47	701792	9/67	Lowestoft 11	
2723	H37/27F	ONY637F	Leyd Titan PD2/37	702476	12/67	Caerphilly 37	
2724	H37/27F	ONY638F	Leyd Titan PD2/37	702477	12/67	Caerphilly 38	
2725	B40D	RFM453F	Leyd Tiger Cub PSUC1/11	751014	9/67	Chester 53	
2726	H43/31F	WEV747F	Leyd Atlantean PDR1/1	702045	12/67	Colchester 47	
2727	H43/31F	WEV746F	Leyd Atlantean PDR1/1	702044	12/67	Colchester 46	
2728	H43/31F	WEV745F	Leyd Atlantean PDR1/1	702043	12/67	Colchester 45	
2729	B51D	HPV71F	Leyd Leopard PSU3/1R	702767	12/67	Caerphilly 16	
2730	B40D	HPV72F	AEC Reliance 6MU2R	6MU2R6319	1/68	Ipswich 71	
2731	B40D	HPV70F	AEC Reliance 6MU2R	6MU2R6320	1/68	Ipswich 72	
2732	B40D	HPV69F	AEC Reliance 6MU2R	6MU2R6318	1/68	Ipswich 70	
2733	B40D	JFA602F	AEC Reliance 6MU2R	6MU2R6317	1/68	Ipswich 69	
2734	H33/28R	JFA600F	Daimler CCG5	20193	1/68	Burton 102	
2735	H33/28R	JFA601F	Daimler CCG5	20191	1/68	Burton 100	
2736	H33/28R	JFA601F	Daimler CCG5	20192	1/68	Burton 101	
2737	H43/31F	NKK243F	Leyd Atlantean PDR1/1	800365	4/68	Maidstone 43	
2738	H43/31F	OKJ844F	Leyd Atlantean PDR1/1	802087	7/68	Maidstone 44	
2739	H43/31F	OKM145G	Leyd Atlantean PDR1/1	802088	8/68	Maidstone 45	
2740	H43/31F	OKM146G	Leyd Atlantean PDR1/1	801821	10/68	Maidstone 46	
2741	H43/31F	KSD661F	Leyd Atlantean PDR1/1	800366	6/68	A1, Ardrossan (Hunter, Dreghorn) 17	
2742	H37/27F	FEK9F	Leyd Titan PD2/37	703016	3/68	Wigan 46	
2743	H37/27F	FEK8F	Leyd Titan PD2/37	703015	3/68	Wigan 38	
2744	H37/27F	FEK6F	Leyd Titan PD2/37	702766	3/68	Wigan 33	
2745	H37/27F	FEK7F	Leyd Titan PD2/37	702855	3/68	Wigan 34	
2746	H37/27F	FEK5F	Leyd Titan PD2/37	702765	4/68	Wigan 32	
2747	H37/27F	FEK1F	Leyd Titan PD2/37	702676	5/68	Wigan 25	
2748	H37/27F	FEK2F	Leyd Titan PD2/37	702677	5/68	Wigan 26	
2749	H37/27F	FEK4F	Leyd Titan PD2/37	702714	5/68	Wigan 28	
2750	H37/27F	FEK3F	Leyd Titan PD2/37	702713	5/68	Wigan 27	
2751	L35/33RD	PAX466F	Leyd Titan PD3/4	703981	6/68	Bedwas & Machen 6	
2752	H43/31F	YWC649F	Leyd Atlantean PDR1/1	801600	6/68	Colchester 49	
2753	H43/31F	YWC648F	Leyd Atlantean PDR1/1	801599	6/68	Colchester 48	
2754	H43/31F	AVX50G	Leyd Atlantean PDR1/1	802455	9/68	Colchester 50	
2755	H43/31F	AVX51G	Leyd Atlantean PDR1/1	802456	9/68	Colchester 51	
2756	H43/31F	AVX52G	Leyd Atlantean PDR1/1	802457	9/68	Colchester 52	
2757	H43/31F	AVX53G	Leyd Atlantean PDR1/1	802496	10/68	Colchester 53	
2758	H43/31F	AVX54G	Leyd Atlantean PDR1/1	802497	10/68	Colchester 54	
2759	B51D	STX217G	Leyd Leopard PSU3A/2R	802538	11/68	Caerphilly 17	
2760	B51D	STX218G	Leyd Leopard PSU3A/2R	802539	11/68	Caerphilly 18	
2761	B40D	XFM54G	Leyd Tiger Cub PSUC1/11	852068	12/68	Chester 54	
2784	H44/33F	LCM163G	Leyd Atlantean PDR1/1	800941	9/68	Birkenhead 163	32
2785	H44/33F	LCM167G	Leyd Atlantean PDR1/1	801187	9/68	Birkenhead 167	32
2786	H44/33F	LCM156G	Leyd Atlantean PDR1/1	800704	9/68	Birkenhead 156	32
2787	H44/33F	LCM157G	Leyd Atlantean PDR1/1	800705	9/68	Birkenhead 157	32
2788	H44/33F	LCM160G	Leyd Atlantean PDR1/1	800847	9/68	Birkenhead 160	32
2789	H44/33F	LCM161G	Leyd Atlantean PDR1/1	800848	11/68	Birkenhead 161	32
2790	H44/33F	LCM162G	Leyd Atlantean PDR1/1	800940	9/68	Birkenhead 162	32
2791	H44/33F	LCM164G	Leyd Atlantean PDR1/1	801176	10/68	Birkenhead 164	32
2792	H44/33F	LCM159G	Leyd Atlantean PDR1/1	800833	11/68	Birkenhead 159	32
2793	H44/33F	LCM158G	Leyd Atlantean PDR1/1	800832	11/68	Birkenhead 158	32
2794	H44/33F	LCM166G	Leyd Atlantean PDR1/1	801186	11/68	Birkenhead 166	32
2795	H44/33F	LCM165G	Leyd Atlantean PDR1/1	801177	11/68	Birkenhead 165	32
2796	H44/33F	LCM155G	Leyd Atlantean PDR1/1	800703	11/68	Birkenhead 155	32
2814	H41/32F	XFM42G	Guy Arab V	FD77081	3/69	Chester 42	33
2815	H41/32F	XFM44G	Guy Arab V	FD77083	3/69	Chester 44	33
2816	H41/32F	XFM43G	Guy Arab V	FD77082	3/69	Chester 43	33
2817	H41/32F	DFM346H	Guy Arab V	FD77107	10/69	Chester 46	33
2818	H41/32F	DFM347H	Guy Arab V	FD77108	10/69	Chester 47	33
2819	H41/32F	DFM345H	Guy Arab V	FD77106	10/69	Chester 45	33

KEY TO BODY LIST NOTES

NOTES:-

An asterisk against the body number denotes true sequence of batch unknown
Rebody
Doubled as a lorry
Demonstrator bought by Huie & Co. Campbelltown
Ordered by Pye, Heswall but did not enter service due to takeover by Crosville
Rebodied as a lorry - originally a charabanc with Whitehaven Motor Services
Demonstrator (possibly KM2742)
Demonstrator bought by Farghers, Richmond
Ordered through North Western Motors, Liverpool
Diverted from Cumberland Motor Services
Ordered through Bamber (Agent), Birkdale
Ordered through Loxhams (Dealers), Preston
Rebody - ordered through County Garage, Carlisle
Possible registration ED5175
Ordered through Garlick, Burrell & Edwards, Manchester
A Tillings-Stevens B10A2 was originally ordered
Sold to Sunderland Corporation 5/30 (Fleet No. 22)
Rebody ordered through Garlic, Burrell & Edwards, Liverpool
Ordered through Garlick, Burrell & Edwards, Liverpool
Ordered through Morecambe Motors as dealer
Sold to Cumberland Motor Services 9/32 (Fleet No. 47)
Ordered by Box, Dewsbury before takeover by Yorkshire Woollen District
Body built to English Electric design
Body overhaul only
Refurbished 1947
Rebuilt following bomb damage
Rebuilt and fitted with streamlined cab
First metal-framed body
Mobile Police Station
Body No. 2412 carried in error
Lengthened to 30 feet giving B45F in 1967/8
Originally ordered by Moores, Kelvedon before takeover by Eastern National
Built by Massey but carried NCME body numbers
Ordered from Massey but built by NCME with Massey style lower saloons and NCME upper saloons.

PRESERVED MASSEY VEHICLES

Bnum	Config	Reg	Make	Chassis	Year	Operator
623	B28R	MN 5105	Leyland Lion PLSC1	45955	7/27	Manxland 27
780	H28/26R	ED 6141	Leyland Titan TD1	71573	9/30	Warrington 42
927	B32R	ATD 683	Leyland Tiger TS7	8925	12/35	Widnes 39
	H30/26R	BG 9225	Leyland Titan PD1	460599	12/46	Birkenhead 105
2018	H30/26R	FDM 724	Foden PVD6	28790	7/49	Phillips, Holywell
2020	L27/26RD	FAV 827	AEC Regent III	9613E4331	9/49	Sutherland, Peterhead 124
2076	DP39F	KTX 631	Leyland PS2/3	501267	4/51	Thomas (Llynfi), Maesteg 59
2083	B35F	LTX 311	Leyland PS2/5	520623	6/52	Caerphilly 1
2093	H31/28R	BG 8557	Guy Arab II	FD26388	5/53	Birkenhead 242
2113	H30/26R	RFM 641	Guy Arab IV	FD71864	6/53	Chester 1
2131	L27/28R	GLX 913	Daimler CWA6	11845	6/54	Southend 263
2148	H33/28RD	RAL 795	Daimler CVG6	18688	8/54	Gash, Newark DD10
2250	H30/26R	TFJ 808	Guy Arab IV	FD73287	11/56	Exeter 50
2252	H30/26R	UFJ 292	Guy Arab IV	FD73680	6/57	Exeter 52
2254	H30/26R	UFJ 293	Guy Arab IV	FD73686	7/57	Exeter 53
2268	H31/28R	FBG 910	Leyland Titan PD2/40	571367	3/58	Birkenhead 10
2280	H32/26RD	DEK 106	Leyland Titan PD2/20	571197	10/57	Wigan 4
2300	H33/28R	DC S616	Daimler CVD6SD	16519	3/58	A1, Ardrossan (Hunter, Dreghorn) 16A
2302	H40/33RD	RDM 200	Guy Arab IV	FD73863	5/58	Lloyd, Bagillt
2303	L35/33R	PHJ 951	Leyland Titan PD3/6	580829	6/58	Southend 312
2304	L35/33R	PHJ 955	Leyland Titan PD3/6	580864	6/58	Southend 316
2305	L35/33R	PHJ 952	Leyland Titan PD3/6	580830	7/58	Southend 313
2306	L35/33R	PHJ 950	Leyland Titan PD3/6	580828	7/58	Southend 311
2307	L35/33R	PHJ 953	Leyland Titan PD3/6	580831	6/58	Southend 314
2308	L35/33R	PHJ 954	Leyland Titan PD3/6	580863	7/58	Southend 315
2309	H41/31F	YTG 304	Leyland Titan PD3/4	571786	7/58	Thomas (Llynfi), Maesteg 72
2310	L29/28R	YNY 922	Leyland Titan PD2/40	581705	11/58	Caerphilly 22
2324	H33/28RD	KAL 579	Daimler CVD6	15227	10/58	Gash, Newark DD2
2361	L34/33R	20 PVX	Guy Arab IV	FD74288	7/59	Moore, Kelvedon
2373	H33/28R	FA 9716	Guy Arab III	FD36252	1/60	Burton 16
2383	H31/26R	974 AFJ	Guy Arab IV	FD74590	7/60	Exeter 74
2422	H31/26R	479 CFJ	Leyland Titan PD2A/30	610091	4/61	Exeter 79
2426	B40F	J 26611	Leyland Tiger Cub PSUC1/5	614353	4/61	Jersey MT 611
2431	L34/33R	373 WPU	Guy Arab IV	FD74911	5/61	Moore, Kelvedon
2436	L27/28RD	260 BAX	Leyland Titan PD2/40	603177	6/61	West Monmouthshire 21
2447	H41/29F	HEK 705	Leyland Titan PD3A/2	610873	7/61	Wigan 57
2459	L31/28RD	YTH 815	Guy Arab IV	FD74812	1/62	Rees & Williams, Tycroes
2460	L31/28R	422 CAX	AEC Regent V	MD3RV565	12/61	Bedwas & Machen 5
2467	H31/26R	484 EFJ	Leyland Titan PD2A/30	620425	4/62	Exeter 84
2505	H37/27F	JJP 502	Leyland Titan PD2A/27	622126	10/62	Wigan 35
2519	H33/28R	918 NRT	AEC Regent V	MD3RV593	1/63	Lowestoft 8
2521	L35/33RD	31 SNY	Leyland Titan PD3/4	629094	3/63	Caerphilly 31

THE VEHICLES LISTED HAVE AT SOME STAGE BEEN PRESERVED, OR EARMARKED FOR PRESERVATION.
THE LIST IS OFFERED IN GOOD FAITH BUT MAY NO LONGER BE FULLY UP-TO-DATE. FOR LATEST
DETAILS WE RECOMMEND THE PSV CIRCLE LIST OF PRESERVED VEHICLES AND THIS CAN BE OBTAINED
FROM THE CIRCLE OR FROM OUR MAIL ORDER DEPARTMENT AT PIKES LANE, GLOSSOP.

num	Config	Reg	Make	Chassis	Year	Operator
27	H31/26R	86 GFJ	Leyland Titan PD2A/30	L00491	5/63	Exeter 86
29	H33/28RD	KAL 578	Daimler CVD6	15226	12/62	Gash, Newark DD1
55	H33/28R	26 YKO	Leyland Titan PD2A/30	L01579	10/63	Maidstone 26
58	H33/28R	25 YKO	Leyland Titan PD2A/30	L01578	10/63	Maidstone 25
59	H33/28R	TFA 987	Daimler CCG5	20060	1/64	Burton 87
62	H37/27F	CTF 627B	Leyland Titan PD2A/27	L03683	5/64	Lytham 70
63	H37/27F	CTF 625B	Leyland Titan PD2A/27	L03681	5/64	Lytham 68
64	H37/27F	CTF 626B	Leyland Titan PD2A/27	L03682	5/64	Lytham 69
72	B42D	RCM 493	Leyland Leopard L1	L04497	5/64	Birkenhead 93
84	H37/28R	ADX 63B	AEC Regent V	2D2RA1606	11/64	Ipswich 63
85	H37/28R	ADX 64B	AEC Regent V	2D2RA1607	11/64	Ipswich 64
86	L31/28R	BWO 585B	AEC Regent V	2MD3RA609	9/64	Bedwas & Machen 8
97	H38/32R	CJN 435C	Leyland Titan PD3/6	L23728	2/65	Southend 335
00	H38/32R	CJN 439C	Leyland Titan PD3/6	L23815	2/65	Southend 339
02	H38/32R	CJN 434C	Leyland Titan PD3/6	L23712	1/65	Southend 334
04	H38/32R	CJN 436C	Leyland Titan PD3/6	L23729	3/65	Southend 336
05	H38/32R	CJN 441C	Leyland Titan PD3/6	L23883	4/65	Southend 341
34	H43/31F	EKP 234C	Leyland Atlantean PDR1/1	L42269	1/66	Maidstone 34
44	H41/32F	FFM 136C	Guy Arab V	FD76128	7/65	Chester 36
45	H41/32F	FFM 135C	Guy Arab V	FD76148	7/65	Chester 35
46	L35/33RD	GNY 433C	Leyland Titan PD3/4	L42818	11/65	Caerphilly 33
47	L35/33RD	GNY 432C	Leyland Titan PD3/4	L42817	10/65	Caerphilly 32
52	H33/28R	OVX 143D	Leyland Titan PD2A/30	L43643	2/66	Colchester 43
80	L27/28RD	UWO 688	Leyland Titan PD2/41	583400	6/66	West Monmouthshire 13
82	L31/29RD	LNY 536D	Leyland Titan PD2/37	L62869	10/66	Caerphilly 36
84	H37/27F	DE K2D	Leyland Titan PD2/37	L62941	12/66	Wigan 139
85	H37/27F	DEK 3D	Leyland Titan PD2/37	L62942	12/66	Wigan 140
92	B43D	DJP468E	Leyland Panther Cub	L72703	7/67	Wigan 20
04	H43/31F	JKE 338E	Leyland Atlantean PDR1/1	L64010	4/67	Maidstone 38
13	H36/30R	GCM 147E	Leyland Titan PD2/37	701235	6/67	Birkenhead 147
18	H36/30R	GCM 152E	Leyland Titan PD2/37	701399	9/67	Birkenhead 152
21	H34/28R	PBJ 2F	Leyland Titan PD2/47	701793	9/67	Lowestoft 12
22	H34/28R	PBJ 1F	Leyland Titan PD2/47	701792	9/67	Lowestoft 11
23	H37/27F	ONY637F	Leyland Titan PD2/37	702476	12/67	Caerphilly 37
24	H37/27F	ONY 638F	Leyland Titan PD2/37	702477	12/67	Caerphilly 38
25	B40D	RFM 453F	Leyland Tiger Cub PSUC1/11	751014	9/67	Chester 53
32	B40D	HPV 70F	AEC Reliance 6MU2R	6MU2R6318	1/68	Ipswich 70
50	H37/27F	FEK 3F	Leyland Titan PD2/37	702713	5/68	Wigan 27
51	L35/33RD	PAX 466F	Leyland Titan PD3/4	703981	6/68	Bedwas & Machen 6
53	H43/31F	YWC648F	Leyland Atlantean PDR1/1	801599	6/68	Colchester 48
14	H41/32F	XFM 42G	Guy Arab V	FD77081	3/69	Chester 42
18	H41/32F	DFM 347H	Guy Arab V	FD77108	10/69	Chester 47

163

MASSEY BROTHERS (Pemberton) LTD.

Annual production for Municipal fleets 1920 - 1969

MUNICIPALITY	20	21	22	23	24	25	26	27	28	29	30	31	32	33	34	35	36	37	38	39	40	41	42	43	44	45	46	47	48	49	50	51	52	53	54	55	56	57	58	59	60	61	62	63	64	65	66	67	68	69	TOTALS
ABERDEEN																							2																												**2**
ACCRINGTON																									4																										**4**
ASHTON-U-LYNE																								3	5	8																									**16**
BARROW																								5												1			1	1		10									**18**
BEDWAS & MACHEN																																						1		1		1			1				1		**5**
BIRKENHEAD												2	10	9	6	5	11	40	10	30	10		3	18			13	13	25	30	30			15		7	10	8	7	13	12	5	15	15	4	15	15	15	13		**434**
BLACKBURN																									7	2																									**9**
BOLTON																3	15	15	2	40	17	30	3																												**125**
BRADFORD																								6																											**6**
BURNLEY, COLNE & NELSON																		2						5	6	3			6	6																					**28**
BURTON																																								3	3	3	3	3	5	2	7	1	3		**33**
BURY											4													3								4																			**11**
CAERPHILLY																																	1		2		1	2	2		2	2	2	3	2	3	2	3			**27**
CHESTER															1		3		4	4	3	3	2	2	5		2	8	3	4	2		1	4	4	8		2	2		2	3	4	4	2	3	4	1	2		**92**
CHESTERFIELD																											6																								**6**
COLCHESTER																				5								4	1					3			4	4	3		4	1		7	3		6	3	7		**55**
COVENTRY																				1			2	2																											**5**
DERBY																							2																												**2**
DONCASTER																							3	1																											**4**
DUNDEE																								4																											**4**
EDINBURGH																								6	1																										**7**
EXETER																													10								1	4			5	5	5	5	5						**40**
GLASGOW																								3																											**3**
GREAT YARMOUTH																				4									10							5	5	5	4	4											**37**
GRIMSBY																									3																										**3**
HULL																				10	10			5	4	10																									**39**
IPSWICH																		11	7		1																								2			4			**25**
LANCASTER																								1	4																										**5**
LEIGH												3	2		6	3		7	5																																**26**

MUNICIPALITY	20	21	22	23	24	25	26	27	28	29	30	31	32	33	34	35	36	37	38	39	40	41	42	43	44	45	46	47	48	49	50	51	52	53	54	55	56	57	58	59	60	61	62	63	64	65	66	67	68	69	TOTALS
LONDON TRANSPORT																										49																									49
LOWESTOFT																										6						2												2				2			12
LYTHAM ST. ANNES																																													3						3
MAIDSTONE																																					6	3	3	3		3	4	4		4	4	8	4		46
MERTHYR																												3																							3
MORECAMBE & HEYSHAM																																					2	3			3		2								10
NEWCASTLE																							2			6	16		8	20																					52
NOTTINGHAM																								4																											4
RAWTENSTALL																								1																											1
ROCHDALE																								1		10	1																								12
S.H.M.D.																								4																											4
SALFORD								12							7	5	5	3																																	32
SHEFFIELD																							5	1																											6
SOUTH SHIELDS																							1	1																											2
SOUTHEND																											3		3	6	6		6		18	3	9	6	6							12					78
SOUTHPORT																		5																																	5
ST. HELENS															11	7			5	12		10																													45
STOCKPORT																									2	7	7																								16
STOCKTON-ON-TEES																												18	25																						43
SUNDERLAND											3													8	9		4		12																						36
TEES-SIDE																						4						2																							7
TODMORDEN										1																																									4
WALSALL																							2		15	6																									23
WARRINGTON											5	3																																							8
WEST BROMWICH											3																																								3
WEST HARTLEPOOL																							1		1		3																								5
WEST MONMOUTH																													1													1	2			2	2				9
WIDNES																																						3	3	4	6	3	2								21
WIGAN																																											9	6	10		2	2	9		102
TOTALS	6	8	4	0	1	1	0	14	0	1	15	18	10	14	20	33	51	94	44	44	41	37	36	76	90	107	48	48	94	60	44	7	8	22	24	24	38	44	25	32	35	37	44	49	35	47	47	39	40	6	1712

165

MASSEY BROTHERS (Pemberton) LTD.

Bodywork supplied to non-municipal operators 1946 to 1969

CUSTOMER	46	47	48	49	50	51	52	53	54	55	56	57	58	59	60	61	62	63	64	65	66	67	68	69	TOTALS
A1, ARDROSSAN													1						3	1			1		6
ALEXANDERS	10	1	9																						20
BAKER, WARSOP	2	1																							3
BARTON						1																			1
BAXTER, AIRDRIE									2	1	4	5	1	4	3	1									21
BEVAN & BARKER, MANSFIELD	1		1																						2
BURWELL & DISTRICT					1	1																			2
CUMBERLAND M.S.		5	10																						15
DAVIES, TONMAWR														1											1
DUNCAN, LAW											1														1
EASTERN NATIONAL																		2							2
FISHWICK, LEYLAND																					2				2
GASH, NEWARK									1				3				1								5
GRAHAM, PAISLEY														1											1
GREEN BUS, RUGELEY							1																		1
GREENSHIELDS, SALSBURGH	1												1												2
HANSON, HUDDERSFIELD	1																								1
JERSEY M.T.																5	5								10
LAURIE, HAMILTON										1				1											2
LLOYD, BAGILLT				1						1			1	1											4
MAINWARING, BIGNALL END		2																							2
McGILL, BARRHEAD										4				1	2										7
MILTON BUS SERVICE		2																							2
MOORES, KELVEDON													2	2	3	2									9
MOZAMBIQUE RAILWAYS									8																8
NAYLOR, STOCKTON HEATH						1																			1
PHILLIPS, HOLYWELL				1																					1
PURPLE MOTORS, BETHESDA		1																							1
REES & WILLIAMS, TYCROES			1							2	1		1		1		1								7
ROWBOTHAM, HARRISEAHEAD							2																		2
ROWLEY, BIGNALL		1																							1
SMITH, BARRHEAD							1																		1
SMITH, UPPER HEYFORD							2	2																	4
STEVENSON, SPATH				1																					1
STOKE-ON-TRENT MOTORS	2	2	1																						5
SUTHERLAND, PETERHEAD	2			2																					4
THOMAS (LLYNFI), MAESTEG		1				1						1													3
TURNER, BROWN EDGE									1					1			1		1						4
WANKIE COLLIERY, RHODESIA													2												2
WEST WALES, TYCROES								1																	1
WILLIAMS, LLANDILO	1																								1
TOTALS	20	16	22	5	1	4	6	3	12	9	6	6	12	12	9	8	8	2	4	1	2	0	1	0	169

NDEX

AFTER THE EXTERMINATION . . .

Builders make a monster 'Dalek' for handicapped children

For many weeks now, a bunch of big-hearted guys at a local works have given up their scant lunch break and spent the ti▮ making a thrillingly lifelike Dalek monster, which is intended as a bumper Christmas present for the handicapped childr▮ of Mere Oaks School. The Dalek, which does everything except cry "Exterminate!", has been made by the men employ▮ as coach-builders at the Pemberton works of Massey Brothers, a subsidiary of Northern Counties, with the kind approval their boss, director Mr Jack Abbot.

Some years ago, the men made a similar machine for the youngsters in Wrightington Hospital, but when they heard of ▮ unfortunate youngsters of Mere Oaks, there was no better excuse for making this Dalek. So the men of Massey Bros. led body shop foreman Joe Bibby who designed the machine set to work with a will to produce a beautifully finished job. Am▮ them were Teddy Gee, Tom Jones, Alan Brightcliffe, Frank Stubbs, Jack Carter, Jim Gore and Frank Brown, the forem▮ painter.

What a Christmas present the Dalek would make for any kid. Standing nearly five feet tall, it is manually propelled, has ▮ electric buzzer, space guns and a door that can't lock, so that no young spaceman should ever feel trapped inside. Six y▮ old Paul Walsh, who lives a few doors down from the workshop and who acted as 'model' while the men measured up, said think it's smashing, I wish its was mine for Christmas". Another little chap who visited the works and saw the Dalek promp offered to exchange his most treasured possession - an electric train - for it.

The presentation of the Dalek to Mere Oaks will take place at Christmas, but before then it is being offered on loan childrens' parties organised by local firms, in order to raise money for the children of Mere Oak.

Workmen picture, left to right:-

Alan Brightcliffe (NCME), Teddy Gee (MB), Joe Bibby (MB), Jack Carter (NCME), Tom Jones (?), Jimmy Gore (MB).

With thanks to the local newspaper which ran the story!